DISCO

The Firth of Forth

DISCOVERING
The Firth of Forth

WILLIAM F. HENDRIE

*For my friend Susan
from Bill Fyfe Hendrie
31 July 2019.
With warmest good wishes*

JOHN DONALD PUBLISHERS LTD
EDINBURGH

ISBN 0 85976 458 3

British Library Cataloguing in Publication Data

A catalogue record for this book is available
from the British Library.

Typesetting and prepress origination by Brinnoven, Livingston.
Printed and bound in Great Britain by Bell & Bain Ltd, Glasgow.

CONTENTS

ACKNOWLEDGEMENTS

My thanks to: Captain Gordon Daly, Captain Alastair Gibson, Colin Aston, Alison Dykes, Margaret Dykes, Tom Dykes, Jim Donovan, Pat Donovan, Roger Banks, Jim Harrower, Leslie Pringle, Bob Jurgensen, Mary Cook, Andrew Strachan, Robert McMurray, Sally Smith, Maureen Handley, Robert Kerr, Allan Hunter and all the other people who so kindly supplied me with information and answered my many questions as I walked the shores of the Firth.

My special thanks to Dr Arthur Down for taking the majority of photographs of places on the south shore.

W.F.H.

INTRODUCTION

Centuries ago, the Vikings sailed across what we now call the North Sea and invaded Scotland. As a legacy they left behind traces of their language in many place names such as Lerwick and Sutherland, which was to them, of course, the Southern Land. One of the most common of these names with a Norse origin is *Firth*, derived from the same root as the Norwegian *fjord*, meaning an inlet. There are eleven firths around the coast of mainland Scotland and another ten in the Shetland Isles. They range from the notoriously rough Pentland Firth separating the north coast of Scotland from the Orkney Islands, to the Solway Firth in the south separating Scotland from England and from the famous Firth of Clyde to the little known Ruff Firth.

None, however, has had such a major effect on the history and development of Scotland as the Firth of Forth. Hundreds of years before the European Economic Community, far less the so-called European Union, was ever thought of, the Forth provided the link, which ensured that Scotland had ready access to the Continent and that it was indeed often in closer touch with the Netherlands and its auld ally, France, than it was with the old enemy, England. Before Christopher Columbus discovered the new world in 1492, the Forth was Scotland's direct route to the then known world, and, as the influence of Europe remained paramount for around another three hundred years, it was its hinterlands in the Lothians and Fife, which flourished throughout the 16th, 17th and 18th centuries. It was not until after the ill-fated economic disaster of the Darien Scheme and the subsequent Union of the Parliaments in 1707 that the Clyde and the surrounding areas of the West of Scotland began to increase in importance, thanks to Scotland's inclusion within the terms of the Navigation Acts, which permitted our merchants to trade with England's colonies in the West Indies and America.

The industrial revolution, with its resultant change from wooden to steel-hulled ships, and the introduction of steam power, continued still further the rise of the Clyde and in particular Glasgow, which rose to become the second city of the whole of the British Empire, at the expense of the Forth and Edinburgh.

Despite this challenge to its former supremacy, the Forth still a remained a major artery of trade and travel throughout the 19th century, with overnight passenger-steamer sailings from Leith, Grangemouth and Bo'ness to London continuing long after the coming of the railways in the 1840s and 1850s. Today, it is strange to think of Edinburgh city businessmen consulting their tide tables and travelling down to Leith to sail south, rather than racing out to Turnhouse to catch the Shuttle; but such was the importance of the Forth.

The two great world wars against Germany helped to continue that importance throughout the first half of the 20th century, with the Forth playing a major role in both war efforts, from the Royal Navy's activities at Rosyth to the building of large parts of the D-Day Mulberry Harbour at Leith Docks. Now, at the end of the 20th century, the Forth has received an unexpected boost from the North Sea Oil Industry, ranging from the coming and going of its supply vessels, to the export of the processed petrol from the Hound Point Terminal and of natural gas from Braefoot. Surprisingly, passenger traffic, which, by the 1970s had all but disappeared, is also on the increase, from the day trippers on the *Maid of the Forth* to the passengers on the steadily increasing number of luxury liners calling at both Leith and Rosyth, adding even further interest to life on the river and prosperity to Scotland's tourist industry.

All in all the Firth of Forth is a fascinating area to explore, from discovering its history to enjoying the ever-increasing range of leisure activities which take place both along its shores and on its waters. *Discovering The Firth of Forth* aims to encourage you to do just that.

W.F.H.

Discovering the Firth of Forth

is dedicated to the memory of my mother and father

Nelson Patrick Hendrie
and
Margaret Fraser Snedden

who, from my youngest years,
encouraged my interest in the Forth,
the river on whose shores I was born and brought up.

Other books by William F. Hendrie, published by John Donald Ltd, include *Discovering the River Forth*, *Discovering West Lothian* and *The Dominie: a Profile of the Scottish Headmaster*.

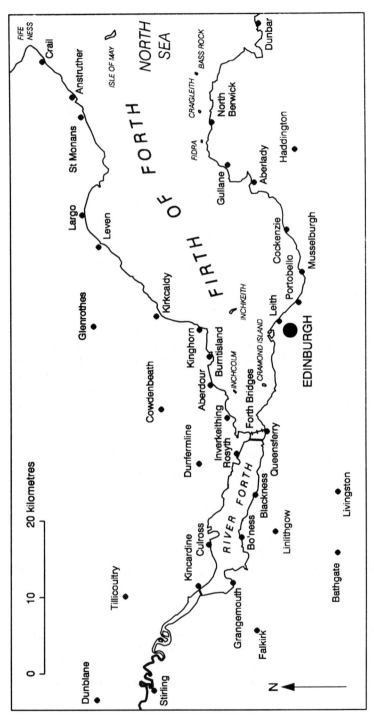

Location Map

CHAPTER 1
A BEGGAR'S MANTLE FRINGED WITH GOLD

'**A** beggar's mantle fringed with gold', is how Fife was described by King James VI. The saying refers not only to Fife's famous sandy shores, but is also an apt reminder of the contrast between its rich and prosperous coastal burghs and fishing ports and the poorer coal-mining towns and farming villages in its interior.

The reason why Fife's coastal regions flourished much earlier than its inland districts was the ease of access provided by the Firths of Forth and Tay, compared with the difficulty of overland transport in the centuries when Scotland's roads were in such an atrocious state that travel was a hazardous adventure.

Fife is also often described as 'The Wee Kingdom', a particularly apt title because of the almost self-contained nature of its long peninsula-shaped territory, which the 'Fly Fifers', as its inhabitants are known, have stoutly defended through two sets of Scottish local government re-organisation, 20 years apart in 1975 and 1995. The Fifers have been wise indeed to shun these disastrous meddlings, which robbed many other places of their pride in local identity. For while Fife has never actually been a separate kingdom, its leaders and its inhabitants often behave as if that is indeed what visitors are privileged to enter as they drive over the Forth and Tay road bridges. With tolls now only at the southern approach to the former and the northern approach to the latter, the Fifers even boast that this truly brings home to travellers how much it is worth paying to enter their proud territory!

And a large and varied territory Fife does indeed occupy within its 115 miles of coastline of which the section from the Forth Railway Bridge in the west to Fife Ness in the East Neuk falls within the scope of this book.

Glimpsed from a train travelling over the Forth Bridge, the first impression of that coast is not a very prepossessing one, as the traveller looks out on what is one of the saddest sights for anyone who loves the sea, a sprawling ugly shipbreaker's yard. This, however, was not just any breaker's, but the site of the famous T.W. Ward's of Inverkeithing, which in its day was one of the largest and most powerful shipbreaking yards in the world, where many fine ships met their end. They included the Royal Navy's famous HMS *Revenge*, HMS *Rodney* and HMS *Royal Sovereign*. Ward's did not only scrap large naval vessels and cargo ships, but also some of the world's finest luxury passenger vessels. These included the White Star Line's twin-funnelled, 774-foot long *Homeric*, which was broken up at Ward's in 1936 when only 11 years old, as a result of the surplus in tonnage brought about by the merger of her owners the previous year with their former rivals Cunard.

Another of the White Star Line's ships, the even more impressive-looking triple-stacked *Majestic*, temporarily cheated a similar fate in May of the same year. *The Magic Stick*, as she was known affectionately to both her crew and her passengers, although she had thousands of miles of steaming capacity still left in her engines and despite the fact that her steel hull was still in top class condition, was sold to Ward's for the similar reason of over-capacity, but after having her three tall funnels reduced in height to allow her to sail under the Forth Bridge, and having arrived off Inverkeithing on what was supposed to be her very last voyage, she was suddenly reprieved. Instead, *Majestic* was ordered to sail on the short distance further up river to the Royal Naval Dockyard at Rosyth, where in the run-up to the Second World War, the Admiralty had suddenly decided that she would make an ideal floating boarding school on which to train 2,000 young cadets from all over Britain.

Ward's had bought *Majestic* from Cunard White Star for the sum of £115,500 but the Admiralty managed to acquire her without any cash changing hands by promising to provide alternative work for Ward's workforce sending 24 old redundant naval vessels to the scrapyard instead. Meanwhile, *Majestic* was quickly refitted for her new role and was then commissioned as HMS *Caledonia*. The 56,551-ton *Majestic* had been the world's largest liner until the launch of the French *Normandie* the year before in 1935 and the launch later the same year on the Clyde of the newly merged Cunard White Star Line's *Queen Mary*. Now having escaped the breakers' hammers, *Majestic* under her new guise as HMS *Caledonia* gained a new claim to fame as the largest vessel of the Gray Funnel Line, as the Royal Navy often used to be known.

For the next three years HMS *Caledonia* proved a highly

successful headquarters for the up and coming officers. Upon the outbreak of hostilities on Sunday 3 September 1939, however, the young sailors were all hurriedly disembarked because the Admiralty feared that HMS *Caledonia* would be one of the enemy's first targets. This was not simply because of her huge size, but because before she became the *Majestic* she had actually been built by the Germans as the Hamburg America Line's *Bismarck* and it had been planned to take the Kaiser on a celebration round-the-world voyage. But the First World War ended in their defeat, his exile and the confiscation of their proudest ship as war reparations, before she ever made her maiden voyage. The Germans had never forgiven being robbed of the pride of their mercantile fleet and the honour of owning the world's largest passenger liner and now their country and Britain were again at war, a revenge air attack by the German Luftwaffe seemed highly possible. This was especially the case as it was known that the Air Attache to the German Embassy, Captain Spiller, had flown low over the *Bismarck* alias the *Majestic* alias HMS *Caledonia* in his Messerschmitt Bf 108B only weeks before on what was at the time described as a summer holiday flight to Scotland with his wife, on which they had landed just up river on the south shore of the Forth at the newly-opened Central Scotland Aerodrome at Grangemouth.

HMS *Caledonia* was therefore hurriedly towed away from Rosyth. It was equally important to ensure that the huge vessel was kept out of the important shipping channel up river to Grangemouth, which for the sake of the war effort had at all costs to be kept clear. So it was quickly decided that HMS *Caledonia* must be beached. She was therefore deliberately grounded. Three weeks later, on 29 September, a mysterious fire broke out on board. The spectacular blaze was seen for dozens of miles around the Forth Valley, making a nonsense of the new blackout regulations. As crowds watched from vantage points in towns and villages along both shores of the river, rumours spread that the Germans had attacked her and set her alight, but there was no truth in this, although for many years some local people claimed that a German secret agent saboteur had managed to get aboard and wartime censorship helped fuel, rather than dampen down, such stories.

Meanwhile, in true British Navy fashion, the work of training the cadets continued uninterrupted and their new shore-based establishment continued to bear the name HMS *Caledonia* until it closed long after the war ended and is still remembered as the name of one of the two function suites at North Queensferry's Queensferry Lodge Hotel. Soon after the fire the Admiralty sold the old *Majestic* back again to Ward's and she was for a second time towed to the yard in Inverkeithing Bay. There the task of breaking up the gigantic vessel proved such a challenge that despite the war demand for metal it took until the summer of 1943 to finally dispose of her huge hull.

The name *Majestic* was also an interesting reminder that all White Star ships had titles ending in 'ic' and that they also owned the ill-fated *Titanic* and the SS *Cedric*, another fine liner which was scrapped by Ward's in 1922. While the White Star Line gave their vessels names ending distinctively in 'ic' their rivals until their merger in 1935, Cunard Line gave all of their ships names ending in 'ia', an equally proud tradition maintained right up until the merger and the subsequent launch of the Queen Mary. It was a Cunarder which was probably the most famous passenger ship ever to end her days at Inverkeithing. She was the mighty 35,000-ton twin-funnelled transatlantic liner *Mauretania* which was withdrawn from service in November 1965. She was the second Cunarder to bear this proud name and interestingly, while the first *Mauretania* was scrapped at Jarrow on the Tyne in 1938, her double-bottomed hull was also eventually towed north to the Forth to be dismantled in 1946.

While the arrival of a large liner at Ward's was always a sad occasion, it was also an exciting one as one of the Forth pilots brought her skilfully into her final berth and her master rang finished with engines for the last time. Soon afterwards there was also the added interest of the auction of all of the fine furniture and fittings from her lounges, dining saloon and other public rooms and local people made many good purchases. Items from the *Mauretania* can still be admired at several places, including the Royal Mackintosh Hotel in Dunbar, and the former Council Chamber in the Town House at Culross, which is now open to visitors as the National Trust for Scotland's information centre in the Royal and Ancient Burgh, while the well-known Woodside Hotel in Aberdour is the proud possessor of the bar from the Royal Mail steamer *Orontes*.

Most ships are now sold to buyers in the Far East, and like

Britain's favourite post-war liner, the Falklands War veteran P & O's *Canberra*, which was known as 'The Great White Whale', meet their end in breakers' yards in Pakistan, India, Korea, China and Taiwan. Ward's is thus reduced even further to the debris-strewn scrapyard of R & M Supplies. The unpolished plaque on their office door states that they are 'Shipbreakers, Scrap Metal Processors and Exporters', but any scrapping which they do is of much smaller vessels than the ones which brought fame to their predecessors, Ward's, in its heyday.

It is, however, through this industrial wilderness that the Fife Coastal Trail winds its way, and it is worth persevering and following the arrows to find the path, which leads up river to North Queensferry and downstream, round the shores of the bay, to Inverkeithing.

It is planned that the Fife Coastal Path will eventually lead right along the shoreline, all the way from the Forth Railway Bridge to the Tay Road Bridge and new sections of this long-distance walk are being regularly developed. To try out the first of them, either take a train and get off at the first station after the Forth Bridge at North Queensferry, with its interesting tiled wall mural erected to mark the bridge's centenary in 1990, depicting ferries, bridges and buildings connected with the famous crossing, or drive across the Forth Road Bridge and take the first exit from the M90 motorway to follow the shore road into North Queensferry.

North Queensferry may not appear to have the immediate charm of its southern neighbour, but the old northern terminal for the ferries does have a lot of history and it is well worth spending a couple of hours discovering it. All three of the local Fife Coastal Walks start at the town's unusual-shaped, stone-built Waterloo Memorial Well, constructed by local sailors to commemorate the end of the Napoleonic Wars in 1815. Water used to gush out of its black wrought iron spout, which is designed in the shape of a lion's mouth. In front is the iron stand which used to hold pails while they were being filled with its fresh water and behind it on the wall of the chamber, where the water used to be stored, there are two other black iron plaques showing a curvaceous maiden riding on the back of a sea creature and a man and woman in each other's arms, but whether they are dancing or squabbling, is hard to decide.

The Waterloo Well also calls for decisions nowadays, because it is the start of three well-signposted and labelled walks. The first guides visitors on a three-quarter mile trail around North Queensferry itself, taking in a view of the town's most famous modern attraction, Britain's top aquarium, Deep Sea World, where visitors enjoy the excitement of walking underwater through a clear plastic tunnel to see the sharks, stingrays and other fish swimming freely above their heads; and its oldest traditional attraction, the Forth Bridge and the old Town Pier, where the ferries originally docked. Later the ferries transferred up river to the Railway Pier, which became famed for its miles of queuing cars, vans and lorries as their drivers swore at the delay while they waited to cross and swithered whether it would really be quicker to abandon the never-ending line of traffic and make the 30-mile detour via the Kincardine Bridge further up river between Clackmannanshire on the north side and Stirlingshire on the south shore of the river.

Today, North Queensferry is much quieter without its waiting ferry traffic and all the pleasanter to explore as a result. Apart from the main features already mentioned the short walk around the town also reveals many pleasant curiosities, ranging from some of the famous Fife forestairs in front of the houses to carved juncture stones above their doors and windows. These old stones bear the initials of the couples who married and made their homes there. One in Post Office Lane is carved with the initials I.M. and M.M. and the date 1776, showing that it has been there ever since this little narrow street was known as North Lane. Around the corner in Helen Place stands Heron House, but it is probably not named after the long-legged bird, but is more likely a corruption of Herring House, a reminder that in the days when North Queensferry was a fishing port, the daily catch used to be stored, salted and smoked in this part of the town.

Another reminder of the fishermen and sailors of North Queensferry is the ruins and gravestones of the churchyard of the chapel of St James, where these very religious, God-fearing sea-going men and their wives and families used to worship. By the entrance gate a carved stone reads: 'This is done by the sailers in North Ferrie, 1752'. Good spelling was obviously not a prerequisite for being a good seaman! The date on the roughly carved inscription probably refers to the building of the gateway in the walls, as the Chapel of St James was already ancient by 1752, as it is known that King Robert the Bruce, of Bannockburn victory fame,

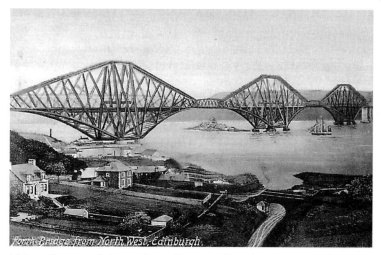

This early view of the Forth Bridge was taken from North Queensferry, clearly showing Inchgarvie in mid-river. The sailing ship appears to have been drawn in by a photographic artist.

gifted it to the monks of Dunfermline Abbey at the beginning of the 14th century. Remnants of the original chapel are built into the north and west walls of the churchyard. A little notice at the gate informs visitors that excavations have revealed skeletons, which, as it leads into the chapel's burial ground, is hardly surprising.

Curving round to the east away from the chapel ruins, the name of Battery Road is a reminder of another of North Queensferry's links to national historic events as it is a reminder of the 17th-century gun emplacement, which Oliver Cromwell's troops had to fight fiercely to defeat, as described later in the chapter on the Inches of the Forth. Battery Road leads right out under the massive girders of the cantilever railway bridge. Standing directly beneath the girders studded with huge rivets, the bridge towers overhead and at one and a half miles in total length, it is easy to appreciate why the Victorians regarded it as the eighth wonder of the world. Just as words beginning in 'S', such as slim, slender, streamlined and silver all seem apt to describe its modern mid-20th century neighbour, the suspension bridge, which now partners it up river, any attempt to describe the railway bridge seems to depend upon words beginning with the solid letter 'M' to capture its appearance, from massive to mighty and from muckle to metal. Finally of course, the words beginning with 'M' must include maroon to give a picture of the red oxide-rich paint which was used for well over a century to paint and protect it up until 1998, when it was finally replaced by a new product originally developed for use out on the North Sea Oil rigs, but which it is promised will maintain the familiar hue. It takes 60 tons of paint to protect the bridge's 145 acres of steel. There are many other famous bridges from London's Tower Bridge to the suspension bridge which spans San Francisco Harbour, but nowhere else in such close proximity can be seen two such fine examples of the distinctive skills of the engineers of two different centuries, as here on the shores of the Forth.

Nowadays directly below the northern cantilever girders, there is a tidy little park complete with picnic tables and a good look-out point. Long before these modern developments, this was the site of North Queensferry's third pier. When bad weather or unfavourable tidal conditions made it impossible for the ferry to dock as it usually did at the Town Pier, this sloping quay and the substantial Railway Pier upstream provided useful alternatives and were known as the catch, or catchment, piers. On stormy rain-lashed days, travellers must have been very relieved to land here.

Behind the pier at the bridge, the green grassy hillside rises steeply and the road leads past two long low modern bungalows to the much older white-harled cottages at the former Royal Naval Signal Station. Today the cottages are in private ownership, but a high unclimbable protective fence still surrounds the signal tower, although it is now disused and has not been operational since the closure on 7 November 1995 of Scotland's Royal Naval Dockyard at Rosyth, when, on an appropriately dreichly mournful day, the ships of the fleet cast off their mooring lines for the very last time and with the rain weeping in sympathy sailed away down river to their new bases at Portsmouth, Devonport and Coulport on Loch Long in the Clyde Estuary. The old naval signal tower is a two-storeyed structure, with the control room on the first floor commanding clear views down river and out over the Firth. On the balconied roof above, the signal lights, which used to control shipping at this narrow part of the river, still stand, but no longer blink out their commands. Down below, the answer phone system at the barbed wired gate still demands that one press it to gain admittance, but now goes unanswered.

North Queensferry's other signal tower is the much more historic stone-built structure known as the Signal House, which has stood sentinel at the head of the Town Pier since it was erected in 1812. The pier itself was designed by the famous engineer John Rennie and was also constructed at this same period, between the years 1810 and 1813. Signal House's eight-sided tower not only provided an ideal look-out position from which to keep watch on the comings and goings of the ferries, its rooms also provided shelter for the boat crews to assemble and for passengers to wait, protected from the weather outside until the next boat was ready to depart to take them across the Forth to continue their journeys to Edinburgh and other places on the south shore of the river. Nearby at the pier head the well-weathered stonework of the little lantern lighthouse, especially on its west side, which takes the full force of the prevailing wind, is evidence of just what wickedly wild conditions these ferry passengers sometimes had to endure.

The fact that there were always travellers coming and going through North Queensferry meant that several hostelries grew up to provide them with hot food and suitably strong refreshments to sustain them on their journeys. A few swift steps inland from Town Pier, on the right-hand side of Main Street, the solidly stone built, grey slate-roofed Albert Hotel still stands and still offers modern visitors a dram or a pint and a suitable snack in its bar or a substantial, well-cooked main meal in its high-ceilinged dining room. Built in 1824 the appropriately old-fashioned looking Albert was renamed in honour of Prince Albert, Queen Victoria's husband and royal consort, after he landed at North Queensferry in 1842. Even earlier than the 19th century, however, it was possible for ferry passengers to obtain food and drink here as the Albert occupies the same site as a much older hostelry, the Hope Tavern. The Hope was often known as Mitchell's Inn, after its landlord, who also owned a fleet of horse-drawn coaches. On the opposite side of the street used to stand the rival Black Cat Inn, which dated back to 1693. Its building, long since converted into private houses, still occupies the site and an initialled juncture stone above one of the windows indicates that its first owners were Thomas Peastie and Bessie Cruach.

North Queensferry continues to be a good place to dine out and in addition to the Albert, the choice includes the attractively traditional Ferrybridge Hotel on the comer of Main Street and, on the shore road leading into the town, the Regent Hotel Group's modernly designed Queensferry Lodge Hotel, whose restaurant windows command panoramic views of the bridges and the river. It also houses a well-stocked tourist information centre operated by Fife Unitary Authority, which offers visitors a full range of services including the intriguingly entitled BABA which stands for Book A Bed Ahead. For those with time to stop and find out more, the Forth Bridges Visitor Centre, on the first floor, is well worth visiting. Set up by a panel of the Historic Engineering Works and Science Associations of the Institute of Civil Engineers, its excellently laid out exhibition provides lots of details about the boats which operated the Queensferry Passage, the bridges, which ultimately replaced them and other plans, including those for a tunnel, which were put forward at different times during the 19th century and first half of the 20th century, as possible alternative ways to cross the Forth.

From all of this food for thought, back to the latest of North Queensferry's eating places, the very innovative Channel Restaurant, situated at 17 Main Street. The brainchild of Andrew Oliver and Sam Taylor, Channel offers an interesting menu of the best of modern Scottish cooking. Open both for lunch and dinner, Channel is particularly pleasant for an evening meal, after which it is an easy stroll down to the pier to see the railway bridge softly illuminated, as it has been by Scottish Power every night since its centenary celebrations, which were attended by Prince Charles, Prince of Wales, in October 1990. His appearance was particularly appropriate as it was another Prince of Wales, Queen Victoria's eldest son, later King Edward VII, who performed the opening ceremony way back in 1890. Unlike his forebear, Prince Charles did not walk on the bridge, but sailed under it aboard P & O Scottish Ferries' *St Clair*, which voyaged south from her usual mainland port of Aberdeen and her usual overnight route to Lerwick in Shetland, especially for the big occasion, which was watched by hundreds of thousands of spectators on either side of the river.

While dinner at North Queensferry allows visitors to admire the lights on the bridge, a lunch-time meal at Channel or one of North Queensferry's other eating places, will set them up well to tackle the two longer Fife Coastal Paths, which, as with the town walk, both commence at the Waterloo Well at the landward end of Main

This First World War postcard view shows the shore of the Forth to the west of North Queensferry, before the construction of the Royal Naval Dockyard at Rosyth. Although the site for what was Scotland's only Naval Dockyard was acquired before the hostilities began in 1914 , it was not completed until the start of the 1920s, so that when the ships of the British fleet visited the Forth during the war years, they were forced to lie off out in the river. Throughout the First World War there was a fear at the Admiralty in London that a German aerial attack by Zeppelin airships, might so damage the Forth Bridge that its naval vessels might be trapped in the upper Forth, unable to reach the Firth and the sea. This worry sometimes led to the ships of the fleet being ordered to anchor downstream off Inchmickery or in Burntisland Bay rather than off Queensferry as they had more usually done in Victorian times before the completion of the railway bridge in March 1890. The fact the bridge survived the war intact, encouraged speedy progress with Rosyth as a naval base in the post-war years. Rosyth Castle was a fortification dating from medieval times and reputed birth place of Oliver Cromwell's mother. Its tower, which still survived being engulfed by the Royal Naval Dockyard, can just be seen in the top quarter of the picture off the tip of the second peninsula. Now with the departure of the navy and Rosyth's return to civilian use, it is hoped that the castle may be re-opened by Historic Scotland, which has carefully preserved its structure.

Street. The walk up the steep brae behind Waterloo Well leads first to another well, this one the Memorial Well. It was restored in 1897 as North Queensferry's tribute to the Diamond anniversary of Queen Victoria's accession to the throne 60 years earlier in 1837 and bears the inscription, 'Restored by Lovers of the ferry for the solace of wayfarers.' North Queensferry seems to have been awash with wells, for although not on any of the signposted walks, a quick walk back down along the foreshore along the intriguingly named King's Way leads to Willie's Well. Immediately behind Queen Victoria's Memorial Well is situated The Water House, which dates from 1787.

The walk then continues to Scaur Hill and Carlingnose Point. The latter is a wonderfully descriptive place name for this quarry-pitted headland, as it means the Witch's Nose! This vantage point offers superb views back up river to the two bridges and south to the Hound Point Oil Terminal. To the east can be seen three islands: nearest the shore just beyond Dalgety Bay is Inchcolm with its historic abbey, much further out due south of Aberdour is Inchmickery with its naval fortifications and in the distance lies the largest of the trio, Inchkeith, topped by its lighthouse. All three are described in the next chapter. On the skyline to the south-east can be seen the rounded green Cramond Island and in the background the silhouette of Edinburgh from the three gasometers on the shore at Granton, inland to the Castle on its rock and beyond to Salisbury Crags and Arthur's Seat.

After admiring all that can be seen, it is worth spending a little longer at Carlingnose Point to look at the rich plant life which has flourished here since quarrying ceased. According to botanical experts, there are many plants not often found on other sites in Fife, including bloody crabesbill, burnet saxifrage and field gentian, as well as the even greater rarity dropwort.

Down below, jutting out from the shore is Carlingnose Pier, which was constructed in 1901 to allow the transportation of ammunitions and other provisions to the gun battery, which had been established out on the island of Inchgarvie to provide protection and defence in case the railway bridge was ever attacked. Today it is the hillside between North Queensferry and Inverkeithing which is very much under attack, as Tilcon is still excavating Cruicks Quarry for the whinstone which it produces and which is in great demand for roadworks and other uses.

There is the option of avoiding all of the quarry action, which is sometimes noisy and dusty, by returning to the main road and taking it across the neck of the headland directly into Inverkeithing, or of sticking to the path which descends and, as it turns, reveals a hidden bay fringed by little Port Laing Beach. It

Smoke belches from the tall funnel of one of the early steam ferries on the Queensferry Passage.

then continues on through a wooded stretch to Cruicks Quarry and on past the wharves where stone and scrap from the shipbreaking yard are loaded, out to the point at West Ness, the latter part of whose place name is derived from the French, *le nez*, meaning 'the nose'. West Ness, as its name suggests, juts out into Inverkeithing Bay and especially in winter is an excellent spot from which to spot the birds which gather there to shelter and feed. Its oozing black muddy slob lands provide a rich hunting ground for waders such as the distinctively feathered oystercatchers and redshank, while out on the water can be seen grebes and goldeneyes in considerable numbers. Walking the entire two and a half mile long path from North Queensferry to Inverkeithing takes about an hour and a half.

Both routes end with a walk up the hill into Inverkeithing itself, which is well worth the detour and the climb away from the shore, as it has a rich and interesting history. Created a Royal Burgh as early as 1165, Inverkeithing flourished thanks to the customs rights which its port possessed. Consisting mainly of two main streets linked by cross wynds, Inverkeithing is a higgledy-piggledy sort of place, but this all adds to its sense of the past. Amongst things of antiquity to be seen are its 18th-century Tolbooth, which contained the local court and jail and the neighbouring unusual

13

eight-sided 14th-century market cross topped by a unicorn, below which those convicted by the court were often punished with a scourging with a long leather lash. Nearby is Fordell's Lodging, the 17th-century town house of the Hendersons of Fordell Castle, which stands between Aberdour and Dunfermline and which in the 1980s gained fame when it was restored by that controversial character, Sir Nicholas Fairbairn, MP.

Of particular interest is Inverkeithing's St Peter's Parish Church, whose somewhat stunted polygonal spire dates from the 14th century. The church actually dates back even further to 1139, when Waldeve, son of Gospatrick, bequeathed it to Dunfermline Abbey, but most of the building to be seen today dates from 1826, when it was rebuilt following a disastrous fire the previous year. The 19th-century church was certainly rebuilt in tremendous style by architect James Gillespie Graham and its Gothic nave and side aisles were reckoned to be able to seat a congregation of one thousand souls. Dating from the original church is the elaborately carved six-sided fount which is believed to have been carefully hidden away at the time of the Reformation to save it from the official vandalism of the Lords of the Congregation who aimed to cleanse places of worship of such Papish ornamentation. The fount was fortunately rediscovered while digging foundations during repair work to the church in 1806 and bears the coat of arms of Annabella Drummond, wife of King Robert II, thus strengthening local claims that Inverkeithing was once a royal residence, possibly from as early as the time of King David I, and that Annabella had her home there when she became a widow.

A plaque in the High Street reminds visitors that Inverkeithing also had links with the Russian royal family through local boy made good, Sir Samuel Greig, whose achievements are illustrated in the town's museum in the 14th-century Priory. Greig was born in 1735 and, as befitted a boy born on the shores of the Forth, took the opportunity offered since the Union of the Parliaments in 1707 to make his career in the British Royal Navy. He served with distinction at the Battle of Quiberon Bay in the great year of British victories on both land and sea, 1759, in the middle of the Seven Years War. Three years later, his bravery was again noted at the successful attack on Havana in Cuba, but although he had by then already gained his master's ticket, the promotion which he sought to being captain of his own ship did not follow. Frustration

The Unicorn, Scotland's original heraldic beast, still looks down from Inverkeithing's ancient Market Cross. Kingdom of Fife Tourist Board.

at continuing to serve as first mate led him to accept an invitation from the Empress, Catherine the Great, for British officers to join her Russian Navy. From being a captain of one of the Russian ships in 1764 his promotion was rapid to the rank of Rear Admiral by 1770, Vice Admiral by 1775 and he became Admiral of the Fleet in 1778. Catherine was delighted with her Admiral from Fife and declared that he transformed what she described as her 'herring fishers' into a modern and efficient navy, in which he found lots of berths for fellow Scottish captains. Catherine rewarded him with the knighthoods of St George and St Anna and, when he paid a short visit to Scotland in 1777, he was honoured by being made a Freeman of Edinburgh, to which he had so often looked out across the Forth from his childhood home in Inverkeithing. In 1788 he commanded the Russian fleet in the war against Sweden. He laid siege to the Swedish navy at Sveaborg and captured the Swedish flagship at the Battle of Hogland. A grateful Catherine honoured him again, this time with knighthoods of St Vladimir and, appropriately, St Andrew. Sadly, he did not have long to enjoy these distinctions, because only three months later he fell ill aboard ship in the harbour at Tallinn in Estonia and died of a fever. Catherine is said to have been devastated with grief at the death of her Scottish hero and ordered that he be given a state funeral at the cathedral in Tallinn and that a gold medal should be struck to commemorate his services to Russia.

While Admiral Greig was abroad in the Baltic, his home port of Inverkeithing declined in importance as its harbour silted up with mud, making it less suitable for the larger sailing ships which were then being built. A contemporary account of the harbour reads:

> The harbour is tolerably good, especially at spring tides, for vessels under 200 tons, but is not now so greatly taken advantage of as formerly. It comprises of an area called the Inner Bay, having an area of about one hundred acres and almost landlocked, the entrance between two small headlands – The East and the West Ness – being contracted to about one furlong (220 yards). At low water this is all an expanse of foreshore, the outer bay broadens rapidly beyond the entrance to the inner bay and measures one and a half miles along a line drawn from North Queensferry on the south west to St David's on the north.

It was to St David's that much of Inverkeithing's former trade moved as it was more conveniently situated for the export of coal from the local pits and one of the earliest railways in Scotland linked it to Fordell Colliery. The rails were made of two layers of wood, one of fir and one of beech, with sleepers underneath at two foot intervals. The wooden coal hutches were hauled by horses and each wagon was capable of handling a load of three tons. When the hutches reached the quayside at St David's the contents were tipped straight into the holds of the colliers which waited to carry their cargoes away down the Firth mainly to London. During the 1830s, however, cargoes of coal from St David's were exported all the way across the Atlantic to the fast-expanding markets in America. According to the Second Statistical

Account of Scotland, the coal shipped from St David's was considered especially good for the new 'steam navigation'.

With this ever-increasing demand for coal, thanks to the development of the Industrial Revolution and the growing use of steam power, the local landowner and owner of Fordell Colliery, Admiral Sir Philip Durham, decided to improve the harbour at St David's to take ships, including the new steamers, of up to 500 tons. An account written at the time describes St David's as having 'a commodious pier at which the loading of coal from pits some distance inland is extensively carried on, the depth of water here being as much as eighteen feet at high tide.'

Admiral Durham's enterprise, however, was not rewarded, rather ironically, because the growth of Scotland's railway network robbed little St David's of its initial advantage, by making it much easier to transport heavy cargoes such as coal overland. The other cargo which Admiral Durham hoped to export through St David's was locally produced salt and to this end he installed a large steam pump to transfer water from the Forth into his pans. Again, however, his timing was wrong, because no sooner was the new pump working than the demand for Scottish sea salt declined, because of the development of the salt mines in Cheshire.

This decline in trade left the area around St David's very cut off. Writing in the Second Statistical Account of Scotland in 1836, the parish minister the Revd Alexander Watt describes the neighbouring village of Dalgety as a very self-contained little community with customs and traditions all of its own. He indicated that this was the case because of the origin of its inhabitants who he suggested had come from Denmark as a result of religious persecution and because many of them had become coal miners, who were thirled, that is bound as serfs to the local collieries. This virtual slavery and the atrocious conditions under which the miners, their wives and their children all worked made them a race apart and according to the Revd Mr Watt they actively discouraged any of the village's young people from marrying outside their own community. This led to inbreeding with its unfortunate consequences and many families shared the same surname, being known simply as the Dalgeties.

At the same time, the neighbouring farm workers who toiled on the surrounding farms were also faring badly because of the new Enclosure System of agriculture which robbed many of them of their jobs. It consisted of the creation of large fenced-in fields, to make room for which many of the farm labourers' cottages were also demolished. At Dalgety the drop in population even led to the demolition of the village school. So determined, however, were the remaining inhabitants that their children should be educated and have the opportunity of a better life, that they clubbed together to open a private school in a house at the foot of the hill near the harbourside at St David's. For every subject which their sons and daughters were taught they paid fees to provide the dominie with a salary, which they claimed proudly was as large as that received by any schoolmaster in the whole of Fife. The local minister had great praise for these parishioners and described them as 'the most sober and civilised of their class anywhere to be found.'

It is intriguing to ponder what these bairns of past centuries from Fordell Estate, who were educated at the little school at St David's, would think about the wonderful opportunities offered to modern youngsters, who come to stay at the Scout Movement's permanent camp site at Fordell Firs, with all of its challenging outdoor activities.

Today the Dalgety Bay area of this stretch of the Forth has thousands of new inhabitants as it is the scene of Scotland's only privately built new town. Rather confusingly, the new houses in the St David's area of Dalgety Bay are being built on the shores of the Forth by a building organisation called Tay Homes. Apart from being blessed with magnificent views across the Firth to Edinburgh, Dalgety is a rather featureless modern development with housing typical of most dormitory commuter towns, the majority of its inhabitants travelling to work each day over the Forth Road Bridge to jobs in the capital. In future it will be even more popular with the completion in the spring of 1998 of its own railway halt on the main line south to Edinburgh and north to Dundee.

Although essentially a very modern development, Dalgety does however still contain some links with the past, including the ruins of St Bridget's Church which was dedicated in 1244 and which had a laird's loft built against its west gable wall in 1610, so that the local laird and his family no longer had to sit amongst their estate workers. Nearby are the remains of Donibristle House or to be more accurate, houses, as it was burnt down and rebuilt on no fewer than three occasions, the last time being in 1858. Donibristle,

The ruins of St Bridget's Chapel, Dalgety Bay, with those of the 17th-century laird's loft in the background. John Docherty.

which can be picked out clearly from the river as consisting of the two older-looking cream buildings, originally belonged to the Abbot of Inchcolm and he and the brothers from the Abbey on the island out in the Firth used to retreat there when their church was attacked by Viking invaders.

At the Reformation, Donibristle and its surrounding lands were given as a secular grant to Sir James Stewart, Lord Doune. It was there that his son and heir, the famous Bonny Earl of Scottish ballad fame was brutally murdered by his enemies, the Earl of Huntly and Gordon of Cluny. Huntly surrounded the house with his men and ordered that it should be set alight. As the blaze swept through the house, the Earl of Moray tried to escape through a secret tunnel. Sadly, he was caught as he emerged on the shore, and was brutally murdered by the water's edge. Today only the chapel, servants' quarters and stables remain, but they give an impression of the scale and the style of Donibristle, when the Morays lived there from the 16th to 19th centuries.

During the Second World War, Donibristle was an RAF fighter

airbase and some of the people who now live nearby claim that the site is haunted. They report that they regularly hear the sound of an aeroplane revving up, taking off and flying out over the Firth, but they never hear it return and suggest that it may be a ghostly reminder of the brave pilots of Donibristle, who sacrificed their lives in missions during the years of the hostilities.

Back down on the coast directly opposite Inchcolm is situated the modern Braefoot Terminal, built in connection with the Mossmorran Gas Processing Plant to which it is connected by a four-mile long pipeline. It has two tanker berths forming an upside down 'Y' shape, running out from the Fife shore, one belonging to Esso and the other to Shell.

One of the pilots who regularly brings the liquid petroleum tankers alongside at Braefoot is Chairman of the Association of Forth Pilots, Captain Alastair Gibson, who has his home in Dalgety Bay. Like all of the Forth Pilots, Captain Gibson is self-employed and since 1988 has worked under contract to Forth Ports Plc. The pilots have their headquarters at Granton, which is manned around the clock, ready to respond to the needs of any vessel sailing into or out of the Forth. Practically all ships sailing up or down the river take a pilot on board, apart from a very small number of vessels, whose captains have passed an examination to prove that they have sufficient local knowledge to navigate these waters. When called out to a ship coming in from the North Sea, the pilots are ferried out on one of three fast pilot launches, each capable of 27 knots, roughly 30 miles an hour. All of the launches are based at Granton, but to save time Captain Gibson is often picked up at Aberdour Harbour just along the coast from his home. As well as providing a swift turn of speed the pilot cutters are also designed to provide a stable platform for the pilots to clamber aboard the waiting ship. This Captain Gibson and his colleagues do by grabbing hold of the Jacob's rope ladder which the ship drops over its side. As law states that pilots must not climb more than 30 feet by ladder, most ships also lower an accommodation ladder for the pilot to complete the boarding procedure.

Once aboard, the pilot goes directly up to the bridge, where he meets the captain and sizes up the condition of the vessel and gains an impression of the experience and ability of the crew he will be working with. While the master of the vessel remains in charge, the Pilot advises on the speed which it should maintain

The Silver Sands at Aberdour are one of the most popular bathing spots on the shores of the Firth and on a fine sunny summer day colourful parasols bring a Mediterranean feel to the Costa Forth. Kingdom of Fife Tourist Board.

and the course it should follow. No doubt it is advice and support which the captains appreciate because the Forth is a tricky river to navigate. Coming in to the berths at Braefoot, for instance, there are several hazards in the shape of rocks, waiting to ensnare the unwary. Those called the Haystack are at least exposed at all states of the tide, but Meadulse Rocks lurk just below the surface. The Haystack is home to a colony of around 100 pairs of cormorants which return every year to nest on it.

For reasons of safety, Braefoot and Mossmorran are strictly out of bounds to the public, but it is possible to resume walking along the coast at nearby Aberdour. At this point the Firth is four and a half miles wide. A Victorian account of the village describes it as 'A sequestered little place with a mild climate. Its good sea-bathing facilities have won for it great popularity as a summer holiday resort.' To this day its famous Silver Sands, to the east of the town out at Hawkcraig Point, are still one of the finest beaches on the Forth and a favourite family attraction each summer. In 1997, the Silver Sands received a Seaside Award from the Tidy Britain group. The waters of the Forth off their shores reached the mandatory standard, according to the Bathing Water Directive, EEC/76/160.

Aberdour has a popular and flourishing boating club which, as well as local members, includes sailing enthusiasts from Edinburgh and further south, attracted over the bridges as much by its friendly atmosphere as by its cheaper rates than those at expensive Port Edgar Marina. Kingdom of Fife Tourist Board.

The Seaside Award slogan is 'Take nothing but photographs, leave nothing but footprints.'

'Aber' means the mouth of the river and Aberdour does indeed stand at the mouth of the Dour Burn, which originally divided it into two distinct burghs, known as Easter and Wester Aberdour. On the bank of the burn stands the historic little St Fillan's Church. It was founded in 1140, from which period the Romanesque chancel dates, while its porch and aisles date from the 17th century. In the 19th century it became a roofless ruin, but it has now been lovingly and beautifully restored. Nearby is the grave of the Revd Robert Blair, who was chaplain to King Charles I. Unfortunately, despite his high position, he fell out with

Archbishop Sharp over his religious views and was banished from St Andrews. He moved to Couston Castle, which used to stand in Aberdour Parish. There he found peace and sanctuary until his death and subsequent burial in the little kirk graveyard.

Adjacent to St Fillan's is Aberdour Castle, which still belongs to the Earl of Morton's family. Unfortunately, the castle was accidentally destroyed by fire in the early 18th century, but even in its ruined state it has a distinctly grand feel about it and is worth visiting. A typically Scottish L-shaped mansion, which was added to the original castle to provide the Douglas Mortons with more comfortable accommodation in the 17th century, survived the 'disastrous blaze and is also worth exploring, but most enjoyable of all on a warm summer's day are the delightfully colourful terraced gardens, one of whose unusual features is a 16th-century bee-hive shaped doocot. It had nesting boxes for around 600 well-fed pigeons, some of whom were culled each winter to ensure that the Morton family could enjoy some fresh doocot pie or pigeon casserole as a pleasant change from the usual winter diet of salt mutton and beef in brine. Conical doocots such as these are amongst the oldest in Scotland and Chief Inspector of Historic Buildings, Mr John Hulme, says that its unusual sharply tapering form makes the Aberdour Castle garden's one of particular interest.

Aberdour seems to specialise in beautiful gardens, because those at the village's immaculately maintained railway station won it the title of best kept station in the whole of Scotland for no fewer than 11 years in succession.

Next stop along the line from Aberdour is Burntisland, whose large stone-built station seems out of all proportion to the size of the little town which it serves. This is, however, a reminder of just what an important port Burntisland was when it was a busy ferry terminal on the main route to the north. Passengers used to disembark at the Prince Albert Pier, built in 1844, right next to the station, cross to its busy platforms and catch the next train on the North British Railway's new line to Dundee and Perth. From 1850 onwards Burntisland even enjoyed the fame of being the Fife port for the world's very first train ferry, with the first roll-on roll-off berth to serve it, until it was made redundant by the completion of the Forth Railway Bridge in 1890.

Burntisland's history, however, dates back much further than the Victorian railway age. It is a Royal Burgh and Mary Queen of Scots stayed there in Rossend Castle, just to the west of the town, in 1563, while she was making the royal progress to St Andrews. It was a night which Her Majesty definitely did not forget in a hurry because it was on that occasion that the infatuated Chastleard rashly forced his way into her bedchamber, an offence for which he was subsequently executed! Rossend, which was formerly known simply as Burntisland Castle, has now been restored and commands superb views across the town's docks to the Firth beyond.

The port of Burntisland is now operated very efficiently by Forth Ports Plc and is equipped with two powerful modern cranes whose grabs unload several small bulk carriers each week. Their cargoes of bauxite supply Alcan's plant on the western outskirts of the town. The factory was founded before the start of the First World War by British Aluminium. It became Burntisland's largest employer with, at its peak, 500 men and women involved in aluminium smelting and turning out aluminium by-products known as superfines which were in demand in the manufacture of goods as varied as toothpaste, pottery and fire retardants. For almost 70 years the works' Red Mud Pond was a familiar local landmark, until it was filled in in 1982, the same year that the factory was taken over in a merger by Alcan.

Burntisland has indeed had a rich industrial past, with quarrying for limestone, coal-mining, whisky distilling and herring fishing all also contributing to the local economy. For a period of just over 20 years at the end of Queen Victoria's reign, Burntisland even enjoyed its own oil bonanza. This came about when it was discovered that the oil-bearing shale rock, the refining of which was pioneered by Scottish inventor James 'Paraffin' Young across the Forth in West- and Mid-Lothian, dipped under the river and occurred again in Fife at Binnend Farm on the outskirts of the town. Mining began at Binnend in 1878 and soon the little farm was transformed into a bustling industrial site with long low lines of brick-built miners' rows to house the workforce and their families. Unfortunately there was a serious fire at the oil works in 1892 and it never regained its former prosperity, production ceasing in 1905.

It was shortly after this, towards the end of the First World War, that shipbuilding, which had taken place on a small scale, for around 400 years, became an important industry in the town and over the next 50 years the Burntisland Shipbuilding Co. won a fine reputation for the trim little cargo vessels which it built at its yard to the west of the Old Dock. A beautiful model of one, the scarlet and black funnelled *Maltese Prince*, which the yard built for the Prince Line of London, today still takes pride of place in the town's museum, situated above the library in the main street.

Once launched, new ships were berthed in the Old Dock for fitting out. During the Second World War the Burntisland yard even turned out several small aircraft carriers as its contribution to the war effort. These small auxiliary carriers were specifically constructed to act as escorts for convoys crossing the North Atlantic and, as well as providing air cover to guard the other ships, were cleverly designed below the flight deck to transport much-needed cargoes of grain to ease the bread rationing in wartime Britain. The Burntisland Museum also has a cut-away model of one of these ingeniously built vessels, *The Empire MacKendrick*, which clearly shows these features.

Once peace returned the yard continued to prosper but during the 1960s, in common with all British shipyards, which were undercut by foreign yards using cheap labour, it found it increasingly difficult to obtain orders. Shipbuilding ended in 1968, but the yard was later bought over by Burntisland Engineering, which carried out work connected with the North Sea oil industry

In addition to all of this industry, throughout the first 60 years of this century Burntisland also managed to establish a reputation as a popular holiday resort and to this day the largest open-air travelling funfair in Scotland takes place on the Links during the summer months and it still attracts large crowds especially during the traditional Glasgow Fair fortnight, from the middle to the end of July. So strong is Burntisland's connections with Scotland's famous show people that a large, well-illustrated display in the town's museum is dedicated to them.

Roll up, roll up, roll up as the showground barkers used to shout, and enjoy a free taste of the colourful amusements of former years. One of the most popular was the 50-foot high lighthouse-style structure of the helter skelter. Indeed, at the shows on Burntisland Links, it was known as the Lighthouse Slip or the Penny On the Mat, from the cost of one of the little coconut carpets on which participants sat to come hurtling round and round and round, to come finally down to earth at the foot of the spiral with a bump. Up until the outbreak of the First World War in 1914, the helter skelter was one of the two largest money spinners on the ground, as the show folks called the seaside site, along with the colourful roundabout with its beautiful individually hand-painted horses, which the showmen called the Gallopers. The first Gallopers ride was built in King's Lynn in the middle of Queen Victoria's reign by the Savage family. They were introduced to the Burntisland fairgoers by two well-known show families, the Burtons and the Lovetts, and these steam-driven rides, or carousels as the Americans called them as in the famous musical of that name, gained great popularity. In Britain, Gallopers always turned in a clockwise direction so that riders could mount their wooden steeds from the correct side and this is still the case with all rides in this country. Particularly appropriate for Burntisland's seashore fairground, sway boats were also a popular attraction.

As well as rides, the shows at Burntisland, just as today, also featured stalls at which 'punters', as the show folk called the public, could try their luck at winning prizes. Many of the prizes were pottery figurines and these were known as 'fairings'. Today these cheap fairground prizes are valued as antiques. The show folk also had their own terms for the differently shaped stalls. The long rifle ranges and other oblong stalls such as darts and throw the ball in the pail were all known as 'sides' as they always lined the sides of the 'ground', thus giving rise to the term, 'side shows', but that was one which the real showmen never used. All round stalls, from the roll-a-penny stall to the circular win-a-gold-fish attraction were known as 'hooplas', not just the one which featured that ever-popular game.

Features of summer fairs at Burntisland in Victorian times and right on until after the First World War were the booths around the edge of the 'ground' featuring live attractions ranging from Paulos Varieties with their lithesomely attractive girl acrobats to freak shows luring in the 'punters' in these much less politically correct times, to see such strange sights as bearded ladies and even mermaids! Particularly popular were the fortune tellers amongst whom one of the most successful at Burntisland was Pheasant Boswell. She was usually billed as 'The Phenomenal Phezzie' and her two younger sisters, Subie and Norah, continued touring Scotland's fairgrounds long after other live acts abandoned life on the road.

Another live attraction, which continued to be a visitor to Burntisland every summer until the start of the Second World War, was the boxing booth, where the more daring of the holidaymakers tried to recoup their expenses by taking up the challenge of the fairground professionals. Amongst the most famous of these fairground boxers was the self-styled Professor James Lavin, who came from Stirling and who continued appearing at Burntisland until 1910 when, at the grand old age of 73, he led a team of veterans ready to take on allcomers.

More safely, try your luck at the coconut shy or linger at the sweet stall. These were the days long before candy floss and ice-cream cones, but fair patrons did not go hungry, because the quaintly named 'panham stall' kept them supplied not with fried ham, but sugar hearts, brandy snaps and gingerbread men. The crowds who flocked to the circus probably bought brown paper bags full of these tasty delights, before taking their seats on the crowded tiered benches to watch the horses, lions and elephants, which had earlier paraded through the streets of the town, as the black and white photographs on the museum's walls still show.

The circus which most often entertained the Burntisland holiday crowds was Ord-Pinders, which, unlike most touring circuses, which moved around the country as an individual attraction, usually appeared alongside the shows. Ord-Pinders was the only Scottish circus with a big top with two king poles and as Pinders Royal Number One Circus, it survived well into the 1960s. The Burntisland shows also often used to feature animals in a mobile zoo called a menagerie and as side-show acts in individual booths. One of the most famous of these was the performing lion brought to the town by the so-called Buffalo Bill. The real Buffalo Bill did come to Britain from the United States during the 1870s, but the huge success of his wild west show encouraged many imitators and the Buffalo Bill who appeared with his lion on the Links at Burntisland was probably Buffalo Bill Kayes.

Burntisland also has a much more solemn and religious side to its history. Originally, the lands on which it stands belonged to the monks of Dunfermline Abbey. In 1541, King James V, shortly before his death the following year at Falkland Palace, decided that he wished to rededicate Burntisland as a Royal Burgh and in order to do so gave the Abbey the rents of some other lands in Fife. One of the conditions which he attached was that Burntisland should build for itself a church. Unfortunately he did not provide the funds for this costly project. In the end, the Provost of Burntisland, John Clephane, went to the Convention of Royal Burghs to seek financial assistance. By the time sufficient money was raised the religious scene in Scotland had changed dramatically and Roman Catholicism had been replaced by Protestantism. Thus Burntisland's new church, when it was eventually built between the years 1592 and 1595, became the first post-Reformation place of worship to be built in the whole country and the different approach to worship resulted in the most unusually shaped parish church, which still stands high on its hilltop site overlooking both town and river to this day. Its square design was deliberately chosen with its pulpit in the middle to stress that, unlike under the old Catholic order which accorded the priest a privileged position before the high altar, under the new Protestant faith, all worshippers were equal in the eyes of God.

The Parish Church is a substantial stone-built two-storey edifice, with a rather Dutch-looking eight-sided central tower and it is, in fact, said to have been modelled on Amsterdam's famous North Church, where the Protestant faith had flourished some years before it took root in Scotland. Six years after the completion of Burntisland's fine new kirk, an unusual distinction came its way, when it was chosen in 1601 to house the General Assembly of the Church of Scotland. Some say that this great honour came to Burntisland because King James VI, who always personally presided rather than entrusting proceedings to the Lord High Commissioner as Her Majesty the Queen does nowadays, had suffered a fall from his horse and because of his injuries did not fancy the long ride to St Andrews; others that he did not wish to make a stormy crossing of the Forth and face an even stormier reception in Edinburgh.

That year's General Assembly in Burntisland turned out to be a very important one, because not only did the King re-affirm his belief in the Solemn League and Covenant, but he went on to call for the revision of the English version of the scriptures. The result was the subsequent publication of the famous Authorised King James Version of the Bible. By the time it appeared in print in 1611, the Union of the Crowns had taken place upon the death of Queen Elizabeth in 1603 and so Jamie had also become King James I of England. It began, therefore, with a pompous dedication to 'The

Most High and Mighty Prince James, by the Grace of God, King of Great Britain, France and Ireland, Defender of the Faith', but thereafter its authors' beautifully phrased passages delighted our ears well until the 1960s, when the production of several stark new modern translations robbed worshippers of any mention even of 'the Babe wrapped in swaddling clothes'.

The Burntisland kirk, which played such a major role in church history, is considered one of the finest post-Reformation churches in Scotland and, for anyone interested in the Firth of Forth, is particularly well worth a visit to admire the Sailors' Loft. All of the ancient trade guilds in Burntisland had their own seats here in the parish church, which is dedicated to St Columba, but, as befitted their status in the town, the Sailors' Loft is particularly impressive. It is reached by an outside flight of stone stairs and above the doorway, as above the front entrance to the church, there is carved in the masonry an upturned anchor, which indicated that its worshippers were truly anchored in God. Inside, there are eight painted panels and each gives a fascinating glimpse into the lives of Burntisland's 17th-century mariners, from the ships on which they sailed to the nautical instruments such as the cross-staff and astrolabe with which they navigated on their frequent voyages across the North Sea to Scandinavia, the Low Countries and beyond. Here it is depicted how sailors in the 1600s coiled ropes into six foot lengths called fathoms and here is shown one of the burgh's master mariners looking splendid in his forked-tailed coat, his bow-tie and his shoes with their decorative rosettes. He is obviously a man of substance and it is not hard to imagine him like Antonio on the Rialto in Venice in Shakespeare's *The Merchant of Venice*, 'many a time and oft' waiting on the Burntisland quayside for his ships to come home at the end of their successful foreign voyages.

Back down in the churchyard there lie the graves of many of the town's sailors, but sadly it is often not possible to examine their interesting tombstones, as on weekdays, as is the case with an increasing number of Scottish churches, not only is the building locked, but the grounds as well, to protect them from vandalism. This is indeed a sad comment on the state of Scottish society and particularly sad that the majority must be denied their right to visit, rather than the authorities catching and having the courage to effectively punish the few whose bad behaviour causes the problem. How very different from the way in which the kirk elders and their church officer, the redoubtable beadle, ensured that miscreants were promptly dealt with at the 'cutty' or repentance stool, in the times when the church was built.

Not all of Burntisland's sailors, of course, were buried in the kirkyard; shipboard life was dangerous and several of the town's vessels were lost at sea. There are even several wrecks as close to shore as the shallow waters of Burntisland Bay. One of the most dramatic of these disasters involved no lesser a person than King James VI and I's son, the ill-fated King Charles I. Charles succeeded his father in March 1625, on the night when a vicious gale swept up the Firth, destroying amongst other things the famous Moat Pit at Culross, which had up until then been considered one of the wonders of the age. This mad March gale was seen as a dark portent for the reign of the new monarch and so it did in fact turn out to be. Similar inclement weather followed King Charles on his first and only visit to Scotland in 1633, by which time Burntisland had been protected by a town wall, a sign of the port's importance at the time. The monarch and his entourage came to the burgh towards the end of his royal progress through his northern kingdom, however, simply as a convenient point to board a fleet of ferries to carry them back south across the Forth. With a wind whipping in from the south-west, the local ferrymen were not at all keen to put out into the Firth, but Charles was tired of his royal tour and anxious to return to the comparative comforts of Holyrood Palace only six miles away in Edinburgh, whose lights he could just make out flickering a welcome on the Lothian shore. He therefore demanded that they set sail. They did, and His Majesty reached the safety of Leith, but one of the accompanying boats, *The Blessed*, carrying several of his courtiers and all of the gold and other rich gifts which he had received at his Scottish coronation, did not, and sank out in Burntisland Bay, thus giving Scotland its own version of England's King Alfred's disastrous crossing of the Wash. Over the years there have been several attempts to recover the royal treasure, but even the most recent high-tech bid in 1995 yielded nothing of value.

Another wreck off Burntisland which also frequently attracts the attention of divers is that of one of the Royal Navy's first aircraft carriers, HMS *Campania*, which sank during a sudden gale on 5 November 1918, just six days before the end of the First World War.

Burntisland's third, and probably best-known, link with tragedy comes upon leaving the town and climbing up to the high point on the hill behind the shore between it and Pettycur. This was the route which King Alexander III followed on a wild and windy March night in the year 1285. His Majesty had been attending a council meeting of his nobles in Edinburgh, but when it ended, affairs of state were replaced in his mind by affairs of the bedchamber. For, following the untimely death of his first wife, Queen Margaret, Alexander had recently remarried. This time he had chosen as his bride the young daughter of the Spanish Count of Dreux, the stunningly beautiful raven-haired, dark-eyed Yolette and it was the talk of the Scottish court that he simply could not wait to be re-united with her at Kinghorn Tower, which was then one of the royal residences in Fife.

So, despite warnings about the weather he left the safety of the castle at Edinburgh and rode to the Queensferry. There he found the ferrymen reluctant to put to sea, but a rich reward persuaded them and, despite a storm-tossed crossing, he safely reached the other side and disembarked at Inverkeithing. From there he spurred his horse and rode through the darkness past Aberdour and Burntisland. At last, tired, soaked and exhausted from the battering wind and driving rain he began the steep climb up the eastern slope of Kinghorn Ness. Then, just as he crested the rise and was almost within sight of the lights of the tower, where Yolette waited anxiously for him, his horse stumbled. In the pitch blackness, Alexander struggled to regain control of his terrified mount, but to no avail. Seconds later, both the horse and its royal master plunged over the cliff to their deaths. The tragedy was not discovered until the following morning, when a local man, Murdoch Schanks, who is said to have been outlawed from Kinghorn for his criminal deeds, chanced to wander along the cliff top, shortly after dawn. Something behind a rock, which ever since has been known as the Black Stane, attracted his scavenging eye. He clambered down and found the bodies of the horse and the king. Six hundred years after Alexander's untimely death plunged Scotland into years of turmoil over the royal accession to the throne, a monument was finally erected beside the coast road. The inscription on it reads: 'To The Illustrious Alexander III, The Last of Scotland's Celtic Kings, who was accidentally killed near this spot.'

DISCOVERING THE FIRTH OF FORTH

With such strong royal connections, it has sometimes been
suggested that Kinghorn takes its name from the sound of the royal
hunting horn, which sounded on days when the royal chase rode
out over the surrounding Fife countryside from Kinghorn Tower.
Although this may have been true and although the little town
was indeed a royal burgh, it is more likely, however, that its name
is derived from the Celtic *Kingorm*, meaning the Blue Headland,
as from a similar derivation the Cairngorm Mountains take their
name. Certainly Kinghorn Ness, the latter word derived from the
French, *nez* meaning 'nose', as in Blackness and Bo'ness further
up the Forth, rising sharply between Pettycur and Kinghorn and
dominating the whole of the coastline of the Firth at this point,
would seem to give strong credence to this view.

Pettycur, with its comparatively sheltered little harbour, was for
long as important as its near neighbour Kinghorn three-quarters
of a mile to the north. For, as several old roadside milestones still
remind visitors, distances in this part of Fife were measured from
Pettycur, because it was from there that one of the Forth ferries
plied across the Firth to Leith. The Pettycur ferry was a small sailing
vessel and the crossing from the little Fife port was long and often
stormy. During Victorian times, therefore, as roads began slowly
to improve, the attraction of a ferry crossing so far down the Firth
began to decrease and travellers preferred to ride on to
Burntisland, where the six mile crossing to Granton was both
shorter and faster, especially after the introduction of a more
reliable steam ferry on this route in the early 1840s. During the
next few years the number of passengers using the Pettycur ferry
declined rapidly and it sailed for the last time in 1848.

Ships, however, continued to put into Pettycur Harbour because
a small glassworks was developed to take advantage of the fine
silver sand on the shores of Pettycur Bay and sea transport
provided a convenient method to transport its products. Today
Pettycur is a popular holiday spot with caravan enthusiasts, whose
mobile homes crowd the slopes of Kinghorn Ness where one of
the two holiday campsites opened a large modern leisure complex
for the 1998 season. Rather than look at the caravans, however,
look back and enjoy the spectacular sweeping view up river and
across the Forth, past Inchkeith Island to the Edinburgh skyline
with the castle and Arthur's Seat both clearly visible. As dusk falls,
the view of the lights on the Lothian coastline is particularly

attractive, with, nearer at hand, the intermittent sweep of the light out in the river on Inchkeith guiding ships through the growing darkness.

Like Pettycur with its large caravan parks, Kinghorn has a reputation for quiet family holidays. It was at its busiest from the 1920s to the 1950s, with families arriving mainly by train at its little railway station high above its tiny esplanade. From the station wealthier holiday-makers took the little town's one ancient black taxi down the steep hill to the Bayview Hotel, whose brochure informed them that its 'dining room is excellently situated with commanding sea views', while the less well-heeled lugged their suitcases to the neighbouring boarding houses, where the Fife landladies provided them with 'bed and full Scottish breakfast'. Those arriving in the immediate post-war years had to remember to surrender their ration books upon arrival to obtain the promised porridge and bacon and egg, but spam and tomato sandwiches were available 'off the ration' at the little seaside cafe situated in a wooden hutted building at the foot of the rocks. From the tearoom, steeply slanting paths led up to the cliff top, where games of tennis and putting could be enjoyed, but the real joy of holidays in Kinghorn lay down on its sandy beach, which had the added attraction of lots of rocky pools in which to catch crabs, hunt for starfish and sea urchins and enjoy sailing model boats and little white-sailed, scarlet and bright blue-hulled yachts.

For those with half a crown to spend there were boat trips round the bay, but the days when one of the paddle steamers of the Forth Towing Company or the Galloway Saloon Steam Packet Company nosed into the old stone pier had been ended by the Second World War. Last of the Forth steamers to call at Kinghorn was the popular *Fair Maid*. Built by McKnight's of Ayr in 1866 and launched as *The Madge Wildfire*, she was already over 40 years old when she began her life on the Forth after being bought by the Forth Towing Company of Grangemouth. For many years the *Fair Maid* was based at the West Pier, Leith, from where she sailed across the Firth to Aberdour and Kirkcaldy and up river to Kincardine and Alloa. But on Saturdays she was often chartered for Sunday school outings from Bo'ness and Grangemouth and many of the older inhabitants of both towns still recall their trips as children aboard her to Burntisland and Kinghorn.

With the outbreak of war in 1939 the *Fair Maid* was taken over by the Admiralty, as she had been during the First World War, and by the time peace returned she was fit only to make her last voyage to the breakers yard at Troon.

Amongst the voyages aboard the *Fair Maid* which are most remembered were those Saturday ones when her decks were crowded with bairns and their parents on Sunday school trips. These summer Saturday church outings did start up again in the late 1940s but were by then made by train, until in the 1950s the relaxation of petrol rationing made it possible for their participants to arrive by bus. Either way, these Saturday afternoon invasions of day trippers were welcomed by the Kinghorn shopkeepers whose High Street premises did a brisk trade in new-style plastic spades and pails, green and red fishing nets on long bamboo canes and little wooden model boats, but were equally detested by the children of the resident holiday families, who deeply resented these temporary intruders.

Saturday afternoons were therefore times to shun the sands and set off on inland expeditions to try to discover the remains of Kinghorn Tower, where Queen Yolette had waited in vain for her ill-fated royal husband. The tower, which was also sometimes known as Glamis Tower, had stood on the high ground to the north of the High Street and had been a royal castle since the time of King William the Lyon, who reigned from 1166 to 1214. In the latter half of the 14th century it was conferred by King Robert II upon his son-in-law, Sir John Lyon, whose eighth descendant became Earl of Kinghorn in 1606. One of his descendants in turn became Earl of Strathmore. Despite such a distinguished pedigree, however, the ruins of Kinghorn Tower were never unearthed by any of the Saturday afternoon explorers, nor by the more serious historians who have since tried to locate them. Where the tower stood and how it disappeared so completely is therefore a mystery, which author and well-known Scottish actor Michael Elder might well have incorporated into one of his stories, as he so successfully did the adventures of the childhood explorers in his book *The Affair at Invergarroch*, which so vividly brings back to life these post-war holidays in Kinghorn.

While Kinghorn is today seen mainly as a holiday and residential town, it did in the past have several small industries, including linen weaving and bleaching, a candle works and a glue factory. Best known, however, was the shipbuilding yard which belonged latterly to Scott and Company. The yard was founded originally in 1863 by John Key of Kirkcaldy, where he owned a large and prosperous engineering works. At Kinghorn, Mr Key used the marine engines, which he produced in Kirkcaldy, to power iron-hulled ships. The largest, which he built in 1867 was a 2,000 ton vessel for the famous Peninsular and Oriental Steamship Company. In the style which P & O still maintains today with *Arcadia*, *Oriana*, *Victoria* and the *Princess* 'Love Boats' of its American division, the Kinghorn-built vessel had luxurious accommodation for 105 first-class passengers, plus slightly less grand cabins for a further 50 in second class. Powered by a 400 horse-power engine she was 280 feet long with a beam of 36 feet and a draught of 28 feet.

In 1868 the Kinghorn yard had the distinction of building the first iron-hulled, steam-powered whaling ship for the Arctic trade. To ensure the 608-ton vessel was as safe as possible for the dangerous business in which she was to engage, in freezing cold northern waters, Key constructed her with six separate watertight compartments and reinforced her hull to withstand the pressures of the ice floes among which she would work. One hundred and forty-five feet long and with a beam of 30 feet and a draught of $18^1/_2$ feet, although she had a coal-fired engine, she was also barque-rigged to allow her to economise by using any available wind on her long northern voyages to whale-hunting grounds as far away as the fjords of Greenland. Once completed on the slipway at Kinghorn she was launched as *The River Tay* for her owners were Gilroy Brothers and Company of Dundee. At first there was considerable scepticism among the experienced whaling experts that the noise of her propeller would scare away the whales before her harpooner could catch them, but in her first season she proved very successful, her speed allowing her to complete two Arctic voyages compared to the sail-powered whalers' one. *The River Tay*, however, came too late to save the Scottish whale oil industry, which declined as a result of over-hunting and the introduction of gas lighting, which reduced demand for its products.

From 1870 on, the ships which the Kinghorn labour force of up to 350 men built were mainly small iron-hulled coasters from one to five hundred tons and figures for the early 1890s show that the yard had an output of up to eight of these little vessels each year.

DISCOVERING THE FIRTH OF FORTH

Behind Kinghorn lies Kinghorn Loch, which was for many years a popular and safe venue for water skiing, with many who learned there eventually progressing on to enjoy their sport on the waters of the Forth.

From Kinghorn the journey by road to Kirkcaldy takes only minutes, but it is tempting to wait at the station to make the journey by rail in order to emulate that most famous of Fife folk characters, the legendary 'Boy In The Train' of Mabel Smith's well-known poem. Its verses appear at the start of the chapter on Kirkcaldy, but now it is time to take to the water to explore the famous Inches of the Forth.

CHAPTER 2

AFOOT ON THE INCHES

The Jewel of the Forth and The Iona of the East are two titles often used to describe Inchcolm, the most easily accessible of the islands in the Firth. Neither name is an exaggeration. Inchcolm is indeed a little emerald gem of an island and, seen on a sunny summer's day, occupies a perfect setting in the surrounding sparkling blue waters of the Forth. It also has a religious past dating back almost as far as that of Iona, but intriguingly much less well known.

To step ashore on tiny Inchcolm therefore carries the promise of adventures to rival the childhood feeling of excitement at discovering a split new Enid Blyton Famous Five novel on the library shelves. It is definitely the kind of island which George and Timmy and the rest of the Five would have felt compelled to explore, starting with its ruined, but well-preserved, abbey on its hilltop site overlooking the harbour cove. Inchcolm's religious links, however, go back even further than the oldest stones of its church or surrounding monastery buildings, whose foundations were laid in the 12th century.

The island takes its name from the Gaelic word *inch* meaning an island and from St Colm about whom the only thing that is known is that he was a contemporary of St Columba. Equally little is known about the early religious history of the island, but from the earliest times it was apparently recognised as a holy place, because the Danes defeated by Macbeth at the Battle of Kinghorn, slightly further down river, paid gold to be allowed to bury their slain warriors on its shores. Could the strange-shaped hog-backed tombstone which lies to the west of the church mark the last resting place of one of these Viking chiefs?

By the time of these burials, Inchcolm was already the lonely haunt of holy men, who found there the solitude and sanctuary to lead the life of hermits. Most famous of the hermits was the one who found himself with a royal guest, when he gave sanctuary to King Alexander I and several members of his retinue, when a fierce gale forced them to seek shelter during a storm-tossed crossing of the Forth. The hermit's cell must have been crowded, as it is less than six metres long and only one and a half metres wide and about the same height. The king and his courtiers were stranded within its narrow confines for three days, during which time the hermit shared with them his meagre diet of shellfish and milk from his cow. In gratitude, Alexander promised to build a monastery, which he subsequently gave to the Black Fathers of the Augustine Order.

Alexander did not, however, live long enough to see the monks installed in his new abbey, because he died in 1124 around the time when work began on its construction on the island. His successor, King David I, placed Inchcolm under the guardianship of Bishop Gregory of Dunkeld in Perthshire and it was dedicated to the memory of St Columba. Its earliest surviving charter is dated 1162, by which time the monks were already in residence under the rule of Prior Brice, and Bishop Gregory transferred the responsibility for the property to him.

The earliest monastic church consisted simply of a little nave and chancel, fragments of which remain in the ruins of the much more sizeable monastery, which grew up around them. These solid stone buildings tell us much about the day-to-day life of this religious community on their island in the Forth.

Start in the perfectly preserved chapter house, because it was here at the start of each new day, immediately after the earliest of the services, that the brothers gathered to read a chapter of the rules of their order as laid down by St Augustine and to discuss the discipline and daily routine of their sheltered lives. Sit on one of the three seats in the east wall from which the abbot, prior and sub-prior conducted the business of the day. Look across to where the dozen to 15 canons and any lay brothers in residence sat on the stone bench raised one third of a metre above the floor, awaiting their instructions about the work and prayer for the day ahead. At this time too, the discipline of the monastery on Inchcolm was imposed, from extra prayers for any brother who had been tardy in descending the night stair from the dormitory at the start of the dawn service, to corporal chastisement for any who had committed a more serious misdemeanour.

On a happier note, climb the dozen or so steps from the dorter, as the monks did, up to the warming house above, which as its name suggests had originally the only fireplace in the entire monastery. Imagine the welcome warmth of its flames and, in the middle of the floor, notice the Polo Mint hole, like the centre of one of the monk's tonsure haircuts through which a light could be lowered. Like the monks, move on to the frater or dining hall, with its pleasant views across the water to the Lothian shore, pausing to rinse your hands in the sink and, as you imagine breaking your fast with the food prepared in the kitchen at the west end, listen to the words of the Bible as it is read from raised pulpit which stood in the alcove lit by the window. Remember again how the monks clearly believed that cleanliness was next to godliness and the need for hygiene, as you follow them out to the reredorter. Originally, this latrine was one of the first real water closets in Scotland as it was regularly flushed by the waters of the incoming tide, but today the waters of the Firth appear to have receded, a 'wee' problem which the early monks appear also to have encountered as there is evidence that they too had to alter the plumbing arrangements at least once during the 14th or 15th century.

But do not linger too long, for now the work of the day is at hand and it is time to clean the guest hall and sweep the outside stair, which was the original means of entry for visitors. The view from the guest hall windows is of the garden to the west, where there are also many chores to be done. Time must also be found for prayer and meditation, for which the covered walk around the stone-flagged cloisters provided suitable shelter. Opposite the east entrance notice the cresset or oil-burning lamp, but before it is lit, as the evening light fades, there is time to step out onto the grass of the garth, perhaps there to enjoy a short game of bowls. But by nine o'clock, even on a June evening, when the white nights, as they are called, are at their shortest and when the clear blue light lingers longest, it is time to go to bed either in the long vaulted dorter or dormitory, or to enjoy the greater privacy of the abbot's lodging with its parlour and its own toilet. No matter which, the bell will toll all too soon for matins. At this early hour of the new morning appreciate the inside night stair which leads down into the church, which was much altered after the English attacked the monastery in 1384. According to a contemporary account, the church was only saved from total destruction by a miracle when the fire, which the attackers had set, was blown back upon them by a sudden and fortuitous change of wind, which ensured that the flames and smoke almost suffocated them and saved the building. Climb the tight turnpike stair which spirals to the top of the tower and you can look out over the entire scene.

Another part of the monastery still to visit, which was changed through the years, was the hospital. Originally one long, draughty ward, it was later divided into four chambers. Fireplaces were also introduced to provide greater comfort for the patients and at the same time the fireplaces were added to the abbot's lodging, the guest hall and the dining room.

Worship continued at Inchcolm monastery until the Reformation in the 1560s and the well-preserved state of the buildings since then owes much to its island site, which made it difficult for plunderers and vandals to carry off its stones, but during its earlier history its isolated island position was also a hazard. Its monks had on several occasions to seek safety on the mainland when the English invaded, including the time when the church was almost destroyed by fire in 1384. The island was last attacked after the Scottish defeat at the Battle of Pinkie in 1547, when it was garrisoned for a time by English troops under the command of the Duke of Somerset.

It seems strangely appropriate, therefore, that the island's other historic remains are of a military nature, being the army defences installed during the First and Second World Wars.

For decades their concrete and brickwork have been allowed to slowly crumble away, but now thanks first to the enthusiasts who set up the Fortress Study and now to the resulting Defence of Scotland Project, which has the full backing of Historic Scotland, they and hundreds of other 20th-century military sites are at last being surveyed with a view to protecting and preserving the most interesting. Thanks to their island setting, the defences on Inchcolm definitely fall into the latter category and so it seems probable that they will be turned into a showpiece attraction. While this is to be welcomed, it will inevitably mean that, because of health and safety requirements and the threat of being sued by a visitor who so much as stumbles, Historic Scotland will have to install guard rails and even, 'no go areas', so in the meantime take advantage of the fact that it is still possible, at your own risk, to explore freely.

Start by walking through the darkness of the cunningly constructed bricklined munitions supply tunnel and at the far end, on the east side of the island, you will find above the entrance a plaque indicating that it was constructed by the soldiers of 576 Cornwall Works Company of the Royal Engineers between 1916 and 1917. At the nearby artillery emplacements there are tracks laid so that the heavy 4.7 and 4 inch guns could be swung round to cover attack from any direction. They were used first during the First World War and then again during the hostilities throughout the Second World War, and it is easy to imagine during the latter manning these guns as enemy German fighter aircraft droned menacingly overhead to attack the Forth Bridge immediately ahead, or the warships in the Royal Naval Dock Yard further up river at Rosyth or to fly on further afield as they did on 13 and 14 March 1944, using the flight path of the Forth to lead them across Central Scotland to launch their deadly blitz on Clydebank.

Search next for the smaller circular tracks. These were for the Pompoms, Twelve Pounders and Befors anti-aircraft guns. From here the lower path leads round to the south-east side of the island, where the searchlight battery is still comparatively intact. Its powerful lamps could not only probe and search the dark night sky for enemy raiders, but could also, if necessary, illuminate the long boom supporting the anti-submarine net, which protected the Firth from underwater attack at this point. Electrical power was provided by a generator and the generator house can also still be seen.

Today the attack on visitors to Inchcolm is led by the flocks of seabirds for whom the island is home and who are particularly territorially defensive during the spring and early summer nesting season. Best advice at these times is not to stray from the marked paths and to wear a hat for protection against the gulls' and terns' swooping raids. Despite the birds' somewhat hostile reception, the breeding period is a fascinating time of year to visit the island, especially now that the puffins have re-established themselves and the number of their burrows is increasing each season. With the bright scarlet, blue and gold markings of their faces and their funny flight, the little puffins well live up to their nickname of the clowns of the sea, but banish any thought that they are silly or stupid as you watch and note how each flight finishes with their descent into the correct burrow from amongst the dozens on the grassy sea pink studded banks.

Much quieter than the swirling, squawking sea birds are

Inchcolm's other popular residents, its herds of placid grey and common seals, who bask and sunbathe on the island's shores and neighbouring rocks. So plentiful and confidently cheeky are the seals that Colin Aston, skipper of the Forth pleasure vessel *Maid of the Forth*, practically gives a hundred per cent guarantee that her passengers will see them, heads a-bobbing, inquisitive eyes darting to and fro, on every spring, summer and autumn season voyage from South Queensferry's historic Hawes Pier. Interest in the wildlife of the Forth was perversely greatly increased by the sad stranding of Moby the sperm whale in 1996. Since all of the nationwide publicity, which the misguided Moby attracted before he was finally stranded on a mud bank further up river beyond Kincardine Bridge off Airth, Colin Aston has also offered special nature cruises and passengers on these excursions have been rewarded with sightings of dolphins and the smaller minky whales for whom, unlike Moby, these are safe waters in which to hunt. The minkies are filter feeders and are tempted into the estuary by the shoals of tiny silver sprats which swim up the Firth at certain times of year.

Just up river from the *Maid of the Forth's* sailing berth below the Forth Railway Bridge, the Seal's Craig Hotel occupies a lofty, rocky perch overlooking the river and hopefully someday in the future the seals will return this far up river. In the meantime, local West Lothian artist Kenneth Raeburn's statues of a seal cow and her pups lie at the head of Hawes Pier and welcome passengers with the promise that the chance to watch the real animals already exists, just down stream on Inchcolm.

As well as the *Maid of the Forth's* regular daily summer service to the island, there are occasional sailings to Inchcolm from Aberdour one and a half miles to the north on the Fife shore. Little Inchcolm is only half a mile long by, at most, just over 200 metres in width, but no matter how you reach it, make certain on your visit to allow as much time ashore as possible, because as well as there being much to see and do, it is also a pleasant spot on a fine day simply to sit back and relax down by the shore on the small sandy strand, or if the wind is not too blustery, high on the green hillside, where an automatic weather station is situated at the west end of the island.

A landing fee and the price of admission to the Abbey is included in the cost of all of the *Maid of the Forth's* Inchcolm

The Maid of the Forth *with the the tower of Inchcolm Abbey in the background.* Courtesy of Colin Aston and the *Maid of the Forth.*

cruises. Other visitors must purchase tickets from Historic Scotland's office at the jetty, where there is also a small shop and covered waiting room and toilets. These are looked after by the custodian of the Abbey who, along with his family, are Inchcolm's only residents. They live in a modern bungalow, built rather jarringly just to the west of the Abbey. On the whole island it is the one discordant note and it is hard to resist the temptation to wish that it had been Enid Blyton, rather than the civil servants of Historic Scotland, who had inspired this equivalent to the cottage in her Famous Five's Kirrin Island adventures.

While little Inchcolm has not yet achieved fictional storybook fame, its charms have inspired a collection of Celtic melodies. They are the work of Scottish composer, William Jackson, who was born at Cambuslang near Glasgow in 1955. After studying at London's Guildhall School of Music, Jackson founded Ossian and was a member of this popular group for 14 years. Available on CD, his music makes an atmospheric souvenir of an island visit.

Most visitors reach Inchcolm by sailing aboard the *Maid of the Forth*, which provides regular sailings from South Queensferry from Easter until late September. After a gap of 20 years following the withdrawal of the ferries in September 1964, filled only by a short-lived attempt to popularise bridge sightseeing cruises by the ferries' former operator Denny of Dunbarton, aboard their little motor vessel, *The Second Snark*, the *Maid* has now successfully re-established passenger sailings on the Forth. Built, as the brass maker's polished plate beside the bar door details, in 1989 by

43

Inchcolm has become a very popular setting for weddings, because of the peaceful charm of this Iona of the East, the sanctity of its ancient Abbey and the ease of access made available by the Maid of the Forth, *whose spacious saloon provides the setting for the bridal breakfast. Here the happy bride and groom are Chriss and Owen Goodacre, who were married on the island on 16 August 1995. So in love have they become with Inchcolm that they returned to the island in 1996 to celebrate their first wedding anniversary and in July 1998 added still further to their romantic association with it, when they brought their baby daughter all the way north from their home in Leicester to be baptised in the church, where, watched by her older brother, she was very appropriately christened, Abbie.* Courtesy of Colin Aston and the *Maid of the Forth.*

David Abels of Bristol, she is the second vessel to bear the name and is now in her eighth year of operation. Twenty metres long and with a six-metre beam and draught of one and a third metres, she is powered by two twin Ford Mermaid engines producing 120 horse-power each and has a top speed of 9 knots with a cruising speed of 7 knots. She has a separate Volvo generator to heat her saloon and provide power for her galley and other domestic needs. Her 5,700-litre fuel capacity gives her an impressive range of 2,000 miles.

A very modern, trim little vessel, the 130-ton *Maid* is equipped with hydraulic steering and, as well as VHF radio, radar and echo sounder, has the latest Global Positioning System, which tracks up to five satellites simultaneously so that she can track her position to within 50 metres anywhere in the world. The VHF radio is used to speak to other ships and keep in touch with Forth Navigation at Leith which controls all shipping in a similar way to air traffic control. The *Maid* under her skipper, Captain Colin Aston, and her crew which often includes his daughters, Claire and Stephanie, working as Jills of all trades from serving in the on-board cafe to working as deck hands, usually stays much closer to home and for her regular voyages to Inchcolm and up and down the Forth estuary she has been licensed by the Department of Trade Marine Safety Agency to carry up to 225 passengers. One of the department's surveyors gives the *Maid* a rigorous inspection every spring, before she comes into service and checks that all of her mechanical, navigational and safety equipment is in first-class condition before issuing her annual passenger certificate.

Unlike its neighbour up river, Inchkeith is not open to the public. Apart from the fact that it is in the private ownership of well-known Scottish business entrepreneur Sir Tom Farmer, of Kwik Fit fame, it is quite a dangerous island to visit, because of the ruinous state of the concrete military installations built on it during the Second World War.

Half a mile long Inchkeith does, however, have many incidents in its historic past which are of interest. Situated approximately in the middle of the Firth, three miles south-east of Kinghorn in Fife and four and a half miles north-east of Leith on the Lothian shore, first written mention of the island occurs in the writings of the famous church writer, the venerable Bede. It takes its name from the Keith family, who were Scotland's hereditary Earls Marischals and from the Gaelic word *inch* meaning an island, which is also found in many other places in Scotland, such as the South Inch in Perth and Inchmahome in the middle of the Lake of Menteith at the entrance to the Trossachs, as well, of course, as amongst the place-names associated with the Forth itself.

One of the most intriguing tales connected with Inchkeith is that at the close of the 15th century it was chosen by King James IV for one of his strange experiments, which led him to be nicknamed Scotland's most curious king. In this case, at a point during what known as Scotland's Golden Age, having encouraged the establishment of Scotland's first printing press in Edinburgh, King

Jamie was most anxious to discover the origins of language. He therefore gave orders for a dumb woman from Edinburgh to be rowed out to the island and marooned on it accompanied by two orphan babies in order to discover what language the children would grow up speaking. There is no documented proof of the outcome of this experiment, but rumour in Edinburgh maintained that the youngsters spoke Hebrew, which one writer at the time delightedly described as 'the language of paradise'.

How long James IV insisted on this royal experiment continuing and the nurse and the bairns being stranded on Inchkeith is also not recorded, but if they remained on the island they could not have stayed for too many years in complete isolation because, in 1497, it was officially declared to be Edinburgh's lazaretto, that is the place to which those of the Scottish capital believed to be suffering from the plague could be compulsorily exiled to prevent them communicating it to other people.

In 1547, following the defeat of the Scottish troops by the English army at the Battle of Pinkie near Musselburgh, Inchkeith was seized by a detachment of enemy soldiers. They fortified it and garrisoned it, holding on to it under the command of the Duke of Somerset for two years, until finally dislodged by a combined force of Scottish and French soldiers in 1549. The island remained under the control of the French troops in support of Mary Queen of Scots until her return to the Scottish court at Holyrood in 1560 and during this time the French soldiers strengthened the island's defences. In 1564, Queen Mary, her ladies-in-waiting and her courtiers paid a visit to the island and a commemorative plaque near the lighthouse records this royal occasion. Perhaps because they remembered only too well how Inchkeith had provided the French with a stronghold in the Firth of Forth, the first of the Scottish parliaments held during the reign of Mary's son, King James VI, in 1568 gave orders for all of the military installations on the island to be completely demolished.

Inchkeith was not fortified again until the beginning of the 19th century when gun emplacements were established on three of its headlands. All three were connected by a military road one and a half miles in length and were defended by 20-foot wide and 20-foot deep dry moats. Four 18-pound guns were installed on the island, two on the southern battery and one each on the northern and north-western emplacements. The guns were deliberately

During the past few years dolphins have returned to the waters around Inchcolm and love to swim alongside passing ships and play in their bow waves. Here the best known of the dolphins, a seven-foot long male, who has been named Donny, frolics in the bow wave of the cargo vessel Stellaman, *which was outward bound from Grangemouth. Donny also often plays around the* Maid of the Forth, *from which this photograph was taken, as if appreciating the applause of her passengers. Sometimes, however, he shuns the limelight and prefers to swim silently alongside a yacht, often adopting one particular craft for the whole season. In May 1997 Donny rather spoilt his good reputation by killing several of the smaller porpoises, which also now often frequent this part of the Firth. Although such behaviour of dolphins had been suspected in the past this was the first time the act was caught on camera and this less appealing side of Donny's character was shown on ITV's* News at Ten *and on the pages of several national newspapers. Courtesy of Colin Aston and the* Maid of the Forth.

designed to fire over the top of the four-foot high parapet walls and not through loop-holes in them, so that in case of attack they could answer fire from any direction as they could each be turned through an entire 360 degrees.

The strategic importance of Inchkeith was recognised again at the beginning of the 20th century when it was garrisoned throughout the First World War. Soldiers were again stationed on the island during the Second World War from 1939 to 1945. Many new military buildings and gun and searchlight emplacements were built during these periods of hostilities and it is these concrete structures which are now crumbling and in a dangerous condition.

The only other building of interest on Inchkeith is its lighthouse, which is still well and regularly maintained. It is situated on high ground at the island's northern end and its beam, at 235 feet above sea level, is visible to ships from a range of 21 miles. It was originally a manned light with lighthouse keepers staying on Inchkeith for four-week periods of duty, but now, like all of the others round Scotland's shores, it is fully automatic. It is kept in good order by the Commissioners of Northern Lighthouses whose tender *Pharos* makes regular routine visits. Its daily operation is however monitored by computer from the Commissioners' Edinburgh headquarters at 84 George Street, which can easily be spotted as it has its own miniature white painted lighthouse situated above the front entrance at first floor level, flashing out its own recognised signal in the heart of the Georgian New Town.

Shortly after the establishment of the New Town, Inchkeith was visited at the start of the 19th century by the Dumfriesshire-born writer, Thomas Carlyle, who in 1817 rowed all the way out to it from Kirkcaldy. He was accompanied on his island expedition by the religious author Edward Irving and their impressions of Inchkeith are recorded in Carlyle's *Reminiscences*.

For a short time during the 1980s an Edinburgh nature lover, Catherine Allan from Gilmerton established an animal sanctuary on the island, but despite attracting support from television personalities, including Noel Edmonds, after a few years she and her animals were evacuated back to the mainland. Now Inchkeith is inhabited by one lone resident, who has his home in one of the former lighthouse keepers' cottages. Apart from him, Inchkeith's large population of seabirds has the island to themselves and from their violent swooping attacks on anyone who dares step ashore, especially during the breeding season, appear to regard it as their own undisputed territory. It is a pity that Inchkeith does not welcome holiday-makers, as it is one of the driest places in Scotland.

Inchkeith has over the years had some unintended visitors, because there have been several shipwrecks on the island. One of the most recent was the Fishery Protection vessel, *Switha*, which

Homeward bound, the Maid of the Forth *sails under the Forth Bridge and draws up alongside the Hawes Pier, where the famous black and white ferries used also to berth.* Courtesy Colin Aston and the *Maid of the Forth.*

grounded on the Herwit Rock. The remains of the hull of the *Switha* can still be seen and the boiler of her engine room is now exposed. Nearby lies a second boiler, which is all that now remains of a much older victim of the Inchkeith rocks, the 909-ton steamship, *Iona*, which was stranded in 1882.

The third Inch of the Firth, Inchmickery, is often called the Battleship Island. It gets this nickname from the fact that the Royal Navy deliberately built the defences on the island to look like a warship, even going to the extent of erecting two tall masts, in the hope that it would lure the Germans into attacking it, instead of the vessels of the fleet. Inchmickery is situated roughly midway between Inchcolm and Cramond Island. There is a pier on the tip of the island, but there are no scheduled sailings to this little island and landing is prohibited. Inchmickery is managed by the RSPB, the Royal Society not for the prevention of birds, as the letters are often mistakenly translated but of course, for the protection of birds, and the island is home to fifty pairs of Europe's rarest seabird, the roseate tern, the only place in Scotland where they breed. To the north of it is the red-painted lighthouse on the Oxcar Rocks. The light is at a height of 54 feet above high water.

The last of the Inches, Inchgarvie, is situated up river, immediately below the Forth Railway Bridge, for whose massive Victorian central cantilever it provides a convenient foundation. This central cantilever very importantly carried at each end of it half the weight of the central girder, so that the entire bridge is equally balanced. The base of the Inchgarvie Tower of the bridge is 100 feet longer than the other two. This feature was incorporated in the design of the railway bridge so that the central cantilever has sufficient stability to bear the weight of any train upon the central girders without the need for the bolts at the base of the central tower, which are only intended to come into play in the event of gale-force winds. All of the piers of the bridge situated on Inchgarvie are 49 feet in diameter. The two northern piers are built on large wrought iron caissons filled with concrete. This arrangement was necessary to ensure that these two piers had sufficiently strong foundations and the wisdom of such precautions has been proved over more than a century of constant use since the bridge was first opened to rail traffic in 1890.

Also clearly visible on Inchgarvie is a range of ruined buildings, whose history goes all the way back to the days when pirates threatened the Forth. The island was originally a royal possession, but King James IV, concerned that peaceful Scottish merchant ships sailing up and down to little ports on the upper reaches of the river, such as Blackness on the south shore and Culross on the Fife side, were being harassed by English privateers, gifted Inchgarvie to the Dundas family, whose castle still stands to the west of Queensferry, on condition that they fortified it to deter these southern raiders. This they did so successfully around the year 1491, that thereafter the privateers did not dare venture so far up the Forth, concentrating their plundering raids instead on vessels nearer the mouth of the river. The remains of that first castle on Inchgarvie can be seen nearest the bridge.

When they were no longer needed for defence, the buildings which had been erected on Inchgarvie were subsequently used at different times for short periods as a state prison and as a plague colony and quarantine station — a Scottish version indeed of

America's famous Ellis Island in New York Harbour. A century later, however, Inchgarvie again became of strategic importance when in the 1650s the Lord High Protector Oliver Cromwell invaded Scotland and the Royalist Scots once again fortified Inchgarvie in their efforts to defy him. A battery of cannon was hurriedly installed on the island by Scotland's General of Artillery, Sir James Hacket. Although heavily defeated at the Battle of Dunbar, the Scottish Royalist General Leslie fought on and, gathering together the tattered remnants of his troops, tried to lure Cromwell into attacking him on the south shore of the Forth at about the same point where the Scots had won their greatest ever victory against the English at Bannockburn in 1314. Perhaps because of his soldiers' superstitious dread of fighting near this site, Cromwell decided instead to attack another of the Scottish Royalist strongholds at North Queensferry, but was prevented from doing so by a determined bombardment from the guns on Inchgarvie.

Always a skilled tactician, Cromwell decided on an outflanking manoeuvre and marched his troops west along the southern shore of the Forth to near Blackness, where he succeeded in acquiring enough small boats to ferry them across the river to near Charlestown. Under cover of darkness they then marched back along the Fife shore and attacked the Scottish garrison at North Queensferry in a surprise dawn raid. The Royalists put up much more of a fight than he expected and although they were dislodged from their fortifications, at what is still known as Battery Road, overlooking the Forth, they maintained a running battle throughout the day. The final showdown came late in the afternoon three miles inland at where Pitreavie now stands. The Scottish Royalist supporters of King Charles II, whose coronation had taken place at Scone, fought bravely, but were heavily outnumbered by the 1,400 Roundhead Republican troops and in the end were defeated, a contemporary account describing the dead as 'lying thick as sheaves in a harvest field'.

The troops on Inchgarvie subsequently surrendered and Cromwell gave orders for the cannon to be removed from the island. Just over a century later, however, little Inchgarvie was fortified for a third and last time. This happened in 1779, when rumours swept through all the towns and villages along the Forth that the Scottish-born founder of the American Navy, the redoubtable John Paul Jones, by then fighting as a mercenary for

France, was about to shatter the famous Auld Alliance into smithereens by launching an attack on his homeland. In anticipation of his naval onslaught four cannon were hurriedly ferried out to Inchgarvie and installed in the old gun emplacements. For a time it looked as if they would definitely be required, as there were reports that John Paul Jones' ships had indeed been spotted off North Berwick, but in the end he was chased off not by Scottish fire power, but by the strength of the Scottish weather, when a gale whipped up and swept him out into the North Sea and well out of harm's way.

Inchgarvie remained in the possession of the Dundas family until the 1880s when, in preparation for the building of the bridge, they accepted an offer of £2,700 from the Forth Bridge Railway Company for the island which they had originally acquired as a royal gift. The building of the bridge made the island an even more important defensive site and it was strongly fortified again during both World Wars.

Another story about Inchgarvie links the little island with the Second World War. The first air raid on Britain shortly after the commencement of hostilities came when an entire flight of German bombers flew up the Firth shortly after two o'clock in the afternoon of the 15 of October 1939 and launched an attack on three ships of the Royal Navy which were at anchor just below the Forth Bridge and just off the shore of the island. The three vessels were the destroyer HMS *Mohawk* and the two cruisers, HMS *Eden* and HMS *Southampton*. Although the enemy Dornier DO 17s and Heinkel HE 111s were effectively harried all the way up river from when they were first sighted off the May Island by the Spitfires of the City of Edinburgh Squadron from RAF Turnhouse, one of the German bombers managed to score a direct hit by dropping a bomb on the bows of the *Southampton*. Although the bomb caused surprisingly little damage to *Southampton* herself, it succeeded in sinking the Admiral of the Fleet's barge and a small naval pinnace, both of which were moored alongside, and three members of her crew were injured by flying shrapnel. Although their ships were undamaged, 25 sailors on the *Mohawk* and three sailors on the deck of the *Eden* were also hit by fragments of bombs, bringing the total list of casualties to 31. Of the German attackers, one was brought down off Port Seton by an RAF Spitfire before reaching its target and

*Excited Primary 5 ten-year-olds from Linlithgow Primary School played
around one of the old iron bollards on the Hawes Pier, Queensferry, as
they waited to board the original* Maid of the Forth, *with which her then
captain and owner, John Watson, successfully re-introduced passenger
sailings on the Forth after an absence of twenty years.*

within minutes of the raid another two were destroyed. One was
brought down in flames by the North Queensferry Anti-Aircraft
Battery and the other was hit to the south of Edinburgh over the
Pentland Hills.

During that first raid the enemy bombers appear to have
honoured an agreement between Germany and Britain which
limited attacks to military targets and so therefore did not aim at
the Forth Bridge itself, but their success in hitting HMS
Southampton alerted the British authorities to just how vulnerable
the bridge could be in the future if the code of conduct was
broken. Very soon, thereafter, giant grey elephant-like inflatable
barrage balloons were moored above the bridge to make a direct
attack much more difficult. This was indeed a wise precaution,
because later in the war the Germans did decide to try to destroy
the bridge as a vital transport link between Edinburgh and the

north of Scotland including the important naval base at Invergordon. Despite several attempts, however, the Germans failed thanks to these precautions and the constant vigilance of the Royal Airforce. As a propaganda exercise, the Germans did however print in their newspapers an out-of-focus upside-down photograph of the bridge and Inchgarvie, claiming that the black mass of the island was actually the explosion caused after one of their fighter aircraft scored a hit on the bridge!

Although Inchgarvie was never hit by a bomb, it has over the years been hit by thousands and thousands of coins, because of the superstition that it was lucky to throw pennies out of the carriage windows of trains crossing the Forth Bridge and make a wish. Any thoughts, however, of a pocket money-raising raid on Inchgarvie must however remain the stuff of which schoolboy dreams are made, because the island is not open to the public.

One way of getting a close-up view of Inchgarvie is to look at it through either the telescope on the terrace of the Two Bridges Restaurant at the Esplanade in South Queensferry or the telescope in the royal and ancient burgh's former council chambers, which is now part of the town's museum in the High Street. The view from the first floor room, with its bay window overlooking the river is an ever-changing scene taking in not just Inchgarvie but the whole sweep from the Road Bridge all the way to Hound Island Terminal which the next chapter looks at. Before moving on, closer at hand, all around the walls of the South Queensferry councillors' former meeting room, are the carved crests presented to the burgh by the many naval vessels which had connections with it.

CHAPTER 3
THE DELIGHTS OF DALMENY

E xploring the southern shore of the Firth of Forth to the east of
South Queensferry is a very pleasant experience as it starts with
a stroll through the grounds of one of Scotland's most magnificent
estates, Dalmeny, the home for centuries of the Rosebery family.

At South Queensferry the path begins opposite the historic
Hawes Inn, where Robert Louis Stevenson set the scene of David
Balfour's dastardly abduction in his famous adventure novel
Kidnapped. Colourful portraits of many of the main characters
from the book decorate the walls of the old black and white
painted hostelry, which is situated directly below the world-famous
Forth Railway Bridge. The name Hawes is a corruption of the
original title, the New Hall's Inn, and it can be reached either by
driving down the New Hall's Brae just as the stage coach used to
do, as described in Sir Walter Scott's novel, *The Antiquary*, or if
coming by train by clambering down Jacob's Ladder, the steep
steps which descend from Dalmeny Station.

Besides the warm hospitality of the Hawes Inn, there is so much
to see and do in the Royal and Ancient Burgh of Queensferry that
there is a great temptation to stop and enjoy all of its attractions
as described in the companion volume to this one, *Discovering
the River Forth*. The views alone, with their ever-changing picture
of life on the river, are an excellent excuse to stop and linger. The
walk along the coastal path is, however, well worth taking, so
press on and you will be well rewarded.

The skirl of the pipes often welcomes visitors right at the start
of the walk, because Queensferry's Caledonian Pipes and Drums
have their headquarters and practice rooms in the long low white-
harled building, which runs parallel with the first 50 yards of the
road. Up until the 1950s, this used to be a restaurant with open-
air tables, where guests could truly enjoy their drinks on the rocks.
Nowadays, the road outside could do with some of these crushed
rocks as it becomes increasingly pot-holed as it curves round to
Longcraig Pier, where vehicle access ends, although unauthorised
vehicles are halted half-way to it.

The approach viaduct of the Forth Bridge towers over the historic Hawes Inn at South Queensferry which is the starting point for the shore walk through Dalmeny Estate to Cramond. The inn was the setting for the abduction of the hero,David Balfour, in Robert Louis Stevenson's exciting adventure novel, Kidnapped.

Longcraig has a history dating back hundreds of years as an access point to the Firth, being originally used as an alternative berthing place for the ferry, when in the days of sail-power adverse winds made it impossible for it to dock as usual at the Hawes. In such conditions the ferrymen had the choice of making upstream to land their storm-tossed-passengers at the Binks landing place, where a plaque on the rocks still marks the spot opposite St Mary's Church, or on the slipway beside the harbour, or of sailing downstream to make a landing at Longcraig. Even after the introduction of steam power on the famous crossing in 1821, Longcraig still retained its importance as a catch pier, as it was known. The first steam ferry was appropriately called *Queen Margaret* in honour of the wife of King Malcolm Canmore, who had established the crossing at this point during her reign way back in the 1070s. Built by Menzies of Leith at a cost of £2,369, *Queen Margaret* was regarded by travellers as one of the wonders of the age. She not only slashed the crossing time to just 20 minutes, almost as fast as her famous Denny-of-Dumbarton-built black and white namesake, which made the final passage of the ferry with Her Majesty Queen Elizabeth as a passenger after the official opening of the Forth Road Bridge on Friday 4 September 1964, but could in addition tow the older sailing boats, which were still required to cope with the volume of traffic. The only problem was that the 19th-century *Queen* could not come alongside the long sloping Hawes Pier at low tide. In those circumstances she had to berth at Longcraig, much to the annoyance of passengers, as at that time it was not suitable to disembark stagecoaches, or indeed any wheeled vehicle.

It was the building of the Forth Railway Bridge during the 1880s which resulted in the improvement of Longcraig Pier and in it taking on its present appearance, as it was required to ship the heavy stones for the building of its piers and pillars, rather than shipping them from the Hawes, which would have disrupted its regular passenger and horse-drawn vehicle ferry traffic. By coincidence, a century later, in 1998, Longcraig is again in use to ship out materials for the reinforcement of the towers of the Forth Road Bridge. The quantities to be transported, however, bear no comparison to the thousands of tons of granite loaded at Longcraig during the early years of the building of the Forth Railway Bridge from 1883 onwards, to construct the bases for the nine piers which carry its southern approach viaduct and the much larger southern cantilever end pier. The massive stone blocks shipped from Longcraig were used to raise each of the approach viaduct supports to a height of 18 feet, after which the girders were placed on the masonry work and thereafter carried up in stages by hydraulic power as the piers gradually rose until their full height of 130 feet 6 inches was achieved. Most ingeniously of all, the bridge's engineer, William Arrol, who was later knighted, utilised the interior of the girders to serve as roadways along which the materials for their completion could be transported and this cunning plan saved both a great deal of time and expense.

Looking back from sea level at Longcraig, the now well over 100-year-old railway bridge makes a truly impressive sight, as it looms up out of the river. The two main spans over the deep water channels on either side of the island of Inchgarvie are each 1,710 feet long, that is about one third of a mile in length. They provide clearance for ships passing beneath at high tide of 150 feet under the central girders, a height sufficient for the safe passage of almost all vessels even to the present day, apart from the very largest passenger liners and multi-thousand ton bulk carriers and oil tankers. The magnitude of these great spans has led to the bridge being nicknamed the Muckle Brig and the enormous strength of its construction makes this a very justified boast.

When, in Victorian times, the rapid spread of the railway network lent urgency to plans to span the Forth, the bridge was originally to have been a girder construction. The Tay Bridge disaster on the dark and stormy night of Sunday 28 December 1879, after it had been in use for only two years, halted these plans in their tracks and forced a complete rethink. In the end it was decided that the only safe way to bridge the even more windswept expanse of the Forth was to use a revolutionary cantilever design. A contemporary 19th-century description of the cantilever principle described it as follows:

> A cantilever is simply a bracket and a very familiar illustration is seen in the metal brackets used to support the luggage racks in railway carriages. The Forth Bridge consists of six cantilevers, or perhaps more properly, of three cantilever girders, each girder comprising two cantilevers and a central tower forming the resting point for the whole and two central girders. Now if we take the case of three railway compartment partitions with a bracket on each side, with two pieces of wood placed between the two brackets facing one another to represent the central girders, and two weights, each equal to the weight of half of one of the pieces of wood, suspended from the outside brackets, we have a fairly close approximation to the conditions obtaining in the bridge. The three partitions represent the central towers, the six brackets, the cantilevers and the weights the counterpoise employed at the shore ends of the cantilevers to balance the weight of the central girders.

The Forth Bridge, whose intricate cantilever structure is recognised as the finest of Victorian engineering achievements. It has a total length of one and three quarter miles and a total height of 361 feet, with a clearance at high tide of 150 feet. The deepest foundation below high water mark goes down a depth of 91 feet. It took 51,000 tons of Siemens-Martin steel, forged by the open fire method and the strongest in the world, plus 6½ million rivets and 140,000 cubic feet of granite to construct at a cost of £3 million and 57 lives to build between the years 1883 and 1890. Ian Torrance.

The enormous task of building the bridge began in 1883 and jetties and landing stages equipped with cranes to lift the huge amounts of materials required were constructed on both sides of the river and out on Inchgarvie. The largest structure, which had to be towed into position, was the large wrought iron cylindrical caisson required for the building of the base of north-east pier at the southern end, whose foundations were at a depth of 89 feet below the high-water mark. This huge 71-foot high monster with a diameter of 70 feet was towed into position under the supervision of Monsieur Coiseau, a French engineer, who was the world expert. When it was in exact position it was sunk by adding thousands of tons of concrete until the bottom edges rested on the river bed. Seven feet above its bottom was constructed a strong iron floor with several shafts running from it up to its top edge.

The workmen then descended into the chamber below the floor and, with the aid of compressed air, which prevented the water from entering, they began excavating the river bed. The material which they dug out was brought up to the surface through the shafts. To maintain the necessary air pressure, air locks were constructed at the top of each shaft. Of particular note at the time was that the men toiling at the foot of the caisson were able to work by the light of what were described as 'incandescent electric lamps'. When all of the work beneath the river was complete, the working chambers and shafts were all filled with concrete and the inside of the caisson was filled with the same material almost up to its upper edge and the granite pier was then built on this solid foundation.

The construction of the great steel columns forming the central towers was achieved by means of moveable platforms surrounding and attached to the columns. These platforms supported the workmen and all of the appliances they needed for placing and riveting the curved steel plates of which the columns were constructed and were raised by hydraulic power as the work progressed. The same type of moveable platforms were used to enable the men to extend the cantilevers out horizontally for 680 feet in mid-air, without any support from beneath.

As soon as the huge cantilevers were completed, the work of constructing the central girders was begun from both ends and at last, after almost seven years of work, they met on 7 November 1889. By February of the next year, the bridge was ready to be inspected by the officials of the Board of Trade. Their report stated:

> This great undertaking, every part of which we have seen at different stages of its construction, is a wonderful example of thoroughly good workmanship, with excellent materials and both in its conception and execution is a credit to all who have been connected with it

Five thousand men worked on the Forth Bridge and 57 of them gave their lives during its construction. They used 55,000 tons of steel and drove home 700,000 rivets The honour of driving home the final rivet went to His Royal Highness the Prince of Wales, later King Edward VII, when he performed the official opening ceremony on 4 March 1890. Stepping down from the royal train, which steamed out to the middle of the bridge, the prince was presented with what looked like a gold rivet, but by this time,

Messrs Tancred, Arrol and Company, the firm formed especially for its construction, were so short of money that it was actually made of polished brass.

Ever since its construction, the painting of the bridge has been the subject of great public interest and, 'It's like painting the Forth Bridge' became a popular description for a never-ending task. With 150 acres of steelwork to be maintained, this was not much of an exaggeration and until Scotrail's financial stringencies of the early 1990s the bridge had its own full-time team of painters. Although they did work all year round, no matter what the weather, the popular tradition that they painted the entire length of the bridge and then immediately started all over again was never actually true, certain more exposed areas receiving more attention than others. At all times, the bridge painters used the same brand of paint, specially created by Craig and Rose, Paint Manufacturers of 172 Leith Walk, Edinburgh, and its maroon hue has become so well known that it is marketed as Forth Bridge Red. In 1997, after the Member of Parliament for Linlithgow, Tam Dalyell of the Binns asked questions in the House of Commons about the state of the bridge, Rail Track contracted out the painting and in February 1998 the new contractors announced that they were going to use a new paint specially developed to protect oil rigs from the ravages of the worst of the weather out in the North Sea, but that the colour of the bridge would be maintained. Another change is that the new firm has introduced girls to their bridge-painting team, including one young lady from Australia, and the newcomers are using abseiling techniques to reach the trickiest parts of the bridge. Some things, however, have not changed and the new painters still stay up on the bridge from the start to the finish of their shifts, using the aerial bothy for their tea breaks, and way down below a safety boat still patrols all the time they are at work.

The bridge safety boat is based at North Queensferry, but from spring to autumn another safety boat is often to be seen off the south shore, because Longcraig is alive with activity at weekends and on evenings, from the beginning of May through to October each year, as it is the headquarters for the Scout movement's watersports activities. The Scouts' new two-storey high, steel-framed, breeze-block boathouse looms up over the pier head and is perhaps best described as functional rather than beautiful, but they are justifiably very proud of it, as it symbolises the tremendous progress which they have made since coming to this site on the Forth 30 years ago.

The Scouts' Water Sports Commissioner for the Lothians, Ian Harrower, recalls how it all began:

> There have been Sea Scouts in the Edinburgh area since 1907 and now there are six troops within the city, plus one serving youngsters in the Currie and Balerno areas, which is now also officially in the city and another troop which has its headquarters on the Union Canal at Woodcockdale near Linlithgow. They all have their own craft and over the years have forged excellent relationships with local yacht clubs from Cramond right along the coast to Fisherrow. During the 1960s, however, a number of Scouting enthusiasts including the very far sighted Leslie Pringle decided that it would be an excellent idea if many more youngsters and not only those in Sea Scout troops could enjoy participating in water-based activities as part of their Scouting experience. The idea was therefore born of a water sports centre, which could both act as a focal point for the Sea Scouts, and also offer well supervised introductory courses for members of other troups.
>
> Until then most Sea Scout activites had centred on Granton Harbour, but it was becoming too busy and commercialised and so the hunt was on for an alternative base, when in 1968 it was suggested that Longcraig Pier might prove suitable. It was decided to try using it for the 1969 season, ferrying out both boys and boats on a daily basis. Longcraig proved so successful that it was decided to approach Lord Rosebery for the lease of a small site to erect a wee hut from which to operate during the following year. His Lordship agreed and Ferranti at Crewe Toll generously donated a building, which was surplus to their requirements. It was a little larger than we had planned as it was sixty feet long and sixteen feet wide, but it was successfully dismantled, transported and erected and got us established on the site. It was later replaced by a former laboratory also gifted by Ferranti, which survived many gales and high seas to serve us for almost 30 years and enabled us to introduce thousands of youngsters to dinghy sailing, yachting and sea canoeing and we are particularly proud to have been one of the first centres in Great Britain to introduce wind surfing as long ago as 1981.
>
> By the 1990s we realised that the days of the old building were numbered and with demand for water sports expanding still further and many more girls eager to participate, it was decided to draw up a master plan to replace it with a purpose-built headquarters. After a great deal of fund raising and a lot of hard work, we now have the

new building erected and when complete it will have a first floor lecture room and even a lounge with spectacular views out across the Forth, where parents can sit and watch our activities on the river and perhaps some of our adult leaders can relax at the end of the day.

Thanks to having this new headquarters at Longcraig, we can now cater for 40 participants at weekends and 25 each weekday evening, depending, of course, on tidal and weather conditions. Using our fleet of six tried and trusted Wayfarer dinghies for beginners and five Toppers for the more advanced, plus 20 decked canoes or kayaks, four sea canoes and 20 wind surfers, our courses can cover a wide range of activities and skill levels leading to qualifications ranging from Scout and Guide badges all the way to Royal Yacht Association certificates. The pride of our fleet at Longcraig is our jolly boat, which is an Uffa Fox designed fast boat and we also have a trendy new fibreglass Buzz complete with trapeze and billowing spinnaker to add a bit of excitement for our older, more experienced sailors. Completing our fleet we have two larger vessels and two very essential safety boats. The first of the larger craft is the 22-foot yacht *Merienda*. Built by Westerly Marine *Merienda* was originally used by the pupils of Cargilfield School, Cramond, from whom we purchased her in 1975. We believe *Merienda* is a Gaelic name whose meaning has been lost in the tides of antiquity, but from experience we know it should stand for 'Slow, Stubborn and Difficult', but she does allow us to introduce the Scouts and Guides to longer cruising with occasionally the opportunity to enjoy the excitement of spending the night aboard. Our second larger boat is the 24-foot *Coho*, which with her 150 horse power engine allows us to introduce new members to the water, ensure older ones learn more about the Forth by taking them on sightseeing voyages to interesting places such as Blackness Castle up river and across to Inchcolm and even sometimes to enjoy deep sea fishing trips or evening outings for beach barbecues.

Every time there is any activity on the water one or other of our safety boats is also out there to ensure all is well. One is a rigid fibre glass craft and the other is an inflatable and at the end of the day as the wind on the Forth has a habit of dying down about nine o'clock in the evening they also often come in useful for towing in any stragglers.

Walking the shore path, it is also wise not to become a straggler because after Longcraig Pier the route enters Dalmeny Estate and a notice-board reminds walkers that the Cramond ferry at the opposite end of the grounds only runs until 7 pm in summer and 4 o'clock on winter afternoons, with a one-hour lunch break for the ferryman every day from 1 pm until 2 pm. Dalmeny is private land and the notice-board also reminds visitors that dogs, prams and bicycles are not permitted and that it is also forbidden to picnic and to pick flowers.

Entrance to the path leading the length of the estate is through an old-fashioned kissing gate and at least there is no injunction against doing that. Like all of the entrances to Dalmeny, Longcraig Gate is guarded by a suitably solidly built stone lodge with the Primrose family coat of arms carved on the wall. Opposite on the landward side there is another stone-built estate cottage. The path then leads through wooded shoreland with a mixture of conifers and deciduous trees, the many beech retaining their russet leaves right through the winter. On the hillside are attractive glimpses of Dalmeny's well-kept farm fields and other substantial stone-built estate houses, but it is the sweeping views out across the Firth, which really demand attention.

The two long berths at British Petroleum's Hound Point Terminal seem much closer to the shore than they do viewed from up river at Queensferry and if, as is often the case, there are giant tankers alongside, the scene is truly dramatic. When the tankers arrive light, that is with their tanks empty, they loom high over the berths, but as loading proceeds they sink slowly lower and lower into the water. The point where the pipelines carrying the petrol cross below the shore path is clearly indicated by a series of small white and black markers on the grass bank on the field side. The fuel can be pumped at up to three million gallons an hour.

The petrol loaded at Dalmeny comes from the huge oil refinery 15 miles further up the Forth on the south shore at Grangemouth. Most of the crude oil, which it processes comes from the North Sea oil rigs and is brought ashore by a huge 300-mile pipeline. The Grangemouth works operate 24 hours a day, and by night, with their fiery scarlet and vivid orange flares and myriad of lights, resemble a year-round Scottish version of the Blackpool Illuminations. Once processed, the petrol again travels by pipeline to the tank farm at Dalmeny. There it is stored in tanks, cunningly hidden below the remains of one of the old shale oil bings, a lasting reminder of Scotland's earlier Victorian oil industry. While the Dalmeny tank farm is discreetly hidden, it can be spotted by motorists travelling along the Forth Bridge approach road, by looking for the unclimbable security fence, which skirts it to

A large tanker loads at Hound Point Terminal One. A million gallons can be taken on board in less than a day. In the background on the hills above Burntisland can be seen the Craig Kelly transmitter, which broadcasts both television and radio signals. Ian Torrance.

protect it from possible terrorist attacks. From the underground tanks at Dalmeny, the petrol is finally pumped down to Hound Point Terminal, each time a tanker arrives to export it.

When tankers arrive empty and ride high above the two berths it is possible to observe many of the details of these massive vessels. Look out for their bulbous bows, built this way to make them more streamlined and thus better at sailing through the waves, thus reducing fuel consumption and consequently the costs of operating them. Even once they have begun loading their cargoes of petrol and the bottom portion of their bows begins to be submerged, bulbous bows can still be identified by looking for the give-away curved white sign, like Keyhole Kate's nose, painted on the hull. A second white circular sign painted on this part of the hull indicates that a vessel has a bow-thrust propeller to make it easier for it to manoeuvre. The tankers always berth facing up river, so up on the bridge deck look out for the red navigation light. An easy way to remember that this is the port side of the ship is that red is the colour of port wine. Another simple way to remember is that port is the left-hand side of the vessel and port, left and red are all short words. On the other hand and the other side, starboard, which is on the right and the green navigation light displayed there are all longer words.

Above the wheelhouse on the bridge deck from which the ship is steered, look out for the long narrow grey radar scanner, which as it turns, provides pictures ranging from a few hundred yards to 20 miles radius for the navigation officer on the deck below. Radar charts are now easier to read as they are in full colour. Some tankers also now have communication satellite domes, which keep them in touch with the shore and, it is said, allow their owners to know to within a metre exactly where their vessel is at any time and, through the ship's computer, the precise amount of petrol in her tanks amongst a myriad of other details.

Next, take a look at the funnel, whose design tells to which shipping line the vessel belongs. Then look up higher still to the masthead, where it is always interesting to look at the flags flying there. They include the house flag, that is the flag belonging to her owners and usually similar to the design on her funnel and, if she is a foreign vessel, a British Red Ensign, red with a union flag in the corner, which is often nicknamed the Red Duster and which is flown as what is known as a courtesy flag, in other words as a sign of good manners and respect while in UK waters. Since the Scottish Devolution Act some visiting overseas tanker masters have been substituting the bright blue and white saltire of the St Andrew's Cross as a courtesy flag. The other flags flown at the masthead are signal flags and may range from red and white indicating that the vessel has a pilot on board, to the famous Blue Peter. This white square on a navy background indicates that the ship intends to sail within the next 24 hours and it is said that this 'P' flag was traditionally flown to warn publicans to ensure that

This 1930s postcard view looks east through the arches of the southern approach viaduct of the Forth Bridge to Longcraig Pier with the wooded Dalmeny Estate in the background.

sailors cleaned their slates, that is paid the drink bills which they had rung up during their runs ashore.

Turn-round time for tankers loading at the berths at Hound Point Terminal is so fast (less than 24 hours) that they spend much less time in port than ships did in the past, but their crews still bring welcome trade for the pubs, bars and restaurants of South Queensferry, with a private ferry service being provided to run them to and from the Hawes Pier. These same small motor launches also transport the oil terminal workers to and from their jobs and their regular coming and going adds life to the river scene.

Larger and enormously more powerful than the little ferries are the terminal's three sleek, streamlined modern tugs, which when not in service ride at anchor between the berths and the shore. The newest of the tugs to join the fleet in 1997 was appropriately named *Hopetoun* at a ceremony performed by the Marquis of Linlithgow whose family home is Hopetoun House, situated just two miles up river. The distinctive green shield with the letters BP in gold on their funnels shows that all of the tugs belong to British Petroleum. Each tug has a bollard pulling power of over 100 tons. There are always two of these powerful little vessels on duty every time a tanker arrives or departs. As well as assisting the safe navigation of vessels in and out of the Hound Point Terminal, they are also fully equipped with fire-fighting nozzles, which can be spotted high above their wheel houses and all of the equipment which they need to cope with any oil spillage. It is good to see BP taking this potential problem so seriously, because the devastating threat from pollution in a tight narrow waterway such as the Firth of Forth has already been demonstrated in similar fjord-type conditions by the tanker *Exon Valdes* disaster in Alaska. While it was a catastrophe for local wildlife, as well as the fishing industry and tourism in this part of Alaska when the tanker grounded on the rocks and ripped open her fuel tanks, contrary to popular belief the *Exon Valdes* was not so badly holed that she was wrecked. After repairs to her hull she soon sailed again and is now a frequent caller at Hound Point Terminal, where she docks not as the *Exon Valdes*, but under her newly registered name of the *Sea River Mediterranean*. So far there have been no major incidents at Hound Point and it has one of the best safety records in the world.

All ships display their port of registration on their stems, where the flag of the country to which they belong is also flown. Walking on along the shore path at Dalmeny to the stern of the tankers you will notice that some of the vessels are registered in Panama, the Bahamas or Liberia. This is usually an example of what is known as 'flagging out', which means that the shipping company to which she belongs, rather than registering her in their own country such as the United Kingdom, has taken advantage of the financial benefits to be gained by choosing a foreign registry, thus enabling them, for instance, to employ seamen at cheaper rates. 'Flagging out' does not necessarily mean that a ship is less well maintained or less efficiently operated, but it is surely regrettable that successive British governments' lack of flexibility in their approach to the shipping industry has resulted in such a marked decrease in ships flying the Red Ensign. It is to be hoped that Britain will in future adopt a more enlightened attitude to greatly increase our mercantile marine. In the meantime, it is a fact of life that shipping is truly an international business and that the Panamanian registered tanker at Hound Point No. 1 or No. 2 Terminal may have been built in South Korea for Norwegian owners, with European officers and a Filipino crew sailing her from Scotland through international waters across the North Sea to Belgium to discharge her cargo at the Spot Oil Market in Rotterdam.

Moving on from Hound Point Terminal the shore path runs north-east and the view across to the Fife shore includes a glimpse of Braefoot Terminal in the shelter of Inchcolm, where Liquid Petroleum Gas tankers berth to export the products of the Mossmorran Gas Plant, another example of how exploration beneath the bed of the North Sea is benefiting the Scottish economy. Braefoot has been mentioned more fully in an earlier chapter.

The path's north-east progress terminates on the tip of Hound Point, the ridge of black igneous basalt rock, which runs out into the Forth and from which the oil terminal takes its name and which is said to be haunted. According to local tradition the ghostly tale begins with Sir Roger de Mowbray, whose family were the original owners of nearby Barnbougle Castle, to which the path leads next. Sir Roger was a knight of the Order of St John of Jerusalem, the oldest order of chivalry in the world. To become a fully fledged Knight of St John, it was required by the Order that all of its members play their part in one of the Holy Wars, which it was waging against the advance of the Moslem Turks. Sir Roger eagerly awaited the call for him to take part in one of these Crusades or Caravans, as they were also known. When at last word came for him to depart for the Holy Land, he went to pray in little Dalmeny Church, whose history is told in the companion volume, *Discovering The River Forth*. Then, having asked God's blessing on his dangerous mission he returned to the shore, because in medieval times the least dangerous method to travel all the way to the Middle East was by sea and a sailing ship was already waiting to take him on his journey to the Mediterranean.

He boarded the galley at Hound Point and just as it put to sea, his favourite hunting dog leapt aboard. Sir Roger did not have the heart to put the faithful hound ashore and so it journeyed to the Holy Land with its master. There, Sir Roger fought bravely in many battles with the dog by his side, but in the end he was cut down and slain. What became of his dog is not recorded, but that is not the end of the story, because on dark windy winter nights as gales rage out in the Firth, the dog's baleful, mournful howls can be heard as it returns to haunt Hound Point, in search of its long-lost master. Usually, the dog returns alone to prowl the rocky

The ancient interior of 12th century Dalmeny Kirk, where Sir Roger de Mowbray went to worship, before setting off for the Crusades in the Holy Land. The church is the best example of Norman architecture in Scotland. The typically Norman 'Z' chevron design is a striking feature of the chancel arch and of the arch separating the chancel from the sanctuary apse in the background. The small lancet window in the sanctuary is now filled by a beautiful stained glass window, depicting St. Margaret, who was responsible for the starting of the Queen's ferry. It was gifted to Dalmeny Kirk by the Polish Army officers who stayed in the area during the Second World War and like Sir Roger centuries ago, found comfort there in praying to God before setting off to fight for what they believed to be right and for the good of mankind.

promontory, but on occasion it is accompanied by a white-clad Arab warrior. The appearance of this Saracen Turk in his flowing robes with his curved sword in his hand is a very ill omen for the owners of Barnbougle Castle, because it is said that he has come to carry off another of his old enemies and that a member of the family always dies soon afterwards.

The ghostly hound dog is not the only visitor in winter to this stretch of the Firth, as its shores also offer shelter at this time year to many seabirds and the chance of spotting an unusual visitor from the continent adds to the excitement of bird-watching.

Another good time for an out of season winter visit to Dalmeny is the one Sunday, usually in late February, but sometimes earlier or later, depending on the coldness of the weather, when snowdrops carpet acres of Mons Hill and it is open under Scotland's Garden Scheme to raise money for various charities such as St Columba's Hospice in Edinburgh. How Mons Hill got its unusual name is unknown. One suggestion is that it acquired it as a result of the fighting during the First World War, but Lord Rosebery says it dates back earlier than 1914. Whatever the case, local children have long nicknamed Mons Hill, Snowball Hill, and that is certainly what it looks like as the snowdrops thickly smother it on its annual open day.

While Mons Hill with its snowdrops promising that spring cannot be long in coming and its fine views out across the Forth, is only open for one day, Dalmeny House itself is open regularly throughout the summer season, usually each afternoon from Sunday to Thursday during the months from May to September. As well as conducted tours there is the opportunity to enjoy afternoon tea with home baking in what used to be the courtyard, but has now been canopied to provide a very pleasant cafe.

Dalmeny is the home of the seventh Earl and Countess of Rosebery. Their family, the Primroses, have owned the estate for over 300 years, but the house was the result of a competition organised at the start of the 19th century by the fourth Earl. The ambitious plans put forward by many of the period's leading architects including Robert Adam can be seen in an exhibition in the house. The one eventually chosen was one of the simplest by William Wilkins and it is his imposing grey Coade stone decorated mansion with its mock castellated battlements along the front facade, which today looks out across the river. He designed it in Tudor Gothic style and it took three years to build, between 1814 and 1817. When completed it was the first house of its type in Scotland.

Dating as it does from the end of the period of the wars with France, when for the only time in its history apart from Five Nation Cup rugby Saturdays at Murrayfield, Scotland broke its ancient

Dalmeny House, the home of Lord Rosebery, with its castellated facade and mock battlements, is an interesting feature of the shore walk from Queensferry to Cramond. The house welcomes visitors during afternoons throughout the summer season and has a superb display of old masters and Goya tapestries, many of the treasures from the Mentmore Collection and among the best displays in the country on Napoleon and the Duke of Wellington. Ian Torrance.

Auld Alliance with France and then only because it was obliged to do so as part of the United Kingdom, it is fitting that Dalmeny is home to one of the world's best collections of items associated with the Emperor Napoleon and with the Duke of Wellington, who eventually defeated him in 1815 at the Battle of Waterloo. The Napoleon Room is hung with paintings of the famous French leader and furnished with magnificent pieces of furniture which he used at the height of his power. The plain little wooden desk and chairs from Longwood, his prison home on the island of St Helena in the remote South Atlantic, to which he was finally exiled after Waterloo, provides a very visual and telling image of his fall from power. Ironically, too, the display features the campaign chair from which the Duke of Wellington planned his tactics throughout the long and hard-fought Peninsula Campaign in Spain and Portugal and which accompanied him to the field of battle and his final victory at Waterloo.

Since 1977, Dalmeny has also been home to many priceless items of 19th-century French porcelain, furniture and tapestries from the Primrose family's English home at Mentmore in Buckinghamshire, which the present Earl personally selected before it and its contents were sold. These items, from the famous Rothschild Collection, came into the possession of the Primrose family as a result of the marriage in 1878 of Archibald, the fifth Earl of Rosebery, to Hannah, the only daughter of Baron Meyer de Rothschild.

Not only the rooms at Dalmeny are magnificent, even the fan-vaulted, lofty ceilinged corridors are lined with art treasures. The collection includes 18th-century portraits by Gainsborough, Lawrence, Raeburn and Reynolds and there are also fine tapestries by Goya. For those interested in Dalmeny itself, however, particularly interesting, because it gives a personal glimpse into the life of the family, is the grand painting of the third Earl and his large family all pictured by the artist Alexander Naismith in the wooded grounds of Dalmeny. In the days before the invention of cameras, only the richest of Scottish families could afford the expense of such an intimate family souvenir. Today, it hangs in the National Art Gallery in Edinburgh, but in the great entrance hall, with its hammer-beamed wooden ceiling, there is a modern work depicting the present family, which brings the story of Dalmeny House almost up-to-date.

Naismith painted this masterpiece before the construction of Dalmeny House, and so it is the Primrose family's previous home, Barnbougle Castle, which is glimpsed in the background. Despite its ghostly associations, or possibly because of them, Barnbougle Castle, which was restored during the 19th century in Scottish baronial style, was one of Archibald Philip Primrose, the sixth Earl's, favourite places at Dalmeny and as a leading Liberal Party politician he often used to retreat to its library to write his speeches. Despite the handicap of being debarred from the house of Commons by his title, he earned the reputation in the House of Lords of being a committed social reformer and distinguished public speaker. During the run-up to the 1890 General Election, Lord Rosebery invited his famous Liberal colleague Mr Gladstone to stay at Dalmeny. During these weeks Dalmeny was constantly in the headlines of the national newspapers as it was from there that Gladstone masterminded his Midlothian Campaign, which

The start of the Tall Ships Race in July 1995, as seen from the shores of Inchcolm. It was a dreich day and lack of breeze delayed the departure of the 100-strong fleet of sailing ships, but nothing could detract from the excitement and atmosphere of this great occasion on the river. The event proved so popular and successful that it returned to Scotland, to Aberdeen, in July 1997 and will visit Greenock, on the Clyde, in July 1999. Plans are being made to stage it again in the Forth, following the Millennium. Crown Copyright. Reproduced by kind permission of Historic Scotland.

entirely revolutionised electioneering techniques, as it for the very first time brought politics to the people, most men — but not yet women — having only recently gained the vote.

Gladstone was not Lord Rosebery's only distinguished house guest. Queen Victoria herself visited Dalmeny before crossing the Forth by ferry from Queensferry on one of her journeys to her favourite Balmoral and when, in March 1894, Gladstone resigned as Prime Minister, it was to Rosebery that she turned to appoint his successor as premier. For the next decade Lord Rosebery battled with all of the main political controversies of the time, including then as now, the Irish Question. On this difficult issue he disagreed violently with his own Liberal colleague, Campbell Bannerman. Thus, when the Conservative Party fell in December 1905 and Victoria's successor, King Edward, asked Bannerman to form the cabinet Rosebery resigned and retired from active party politics. He retreated to Dalmeny, where he spent much of his time writing, including a detailed biography of his friend Lord Randolph Churchill, father of Sir Winston.

Lord Rosebery's study at Dalmeny has been left just as it was in his day. Much less formal than any of the other rooms in the house, this den, with its comfortable easy chair and its scatter of his Lordship's favourite magazines, is very popular with visitors. Also on show are his famous Primrose pink racing silks. Lord Rosebery was a passionately enthusiastic supporter of the sport of kings and no fewer than three of the horses from his Mentmore Stables carried his colours to victory in the Derby, twice running in 1894 and 1895 and then again in 1905. Fittingly, right outside the front door at Dalmeny there stands a full-size statue of one of Lord Rosebery's favourite horses, King Tom.

Out-of-season visitors to Dalmeny must stick to the shore path, but when the house is open, paying guests are allowed to explore the sheltered garden and to walk through the rhododendrons, colourful azaleas and trees brought home by members of the Rosebery family from all over the world and planted here. The walk leads to the garden valley.

Back on the shore, the path continues past the lawns of the house and the links of its private golf course, providing a walk of four and a half miles in total to the ferry at Cramond. About a quarter of a mile before reaching the ferry is the famous Eagle Rock. By tradition the rock was carved by a Roman centurion with the outline of the eagle symbol of his legion.

Off-shore at the far end of the walk out across the view over Drum Sands lies Cramond Island, which also belongs to the estate. It is linked to the mainland by a narrow causeway and is open to visitors throughout the whole year, but take careful note of the tide table before venturing across, because at high water the island is cut off. There is little shelter on the island and it can be a long and rather cold stay, waiting for the tide to turn and each year when the weather deteriorates some ill-prepared visitors have to suffer the embarrassment of being rescued by Queensferry's in-shore lifeboat!

CHAPTER 4
EDINBURGH'S SEASIDE

Edinburgh's seaside stretches all the way from Cramond up river to the west to Portobello down the Firth to the coast.

Devotees of well-known Edinburgh writer Muriel Stark's popular novel *The Prime of Miss Jean Brodie* will recall that genteel little Cramond offered the seclusion at a suitable distance from the city for her school-teacher heroine to entertain both Sandy and the other girls, who were her *crème de la crème*, and her music-master suitor and it is still difficult today to imagine the village as anything else but a refined wee backwater.

Cramond's history, however, reveals a very different past, because many archaeological finds confirm it as the Roman army's most important harbour in Scotland. Roman, long-oared, wooden galleys berthed here regularly in the natural harbour where the River Almond flows into the Firth. They brought not only the Roman centurions and their auxiliaries to garrison the forts all along the length of Antonine's Wall, which stretched right across the whole of Central Scotland from Bridgeness 11 miles up river on the Forth to Bowling on the Clyde, but also all of the supplies necessary to maintain life on this the outermost frontier of their mighty empire. Recently, the importance of Cramond as a port has been emphasised by the discovery of a magnificent carved white sandstone statue of a lioness. The 1,700-year-old lioness was spotted lurking in the mud by Cramond's eagle-eyed ferryman, Rab Graham, as he navigated his little craft into the village quayside on one of its many daily crossings to and from Lord Rosebery's Dalmeny Estate on the opposite bank of the River Almond. It is possible that the lioness, which has been declared treasure trove and which will, after cleaning and preservation work, be put on display in the new Museum of Scotland in Edinburgh's Chambers Street, was originally one of a pair erected by the Romans to mark the entrance to Cramond Harbour in a suitably impressive manner. Did she perhaps have an equally proud stone carved lion as a mate and does he still lie waiting to be discovered beneath the waters of the Almond? Another suggestion is that the lioness, which has earned its ferryman finder £50,000 as a treasure trove reward, may have accidentally fallen into the harbour while being shipped ashore from a galley to mark the grave of an important Roman official who had died in this far-flung foreign land.

One thing which is certain is that the place-name Cramond is derived from the Celtic for the Fort on the River and, as well as the lioness, there have been many other interesting Roman finds in the area, including coins from the reigns of no fewer than 11 emperors, altars and mosaic pavements, especially during the extensive excavations which took place during the late 1950s and early 1960s. The remains of a Roman bath-house were uncovered in the 1970 excavations and many more discoveries may be waiting to be made, but unfortunately much of the headquarters of the Roman Camp lies buried immediately below Cramond's picturesque parish church, which makes further archaeological work difficult.

It is possible that the kirk actually originated within the ruins of the basilica which served the centurions and officials of the Roman camp, but the oldest part which still survives is the 15th-century tower and the rest of the cross-shaped thick stone-walled church dates from 1656, when the ruins of the pre-Reformation buildings were demolished to make way for its construction. Older than the kirk is Cramond Tower. This rather stern-looking, tall four-storey building was the summer palace of the Bishops of Dunkeld who were given the rights to Cramond as a retreat by King David I in 1160.

Another Scottish monarch with a link with Cramond was King James V, who loved to learn what his subjects truly thought of him by travelling amongst them disguised as the Gude Man o' Ballengeich. Dressed thus, he was attacked by robbers at Cramond Bridge, but was fortunately rescued from these thieves by local farm labourer, Jock Howieson. In gratitude the king insisted that Jock must come to Holyrood Palace so that he might receive his just reward. 'But how will I ken ye amongst all these fine folk,' queried Jock. 'When you enter just look for the only person who is wearing a hat,' replied the Gude Man and, of course, when Jock was ushered into the presence chamber at Holyrood he immediately spotted King Jamie, seated on the throne of state and this time wearing the royal crown. Jock's journey into the city proved well worthwhile, because in gratitude for his bravery the king granted him the lands adjoining the bridge of Braehead for himself and his descendants to farm, with only one condition attached — that a basin of water and a napkin be produced every time a monarch crossed Cramond Bridge. The original wooden brig where King James was attacked in the 16th century was replaced with a sturdy little humpbacked stone bridge in 1622 and today a modern flyover carries the traffic, heading to and from the Forth Road Bridge, high overhead.

Down on the banks of the River Almond, it is still possible to turn history detective and find out about Cramond's varied historic past. During the 18th century, the availability of water power from the river, with direct and easy transport links with the sea, transformed Cramond from being a quiet farming village into a bustling little industrial community at the very forefront of the industrial revolution. Cramond Iron Works was established in 1751 at Cockle Mill and was taken over in 1759 by the newly established Carron Iron Company of Falkirk, whose products from kitchen ranges to short muzzled cannon called Carronades, which helped ensure British victories at the Battle of Trafalgar in 1805 and the Battle of Waterloo in 1815, ensured its world-wide fame. Amongst the partners in that iron works established on the shores of the River Carron, further up the Forth, were the Cadell brothers of Cockenzie, who already had a small iron works near their East Lothian home. In 1770 they bought Cramond Iron Works and were soon so successful in the village that they had over 100 workers labouring in four mills along the shores of the Almond including the forge at Fairafar. The first crude steel produced in Scotland on a commercial basis was manufactured at Cramond and the stone-lined quays built by the Cadells for the ships, which brought in the iron ore and other raw materials and sailed out again with the finished products, can still be seen.

Today, instead of cargo vessels it is pleasure craft which moor along this stretch of the Almond, where the local yacht club has its riverside premises. Walk on past and you come back to the harbour from which the ferry sails six days a week across to the Dalmeny Estate. A ferry has plied across the Almond at this point since the 16th century and has been operated by the estate's owners, the Rosebery family, since 1622. The ferry provides free access to the coastal footpath which runs all the way through the estate past 19th-century Dalmeny House to South Queensferry, but the crossing itself is not free. The ferryman has to be paid before passengers are dropped off on the far shore in front of his old stone-built cottage home, which is a tied house belonging to the estate.

It was near Cramond that Robert Louis Stevenson placed his imaginary House of Shaws in his famous tale of adventure, *Kidnapped*, and it was to this gloomy mansion that he had his hero David Balfour come to seek his miserable Uncle Ebeneezer, the old miser who almost sent him to his death by plunging in the pitch darkness of the night from the top of the house's ruined turnpike stair, a fate from which he was only saved by a fortuitous flash of lightning.

In real life too, the parish of Cramond had many interesting residents including, appropriately considering the village's literary connections, Archibald Constable, the famous Edinburgh publisher. Others included Francis, Lord Jeffrey, the celebrated early 19th-century critic, Andrew, Lord Rutherford, the eminent judge of the Court of Session and Archibald, younger brother of John Napier, inventor of every school pupil's nightmare, logarithms, whose home Lauriston Castle stands within its bounds and which is open to the public, while its lawns are well utilised by the players of the Scottish Croquet Club. One phenomenally and precociously bright young Cramond resident was Marjory Fleming. Born in 1803, this little child prodigy, who charmed Sir Walter Scott with her witty humour and early writing ability, was nicknamed Pet Marjory by Victorian essayist Dr John Brown, who told the story of her short eight-year life.

Youngsters growing up in Cramond nowadays have the choice of two schools within the bounds of the parish. One is the local primary, whose Victorian stone-built classrooms stand on a corner site at the top of the brae and whose maroon-blazered pupils add a lively splash of colour to the village scene. The other is Cargilfield Preparatory School, which was the setting for the filming of the James Bridie short story, *Dollar Bottom*, starring Scottish comedian Rikki Fulton, telling the tale of a group of pupils' efforts to organise their own insurance scheme to give them some cover from the risk of receiving corporal punishment

Best known of the present homes in the village is Cramond House, which was built in 1680 by Edinburgh merchant and well-known supporter of the Covenanters, John Inglis. It was enlarged in 1771 by his descendant Sir John Inglis whose daughter Lady Anne Torphichen, later completed it as it stands today overlooking the Firth. Perhaps it is in its sheltered garden that we can best imagine Miss Jean Brodie picnicking with her girls.

Walking on from Cramond, a path leads above the shore east to the impressive esplanade at Silverknowes, which was built during the 1930s to provide work relief for hundreds of Edinburgh labourers who were unemployed because of the results of the Great Depression. The esplanade provides opportunities to admire seascapes out across the Firth and clear views of the ships waiting down river to enter Leith Docks.

Before Leith, however, lie the smaller ports of Granton and Newhaven. Granton cannot be missed as its tall gasometers, rising above the shore of the Forth, are well-known local landmarks. Granton harbour was a bold Victorian enterprise begun by the Duke of Buccleuch, who owned the site at Wardie Muir and who hoped to rob neighbouring Leith of its trade because of the difficulty which ships were at that time experiencing in entering and leaving at anything but high tide. His ambitious plan, as well as the large new dock itself, included the fine hotel and offices for the expected passengers and the shipping lines to serve them, which well-known Scottish architect Williarn Burn designed at Granton Square. Work on the new port was sufficiently far advanced for it to be officially partially opened with great ceremony on 28 June 1838, the day of Queen Victoria's coronation in London. The impressive new stone-built Granton pier was completed by 1845. It cost £80,000 and was built entirely from stone hewed from the local Granton Sea Quarry. Work then continued on the even longer East and West breakwaters. The East Breakwater was the longest at all of 3,170 feet, while the West Breakwater, which was completed in 1855, stretched out into the Firth for a distance of 3,100 feet. The new port's great advantage was that, unlike at Leith, vessels did not have to pass through dockgates to enter or leave it. As there was a depth of 30 feet of water available at the entrance, ships could sail in and out safely without waiting for high tide and so, although at first Granton was classified as a sub-port of Leith, in 1860 its popularity with shipping lines led to its official recognition as a head port in its own right.

As a new port it was also very well equipped from the very

beginning, the New Statistical Account of Scotland in 1846 stating that Granton Pier offered 'ten jetties, two low waterslips, eleven warehouses and ten cranes'. The enterprise of the Granton port authorities led to the North British Railway Company choosing the port for the introduction in 1848 of the world's first train ferries. They employed Sir Thomas Bouch of ill-fated Tay Bridge fame to devise an ingenious system of moveable stages and powerful stationary steam engines, so that fully laden waggons and passenger carriages could be loaded and unloaded at all states of the tide onto steamers with long flat decks and transported across the Firth to Burntisland, where a similar system enabled them to continue their journey without delay by joining the company's Northern Trunk Line.

The Granton to Burntisland train ferries were discontinued when the Forth Bridge made them redundant in 1890, but passenger and later car ferries continued to ply to and fro between the two ports until the service was ended in 1940 by the Second World War. The service was resumed after the war in March 1951 using four converted former naval tank landing craft. Although these were given romantic names such as *Flora MacDonald*, *Bonnie Prince Charlie* and the *Thane of Fife*, their shallow, flat-bottomed hulls often gave passengers a bumpy ride in rough weather and the crossing failed to make money and was discontinued again. Its last revival to date came in 1991 when Forth ferries introduced what was described as 'a fast passenger catamaran'. According to the company's glossy publicity leaflet the *Spirit of Fife*, as she was christened, offered 'a unique new experience cruising across the Firth of Forth.' The 70-foot long twin-hulled vessel had a passenger seating capacity of 250 and made ten crossings in each direction every day, each arrival and departure connecting with a shuttle bus service to Edinburgh city centre. With a first sailing on weekdays from Burntisland at 6.55 am the 20 minute high-speed crossing was aimed to appeal to city-bound commuters, for whom free car parking was provided. On Thursday, Friday and Saturday evenings, throughout the summer and autumn, the *Spirit* offered attractive regular cruises with entertainment ranging from ceilidhs and discos to 'river boat jazz shuffles' as they were advertised, but despite considerable initial interest in both her routine ferry crossings and these special extra events, she sadly did not generate enough business and was in the end withdrawn from service and laid up at Port Edgar Marina in the shadow of the Forth Road Bridge, from whose congested traffic jams she had hoped to profit.

During its Victorian heyday, Granton's exports consisted chiefly of coal, pig-iron, castings, wrought iron, Scottish shale mineral oil and paraffin from the same source, paper, beer and malt. Its imports were equally varied, including American, European and British timber, esparto grass for paper manufacture, rosin, cork, fruit, lead, turpentine, bottles, china clay, bark, woodpulp, grain and tobacco. For the last, Granton had large bonded warehouses which also housed cargoes of whisky awaiting export. The customs revenue for Granton in 1890 was £137,653. Total imports that year were estimated to be worth £400,000, with exports at a quarter of that sum. Shipping companies regularly using Granton at that time included the famous Salvesens, the General Steam Navigation Company, the United Steamship Company of Copenhagen and Nalvorsen and Company whose Norwegian royal mail steamers provided a passenger service across the North Sea to Scandinavia.

Granton was also the headquarters of the Forth Steam Trawling Fleet. The trawlers took advantage of Granton's excellent rail links provided by both the Caledonian and North British Railway Companies to transport their catches of haddock, cod and whiting swiftly to fishmongers all over Scotland, but especially in Glasgow. At its peak the company had 15 powerful steam trawlers operating out of Granton. A patent slipway at the west end of the harbour allowed these fishing vessels of up to 1,400 tons to be repaired in the port.

At one time there was also shipbuilding at Granton, but this died out in the second half of the 19th century as the focus of that industry moved from the Forth to the River Clyde. Other industries in Granton included a large timberyard and sawmill, a foundry and a forge, a rope works, a chemical works and one of Britain's largest ink manufacturers, which supplied not only Scottish printers and newspapers, but also the major London dailies and even the foreign press.

While Granton did have an early shipbuilding trade, it was its neighbour Newhaven just over a mile along the shore which gained national fame as the birth place of the mightiest vessel the Scottish navy ever possessed, the appropriately named *Great Michael*. Some say that Newhaven was given its name in contrast to the old haven of Blackness, further up the Forth between Queensferry and Bo'ness, which was throughout the middle ages the country's second most important seaport, second only to Leith. The New Haven owed its rapid growth at the beginning of the 16th century to the royal patronage of King James IV because it was there, rather than at either of the established harbours of Leith or Blackness, that he chose to build his huge wooden hulled man o' war, which he was certain would allow him to 'ding doon' his enemies, the English, and allow Scotland to exert her authority over the seas. Leith was deemed unsuitable for his magnificent enterprise by His Majesty the King on account of the sand bank at the mouth of the Water of Leith, which had already resulted in the stranding of Scotland's other great warship, Sir Andrew Wood's, *Yellow Carvel*, which had had to be stripped of all her furnishings and even her tall masts before she could be refloated on the highest tide of the year. Such a fate could on no account be allowed to befall his *Great Michael*. Blackness was ruled out because James considered it too far to ride to keep as close an eye on the construction of the new vessel as he definitely intended to take.

The ambitious king therefore decided the only alternative was to construct an entirely new shipbuilding yard and that Newhaven was the ideal place. Until that time it had been simply a tiny little sandy harbour in a sheltered bay. The King therefore approached the Abbot of Holyrood, who owned the area, and offered to swap it for a richer site close to his royal palace at Linlithgow. The Abbot accepted and so the few fishermen and their families who had their humble cottage homes along the coast to the west of Leith and worshipped there suddenly found themselves with a new royal landlord.

Almost overnight during the year 1504, their little hamlet was transformed into a bustling construction site with 163 large trees from along the shores of the Water of Leith chopped down and brought in to build a hurriedly constructed village along one long main street to house the incoming craftsmen. At the same time, a dock was dug and the rubble used to form a protective breakwater and to form the foundation for a pier. Even at this early stage all of the work enjoyed the personal supervision of the king. Always a very religious man, he also gave instructions for the building of a stone chapel to be dedicated to St Mary and St James and the ruins of it can still be seen in the shadow of St Andrew's Church.

From the chapel the new port at first became known as St Mary's Port and, even after the name Newhaven started to be used, it was often described, because of the dedication of its place of worship to the Virgin Mary, as Newhaven, Port of Grace.

By 1507, a royal naval dockyard complete with workshops for its carpenters and other craftsmen, warehouses for all the chandlery they required and a very vital rope works had been constructed and all was ready for the laying of the keel of the *Great Michael*. To find exactly the right oak tree which was long and straight and strong enough for the keel, Sir David Lindsey, the author of the famous *Satire of the Three Estates* described how 'she waisted all the woods in Fyfe, except the woods Falkland Wood'. which was left standing as it formed the royal hunting estate. In addition, more timber was imported from Norway and canvas for sails from France, while the whole of the rest of Europe was scoured for all the other maritime essentials needed to fit out such a massive ship from anchors to lanterns and from compasses to guns.

For the next four years the royal dockyard at Newhaven became the largest employer of labour which Scotland had ever known. As she neared completion the *Michael's* four tall masts became a local landmark. Then, at Michaelmas in October 1511, all was ready for her launch and in front of King James and his young English Queen, Margaret, she took to the water, but disappointingly there is no actual description of her launch. We do know, however, that on the evening of the launch the king and the royal party were rowed out to the great ship as she lay at anchor close to the shore off Newhaven and that they entertained those who had worked on her to wine served on her lantern-lit decks.

For the next six months, James took obvious pride in visiting the *Great Michael* every day as the work of fitting her out began. By March, the work was sufficiently far advanced for her to be towed all the way up the Forth to Airth for further work at Scotland's other royal naval dockyard and this was done by the fishermen of Newhaven, who in their small sailing boats towed her all the way up river.

Almost exactly a year later, in March 1513, the *Great Michael* paid her first return visit to Newhaven for drydocking. This was done by sailing her into the dock, then damming the entrance behind her tall stem and painstakingly baling out all of the water. Once this first overhaul was complete, she sailed out of Newhaven and into the Firth to take up station for the first time in the lee of Inchkeith, ready and very able to deter any English invader which dared to enter her territory. It was good that James IV saw her in service because sadly, shortly afterwards he and all his Scottish nobles were slain by the English at ill-fated Flodden field.

It is interesting to note that it was the fishermen of Newhaven who had the honour of towing the *Great Michael* up river to Airth, because from then on the devastating defeat at Flodden and the death of the king meant that there was no further call to strengthen the Scottish navy and so no more work building ships, and so it was upon them that the port depended for its livelihood. For almost 300 years the main catch was shellfish, especially excellent oysters, but in the 1790s the emphasis changed to drift net fishing for herring and line fishing for haddock and other white fish

In Victorian times, the Newhaven fisherwives with their distinctive cries such as 'Who'll buy my herrin', bonnie fish and halesome farin' ', and their even more distinctive dress, became a notable feature of the Edinburgh scene as they sold the day's catch on the city's streets and even down on the platforms of the new Waverley Station as the crowds rushed for their homeward trains. It was from Waverley Station that an invited group of the Newhaven fisher lassies travelled south by train to be the star attraction at the London Fisheries Exhibition in the spring of 1883. With their wickerwork creels on their backs and their uniform of red- and white-striped dresses, they caused a sensation in the capital because they wore their skirts and petticoats girded up almost to the knee, at a time when even a glimpse of ankle was considered something shocking! One London writer who was attracted by the Newhaven girls when he visited the exhibition, noted, 'The Scotch lassies look well dressed in this fashion because they have fine legs and are not afraid to show them!' The fame of the Newhaven fisherwomen even attracted a visit to their display by some of the younger members of the royal family, who were reported to be surprised by the way in which the girls addressed them and by their ready tongues. No offence, however, was apparently taken because on a Sunday in May they were all invited to Marlborough House to meet the Prince and Princess of Wales.

Seagulls wheel above a fishing boat at Newhaven Harbour in the 1950s as she unloads her catch.

Even greater fame awaited them because before the exhibition closed and they returned to Scotland, the Newhaven fisherwives were honoured by being received by Queen Victoria at Windsor Castle.

The fisherwives used to vie with each other running up the whole length of Leith Walk, despite the weight of their creels, which usually contained over 150 lb of fish, to be the first to sell the day's catch on Princes Street and thus get the best price. Sometimes, they formed relay teams to get their fish on sale even faster and shared the profits. Others increased their takings by walking all the way to inland towns such as Haddington and Falkirk to sell their wares. Many had regular customers whom they visited faithfully each week, usually with fine fresh herring and firm white haddock, but never being abashed at suggesting a wee bit of more expensive sole as a special treat.

The fisherwives purchased their fish right on the quayside at the long stone-built Newhaven Fish Market. Today, it is possible to sample haddock in the fishmarket building as the part of it nearest the shore road has been attractively converted into a busy restaurant by the famous Harry Ramsden chain, but sadly the fish which it cooks are not landed there. Although very tasty, as in all of its worldwide branches as Hong Kong, in order to maintain portion control and, it is claimed, top-class quality, the fish it fries are not fresh, but frozen. Fresh haddock and chips is, however, still available in Newhaven as a sign directly opposite at the much older eatery, the Peacock Inn, proudly proclaims. A 19th-century guidebook mentions the Peacock as 'famous for its fish dinners' and today there is fierce competition between it and its upstart English Yorkshire rival across the road as to whose fish suppers taste more delicious. Perhaps the best idea is to sample both. Ramsden's and the Peacock often have waiting lists for tables, so happily there is obviously a place for both on the shores of the Forth and it is good to know that old-fashioned fish suppers can still hold their own against all of the other fast foods which have invaded the modern Scottish culinary scene.

Goodness knows what the fisherfolk of past generations in Newhaven would have made of Balti curries and Chinese carry-outs, but much else about their lives may be discovered by walking along the quayside to the far end of the fishmarket building, which has now been converted into an excellent local history museum. It is a particularly good place to take children to explore, as many of its displays are hands-on exhibits, from identifying different North Sea fish to tying knots in nets and they cover not only work, but what it was like to grow up and go to school in a tightly-knit fishing community. One of the most interesting stands tells the history of the Society of Free Fishermen, which provided the poor of the village with many benefits, as well as looking after its members' interests, from protecting their fishing rights to supplying a mortcloth for their funerals. Its funds, contributed by its members after every successful voyage, were kept securely in a solid wooden sea box, which was 'double lockit'. The key for one lock was kept by the Boxmaster, while the other was deposited for safe keeping with the treasurer of the local kirk session, whose members had to be present before both locks could be opened and any money removed from the kist. The Society of Free Fishermen's records date right back to 1572 and it is still in existence. Another stand tells of Newhaven's three famous choirs, of which the oldest, the Fisherlassies began singing in 1896.

The only trace nowadays of another Newhaven institution, the

Chain Pier, is the Old Chain Pier Pub, which marks the spot on the shore where it used to stretch out into the Firth. Constructed in 1821 at a cost of £4,000 it was built to serve the recently introduced steamers. Appropriately, the first steamer to operate a regular service on the Forth was the *Stirling*, because passengers could indeed travel all the way up river to that town. Built on the Clyde at Greenock she was brought to the east coast through the Forth and Clyde Canal and began operating in 1813, only two years after the launch of the world's first practical sea-going steamship, the *Comet*. Despite the novelty of steam propulsion, or perhaps because of it, the little *Stirling* proved an immediate success, so much so that her owner, a Stirling businessman called Bell, in 1815 ordered the first two steamers to be purpose-built on the River Forth. They were both built at Newpans, or Kincardine as it is now known, and were also both launched on the same day. The new *Lady of the Lake* and the *Morning Star* soon both joined the original *Stirling* on the route between Newhaven and Stirling with calls at Queensferry, Bo'ness, Grangemouth and Alloa en route, but Mr Bell had been over-ambitious. There were insufficient passengers to keep all three steamers busy and so he was forced to sell his pride and joy, the *Lady of the Lake*, to a German shipping line. Three years later, however, passenger business on the Forth had increased sufficiently for him to be able to buy back the *Lady* and she sailed safely back from Hamburg, down the River Elbe and across the North Sea to Newhaven, from where she resumed service on her original route.

Eight years later, in 1826, Mr Bell sold his fleet of three vessels for the sum of £4,500 to the newly-formed Stirling, Alloa and Kincardine Steamboat Company, which was also owned by a consortium of Stirling businessmen. They did not buy any new steamers but continued to operate the original three and enjoyed a monopoly of passenger sailings on the Forth until 1835. From then on, more steamers came onto the river and in 1840 the Chain Pier at Newhaven was purchased by one of the new steamer owners, the Alloa Steam Packet Company. During its Victorian heyday the pier was busy not only with steamer passengers, but with many summer visitors who enjoyed walking its wooden deck to get a whiff of the brine and who even used it as a diving board to swim in the river. At one time, there was even a gymnasium at the end of the pier, where the swimmers and other holiday-makers could enjoy their exercises. Even Edinburgh city businessmen could enjoy the pleasures of a swim from the pier and an hour toning up in the gym before the strains and stresses of the working day, as a special train ran from Waverley Station down to Newhaven at 6.15 every morning to cater for the early bathers. The Edinburgh, Leith and Newhaven Railway Company's line ran from the north-west end of Waverley Station directly under Princes Street and St Andrew's Square, the tunnel continuing all the way to Scotland Street, where the line re-emerged into the daylight. The line was later bought by the North British Railway Company. Later, there was also a rail service to Newhaven from Princes Street Station, where the impressive red Dumfriesshire sandstone railway hotel, the Caledonian, still marks the spot. In late Victorian times the fares for the two and a half mile journey were first class threepence, third class tuppence, with return tickets available at fivepence first class and only threepence for third. There was no second class.

During the latter half of the 19th century Newhaven became a popular place for city families to take the sea air and its Annfield Promenade and the beach in front of it became a favourite picnic spot, before a land reclamation scheme pushed back the sea. At the peak of its popularity, Newhaven's three-storey Marine Hotel at the West End was considered a very fashionable place to stay at the seaside and horse-drawn trams plied to and fro carrying holiday-makers along the promenade outside. Before long, the horse-drawn trams were replaced by cablecars, which were eventually in their turn replaced by the electric trams, which served Edinburgh well until the city councillors misguidedly did away with them 40 years ago, a decision which has always been regretted with many plans for lines for light railways to replace them being put forward but never acted upon, despite ever-worsening city road traffic congestion.

From Newhaven it is, however, comparatively easy to drive the three-quarters of a mile east into Leith, which since the 1920s has officially been incorporated into the city of Edinburgh, but still likes to display its independence. Leith Walk, which links it with the east end of Princes Street, was first made into a proper road by the soldiers of General Leslie in 1650. Long before then, however, on Tuesday 19 August 1561, this was the route which Mary Queen of Scots followed when she returned to Scotland for the first time after spending the whole of her childhood in France, marrying the French crown prince the Dauphin Francis and being left a widow by his tragic death at a young age. Mary's arrival at Leith took the Scottish nobles and other leaders by surprise as a thick, damp North Sea haar blanketed the river as her two galleys nosed their way up the Firth, John Knox noting gloomily that the fog on the Firth symbolised 'the sorrow, dolour, darkness and impiety', which he declared Roman Catholic Mary was bringing back to his proud new Protestant Scotland.

Despite the fog, which became known as the Protestant Mist, and the lack of a suitable welcoming committee, the young Mary, although still wearing mourning black, is said to have been surprisingly cheerful as she set foot again on Scottish soil at Leith. As Holyrood Palace was not ready to receive her and as there were in any case no horses available for her and her French courtiers, she was escorted into what must have been one of Leith's finest houses, the home of merchant Andrew Lamb. Lamb's House is still one of Leith's best-known landmarks, but whether it is the same building where Queen Mary rested throughout the morning and was subsequently entertained to lunch by her half-brother, Lord James, Earl of Moray, is not certain.

By the time the poor ill-fated Mary landed at Leith the town was well used to royal comings and goings. James I brought his queen, Jane, to Edinburgh by this sea route and their baby, James II, was smuggled here in a wooden kist from Edinburgh Castle and taken up river by boat to Stirling. Mary of Gueldres landed here on her way to wed King James II and Princess Margaret of Denmark followed her to marry their son when he grew up and became James II, James IV was a frequent visitor. Then his son and heir, James V, welcomed both his first and second wives to Scotland as they stepped ashore here at Leith. First came the bonnie young Madeleine, whose good looks and equally captivating manner so charmed the Scottish people, that when she died, only months later, they are said to have worn black in mourning for the first time. Soon her royal place was taken by Mary of Lorraine and Guise, and again she received her first impressions of Scotland when she landed here.

Most spectacular of all the regal arrivals at Leith, however, was undoubtedly that of King George IV in 1822. There are two plaques to mark the occasion. One is a simple iron plate on the edge of the quay, known to this day as the King's landing, which merely reads 'George IV Rex, o Felicem Diem'. The other, out of sight on the wall of the quay is much more expanisve, recording in detail that 'Here our most gracious sovereign George IV first touched Scottish ground on Thursday 15th August, 1822'. It goes on to detail those who welcomed His Majesty as 'William Child, Admiral of Leith, John Macfie, James Reoch and Abram Newton, Magistrates, Hugh Veitch, Town Clerk'. George IV's royal visit to Scotland was the first since the more troubled one of King Charles II, in 1650, and that godfather of Scottish tourism, Sir Walter Scott, stage managed the whole event quite brilliantly, as the famous Turner oil painting of the scene at Leith records. A contemporary description of the royal arrival states:

> As soon as the royal barge came within hail of the pier the Royal Standard was hoisted on the lighthouse; an immense cheer accompanied by the waving of hats and handkerchiefs burst from the multitude. The noise at once subsided into perfect calm, as if the breathless interest of the people, the palpitation which they had endured to a degree almost painful, had for the instant choked all power of utterance. The royal barge passed the pierhead, when three young men as pipers struck up some national airs. The King bowed and a great cheer rent the air.

Sir Walter had even managed to persuade His Majesty to wear the kilt for the occasion. What he had not reckoned with was the fact that George had donned a mini kilt and teamed it up with of all things, pink silk tights. The official royal portrait of King George in his wee kilt and pink silk tights can still be seen at Holyrood Palace, although the fine stone statue erected to officially mark his visit at the junction of George Street with Hanover Street shows him more decently garbed in his flowing royal robes.

By the time the king landed at Leith, it was already expanding as a port. Originally simply a tidal harbour, where the Water of Leith joined the Firth, in 1799 the magistrates commissioned the eminent civil engineer Robert Rennie to draw up plans for enlarged piers and proper docks. The magistrates obtained an Act of Parliament authorising them to raise the then considerable sum of £160,000 to put them into effect and in 1800 the digging of the first of two wet docks, parallel with Commercial Street was begun. It was completed in 1806 while the neighbouring West Dock, sometimes called the Queen's Dock, was begun in 1810 and opened in 1817. Together they covered an area of ten and a quarter acres and were capable of accommodating around 150 of the small sailing vessels which at the time most frequently berthed at the port. Rennie's ambitious scheme also included three graving docks and several drawbridges. The total cost eventually came to £285,100 plus a further £8,000 spent in erecting the new bridge across the Water of Leith.

In 1824 the port of Leith was further improved by extending the already existing East Pier and by building a West Pier and a breakwater. All of this work was completed by 1826 at a cost of £240,000. Twenty years later, more improvements were begun and over the next seven years, between 1848 and 1855, piers were again extended, the approach channel was deepened to a depth of at least 20 feet at high tide and the fine new Victoria Dock was opened immediately to the north of the original West Dock. A contemporary account notes that:

> The new Victoria Dock has an area of four and three-quarter acres and is 700 feet long by 300 feet broad with a depth of twenty one feet at low water and an entrance of sixty feet. Its wharfage amounts to 1,900 feet in length by 100 feet broad. The whole of the improvements cost £135,000.

During the 1850s and 1860s Leith Dock's prosperity continued. To cope with the continued expansion in trade, the Prince of Wales Dock was opened in 1858, while the end of the 1860s in 1869 brought the opening of the Albert Dock, named after Queen Victoria's royal consort. Covering an area of over ten acres and all of 1,100 feet long and 450 feet broad, its hydraulic equipment was amongst the first of its type in Scotland. It occupied the former low-lying sands where Leith race-course had formerly been situated.

Leith's innermost dock, the Edinburgh Dock, to the east of the Albert, to which it was linked by a broad channel, was officially opened in July 1881 by appropriately, the Duke of Edinburgh. The total masonry needed to construct this $16\frac{1}{2}$ acre basin was estimated at 900,000 cubic feet, most of the stone being hewn from Craigmillar Quarry. By 1890, no fewer than 181 vessels were registered at Leith. Thirty of them were steamers belonging to the famous Currie Line and it is interesting to note that they carried not only cargo but passengers, with regular twice-weekly sailings

This 1960s aerial view of Leith Docks looks west over the Western Harbour, with the piers of Newhaven Harbour in the top left-hand corner. Forth Ports Plc.

to Hamburg and once weekly departures to Copenhagen, Kristiansand and Stettin and a ship once a fortnight to Bremerhaven. Another well-known name in Leith shipping circles, George Gibson and Company, owned a fleet of 12 steamers and maintained regular cargo and passenger services twice weekly to Rotterdam, once weekly to Dunkirk and Antwerp and fortnightly to Amsterdam. Leith's most frequent service was, however, with London and a contemporary travel book described 'the fleet of magnificently appointed and swift steamers of the London and Edinburgh Steam Shipping Company' which operated these thrice weekly sailings to the Thames. These overnight journeys by sea were preferred by many passengers to travelling by rail.

Leith's other important passenger routes were to Aberdeen, Orkney and Shetland and these continued even after the Second World War well into the 1950s, when they were relocated to Aberdeen from where they are still operated by P & O's car ferries, all of which, like the *St Clair*, happily still maintain the tradition of bearing the names of Scottish saints. One of the last of the Saints

One of the largest cargo ships ever to work the Port of Leith, the 40,000 ton New Prospect *discharged pipes for the North Sea Oil Industry on 29 July 1991.* Forth Ports Plc.

to carry passengers all the way from Leith to the northern islands, before people preferred to save time by driving up to Aberdeen, was the popular sleek streamlined *St Ninian*, which was eventually sold to Canadian owners and went on to enjoy a long career sailing to and from Newfoundland.

About the same time that Leith lost its sailings to Orkney and Shetland, it also lost the last of its international passenger services, when the *Gulfoss*, which had previously operated a weekly service to Copenhagen and Iceland was withdrawn. Now, however, in the late 1990s Leith is enjoying a revival in its passenger sailings because it is becoming an ever increasingly popular cruise-liner port of call with tourists eager to explore Edinburgh. A fine new cruise terminal is planned and will be able to cope with liners of up to 40,000 tons while the former Royal Yacht *Britannia* may also be moored alongside it, as a major tourist attraction.

One of the largest passenger liners ever to dock at Leith, Cunard Line's five star luxurious, 37,845 ton Royal Viking Sun *which visited the port in August 1994. Forth Ports Plc has done much to encourage the development of passenger trade and plans to build a modern new terminal to further enhance this important aspect of Scotland's tourism industry. The plans include a permanent berth for the former Royal Yacht,* Britannia, *which as well as being a major visitor attraction, will be very much at home so close to the royal palace at Holyrood.* Forth Ports Plc.

Forth Ports Plc can also now accommodate even larger passenger vessels further up river at the former Royal Naval Dockyard at Rosyth, whose port facilities it is developing. Adding the seal of success to Forth Ports Plc's campaign to make Edinburgh a popular cruise destination, the world's most famous liner *Queen Elizabeth II* made two calls in the Firth during the 1998 summer season. The great 70,000-ton Clyde-built Cunarder had only previously visited the Forth twice during her 31-year-long career so the 1998 double event was a particular cause for celebration on the river.

Queen Elizabeth II's first ever visit to the Forth was very unusual because she was given special permission to berth alongside the quay at the Hound Point Oil Terminal off the shore at Dalmeny. Her second visit was equally high profile as she lay at anchor for two days at the Admiralty Buoy in Dalgety Bay, ready to lead the Tall Ships out of the Firth on the first leg of their 1995 race across the North Sea. For the previous four days the sailing ships, dressed all over with flags and bunting, had lain alongside in Leith, whose quays teemed with sightseers who had travelled from all over Scotland to catch close-up views and in many cases to go aboard to meet the young crews of these graceful ships of a past era. On the eve of their departure, the night sky over Leith was illuminated with an impressive firework and laser show, which could be seen from vantage points along the river for up to 20 miles around.

The spectacular visit of the Tall Ships focused public attention on the new image which Leith has achieved during the 1990s as a lively and attractive place for city dwellers to make their homes and in 1997 the opening of the new Scottish Office, with all the civil servants which it has brought to work in the area, has added still further to this trend. To cater for them, many fashionable places to eat and drink have opened up and, after some years of neglect, Leith's waterfront has been transformed. Particularly pleasing is the atmosphere in Shore Street on the banks of the Water of Leith, where a line of pubs and restaurants make it comparable year-round with Copenhagen's colourful Nyhaven, while on summer evenings their open-air tables bring a flavour of a French harbour town such as La Rochelle. As befits a port with such an international trade, eating out in Leith is truly a cosmopolitan experience. Particular favourites include Skipper's Bistro at 1a Dock Place, the Waterfront next door at 1c; for the freshest most succulent oysters, Oyster Bar Enterprises at 1 Quayside and the Leith Oyster Bar at 58 The Shore, the Ship on The Shore at appropriately 24 to 26 The Shore, Malmaison Brasserie in Tower Place, The Rock, 78 Commercial Street and, though not famed as a seagoing nation, for excellent Swiss cuisine, Denzler's 121 Restaurant in Constitution Street. The list of enticing hostelries in Leith is almost endless and it is even possible to go aboard ship to eat and drink at a vessel moored picturesquely alongside the quay at The Shore. For whisky connoisseurs, Leith boasts the headquarters of the Scottish Malt Whisky Society Ltd, whose premises are appropriately situated in the Vaults at 67 St Giles Street.

To work up an appetite or a drouth take a walk through the old port area, where fortunately some of Leith's fine old stone-built buildings have survived. Start at the Customs House, just across the bridge from The Shore, in Commercial Street. It was built by Robert Reid in 1812 and as a sign of its authority still has the royal coat of arms above the entrance. The entrance stair and the wings to the side were designed by distinguished Scottish architect William Burn and added in 1824. Burn also designed the stable block to the rear, which is a reminder of the days when the scarlet coated, sword-carrying excisemen went about their duties on horseback.

Look to the end of the street opposite and there is a glimpse of an even earlier period in Leith's history, in the form of the last remnants of the fortress constructed during the 1650s by Oliver Cromwell's soldiers under General Monk, while they occupied the port, which provided a vital link in their supply chain. On the corner of Commercial Street with Quayside Street stand the remains of Old North Leith Parish Church, which was dedicated to St Ninian. It dates back to the end of the 16th century and its spire has remained unaltered since it was added in 1675. The church was last used for worship as long ago as 1826. The North Leith Churchyard round the corner in Coburg Street, where burials date from 1664, includes the graves of Prime Minister William Gladstone's grandparents. The kirk built to replace the one originally dedicated to St Ninian, the present North Leith Parish Church, is further west in Madeira Street. It is another example of the work of architect William Burn and its spire is a well-known Leith landmark.

Cross the bridge over the Water of Leith and walk along Great Junction Street and in Mill Lane, which runs off it, can be seen the remains of the schools, which William Gladstone's father, Sir John Gladstone, set up in 1840 to educate the poor children of Leith. There was a school for boys and a separate one for girls and he also opened an asylum for what were at the time described as 'female incurables'. Further along Great Junction Street stands the premises of another pioneering Victorian school. Founded in 1840, it was always known as Dr Bell's after its benefactor, who founded the Madras System of teaching. Madras College in St Andrews and Bell Baxter High School in Cupar are other reminders of this early educationalist. Leith's Dr Bell's, with its separate playgrounds for boys and girls, separate entrances and even intricately devised intertwining wrought iron stairs to guarantee that the two sexes crossed paths but never bumped into each other, continued as a school for well over a century and later, when replaced by more modern premises, it still rang with children's voices as it became the local education authority's drama centre.

From Great Junction Street turn into Kirkgate. Although spelt 'gate', the latter part of this place-name does not refer to an entrance or archway, but is derived from the old word *gait*, meaning a step or stride and, as in so many Danish, Norwegian and Swedish seaport towns, means a street. This street leads appropriately to South Leith Parish Church which was founded as St Mary's way back in pre-Reformation days in 1483 as a guild kirk, but whose exterior was altered very extensively in Victorian times in 1842.

On the opposite side of Kirkgate stands the jewel in the crown of Leith's historic buildings, Trinity House. A neo-classical style building it dates from 1817, but the organisation which it represents goes back much further to 1555. Leith's Trinity House is proud of the fact that it pre-dates by several years the similarly named organisation in London. Leith's Trinity House owes its origin to the custom of the town's skippers levying dues on every vessel coming into the port and using it to provide a sort of very early local version of the welfare state, centuries before such an idea was thought of nationwide. They called themselves the Corporation of Shipmasters of the Trinty-House of Leith and, in the middle of the 1500s were given the legal right to use the dues to pay for a hospital to care for 'poor, old, infirm and weak mariners'.

In 1797, Leith's Trinity House took on the very important task of licensing all pilots for the Firth of Forth, a duty which it faithfully undertook for almost 200 years until this responsibility was transferred in the 1980s to the Forth Ports Authority, which has now become Forth Ports Plc. All vessels above a few hundred tons navigating the Firth of Forth must either take on board a pilot, or have a captain who has passed the same very strict examination which Forth Ports Plc sets for the pilots. The Forth pilots are all very skilled, highly trained mariners, who all already possess their masters' certificates and have to resit and to pass their pilots' test every year in order to retain their licences. While the owners of some smaller vessels which regularly ply the waters of the Forth try to persuade their masters to sit the examination and thus save them spending money on pilotage fees, most captains are much happier to have the up-to-date advice of one of the local pilots, although, of course, all skippers are ultimately responsible for their vessels, the Panama Ship Canal being the only place in the world where the pilot takes over control. Having a pilot on the bridge as a ship enters or leaves the Forth also has the added advantage that the navigating officer does not have to remain on duty as he has legally to do if his captain is also acting as pilot, which is a great consideration in these days of reduced crewing and faster turn-arounds.

From their heyday in the 1950s when there were 45 pilots at work on the river, with 18 each at Leith and Grangemouth, six at Methil, two at Burntisland and one at Bo'ness, the total number of pilots has now been reduced to 33, but this does not mean that they do less work, simply that they are more efficiently organised thanks to more modern means of communication with the ships coming into the Forth and also more flexible working patterns. The pilots, who are all self-employed, now undertake their own organisation from their headquarters in Granton and take vessels in and out of all of the Forth ports. The number of calls which they make to each of them ranges from arrivals and departures on every tide at Grangemouth, which deals with an impressive 50 per cent of all of Scotland's sea-going traffic, to occasional visits to one or other of the two jetties at Inverkeithing.

While Leith's old Trinity House no longer has the direct contact with the river which it formerly enjoyed, it still retains many interesting relics, including several impressive oil paintings ranging in subject from an early view of Leith and portraits of famous people connected with the port, to one of the explorer Vasco da Gama's sailing ship rounding the Cape of Good Hope near Cape Town in South Africa. Another place in Leith with interesting artwork is the famous King's Wark pub with its stained glass windows depicting scenes from the district's history including a fisherman handing over some of his catch to a priest and the famous man o'war, *The Great Michael*, described earlier in this chapter.

Street names, too, are a reminder of Leith's links with the sea and ships. Some are immediately obvious such as Water's Close, Shore Street, Commercial Street, Baltic Street, Cadiz Street and romantically named Salamander Street. Others need more searching out, such as Timber Bush Lane, which takes its name not from a wee tree, but from a corruption of the word *bourse* meaning that it was here that the cargoes of wood from across the North Sea from the Baltic countries and from as far away as the tropical forests of Africa and South America were bought and sold.

Another Leith Street with an intriguing tale behind its name is Tower Street, which runs parallel with the docks. The tower from which it derives its name was originally built in 1696 as a windmill and was two storeys higher than it is now. A century later, during the Napoleonic Wars, the timber-built windmill was demolished and it became a signal tower from which messages were sent to naval vessels in the Forth by the use of flags. For navigational reasons, the ships also required very accurate time checks to set their chronometers, and so the Leith Signal Tower was developed into what was known as a ball tower. This meant that, shortly before one o'clock each day, a black-painted wooden ball was hoisted to the top of the flag pole from which it was dropped exactly on the stroke of the hour. As sight travels faster than sound, this allowed the navigating officers on the vessels in the roads, as the waters off Leith were known, to set their ships' clocks to within a fraction of a second. Edinburgh still has its ball tower, now situated on top of the inverted telescope-shaped Nelson Monument on the summit of Calton Hill. Nowadays it is synchronised by an electronic link with the firing of the famous One o'Clock Gun from the Argyll Battery of Edinburgh Castle. When the blank shell is fired by the modern 25-pound artillery piece, as it is every day apart from Sunday, because it is said that the douce inhabitants of the capital refused to have the traditional silence of the Scottish Sabbath shattered, the black, zinc-clad, five foot six inch signal ball drops simultaneously down the white pole on top of the Nelson Monument and ships in the river still see it fall, before they hear the loud bang of the castle's gun. Many visitors to Edinburgh ask why the One o'Clock Gun? Why not the Twelve Noon Gun as in Hong Kong? They are always told that it is because this is Scotland and it would appal our traditional sense of thriftiness to waste twelve shells, when one does the job perfectly adequately. The truth, however, is that the castle gun is fired at one o'clock because the descent of the single ball from the signal tower indicated that hour to navigators out at sea. The signal tower on Calton Hill, whose operation is still financed by

Forth Ports Plc, is one of the last remaining ones in the world. Others still working are those at Greenwich on the River Thames, from where longitude is measured from the Meridian Line, which passes through it and the one at the city of Christchurch's Lyttelton Harbour on the east coast of New Zealand's South Island.

Leith's trade with such far-distant parts of the world is recalled by two of the port's historic buildings. One is the Corn Exchange on the corner of Constitution Street, which was built in 1863 and whose carved stone frieze depicting the cultivating and export of grain crops is a reminder of the trade which used to be conducted there. Its offices are to the front and its trading hall, once noisy and busy with the shouts of traders, is to the rear. The other is the impressive Exchange Building, which stands opposite facing down the imposing breadth of Bernard Street. Its classical facade dates from 1810, but it also incorporates the older Assembly Rooms of 1783, from which Leith's Assembly Street takes its name.

Many of the port of Leith's most fashionable social events from soirées to grand balls took place at the Assembly Rooms and it is interesting to imagine the ladies with their high-piled hair and flowing gowns and the gentlemen with their white-powdered wigs and brocade suits, wining, dining and dancing the night away. No doubt there was always time between the courses and the dances to give the Exchange Rooms an entirely different meaning as the guests swapped the latest stories and gossip. Certainly, in 1779, they must have had plenty to chat about, because the revolt by the American Colonies, which the rebels deigned to dignify with the title of the War of American Independence suddenly impinged on their everyday lives with the news that the Scottish-born turn-coat privateer, John Paul Jones, had arrived off the Leith shore and was threatening to shell the port. Fortunately, a gale swept his ship out into the Firth and he never returned, but the incident was enough to panic the inhabitants into demanding better protection. This resulted in a contract for James Craig, the young architect, who had won the Edinburgh Provost George Drummond's competition to build the New Town, but had had little work ever since, because of his conceited pomposity. Now, instead of designing the broad streets and curving crescents and circles of the Georgian New Town, he was called upon to build Leith Fort. Situated overlooking what was then the water, before so much land was reclaimed from the Forth, the resulting tower was similar to the Martello Towers, which were hurriedly erected around the coasts of England a few years later when the French Emperor Napoleon threatened to invade. Only some of the walls and two guard houses survive, since the area around it, off Ferry Road, was redeveloped as a disastrous local authority housing scheme in the 1950s.

Some earlier Leith defences can also still be seen on Leith Links, the green sward, which is an attractive feature of the east end of the port. These were earthworks thrown up in 1560, when, as the last Roman Catholic bastion in Scotland, Leith was besieged by both the Scottish and English armies. One is called the Giant's Brae and, according to local tradition, is said to have been raised to form a gun battery for the Earl of Somerset's English guns, so that his cannons could fire over the top of the town wall at Constitution Street. The other is known as Lady Fyfe's Brae and is claimed to have been the site of Pelham's Battery. Although the siege ended peacefully after the death of Mary Queen of Scot's mother, the French Mary of Guise, much of Leith had in the meantime been destroyed by the gun fire from these two defensive positions.

In more peaceful times, Leith Links were a popular place with the local inhabitants to enjoy their recreation, especially by playing golf. The earliest mention of the sport in Scotland mentions Leith Links, but it might also have been its last as it was an edict from King James II forbidding both golf and football, because they were interfering with his army's archery practice. Fortunately for Scotland's sporting future, his ban was ignored and the people of Leith continued to enjoy wielding their wooden-shafted golf clubs on the Links. The first proper course, consisting of five holes, was opened in 1744 and a cairn in the middle of the grass commemorates its construction. That same year, in order to ensure fair play, the first 13 rules of golf were drawn up by the players at Leith and ten years later it was these same rules which were adopted at St Andrews, thus enshrining them in the story of the sport. For almost a century from 1777 to 1867, Leith Links played host to an annual all-comers golf tournament, which became the Scottish Open. In 1907, however, it was decided that it was becoming dangerous to allow golf to be played in the heart of Leith and so the greens, fairways and sandy natural bunkers of the dunes were all levelled and turned into the public park which exists today.

Apart from its claim to be the birthplace of golf, Leith has many other claims to fame. Some of these connected with transport include the opening in 1720 of Scotland's first dry dock for the repair of ships on the site of what is now the open grass land between Commercial Street and Sandport Place; the building of the SS *Sirius* in 1837, which became the first steamship to successfully cross the Atlantic Ocean; the opening of Scotland's first passenger railway station the following year in 1838; the opening in 1905 of one of Scotland's earliest electric tram systems, 17 years before the then rival Edinburgh succeeded in electrifying its network. Leith can also claim a 'last'. Its Western Harbour was the last dock in Britain licensed as a passenger flying boat base. The story of the seaplanes began in 1949 when a flying boat from Norway landed bringing the ship's company for a new vessel, which had been built and launched at Burntisland. Following this successful visit, Aquila Airways asked the Dock Commissioners for permission to schedule a regular service from Leith to Falmouth in Cornwall. The required licence was obtained from the Ministry of Civil Aviation to register the docks as an airport, but the Aquila service failed to take off because of lack of bookings. During the next few years, occasional seaplanes on charter flights did land on the waters of the Western Harbour, but flying boats went out of fashion and in 1959 the airport licence was allowed to lapse.

Earlier in its history, the Western Harbour played an important part in the war effort, when towards the end of 1943 work began in top secrecy on the construction of piers and pontoons for a project code-named Mulberry. At a construction yard hurriedly built on the land reclaimed by the Western Extension, hundreds of men worked round the clock. In under six months they produced 13 piers and 16 pontoons, which on 5 June 1944 made up a major part of the Mulberry Harbour, whose facilities contributed much to the success of the D-Day Normandy Landings.

After the war, many of the men involved in the Mulberry Harbour project found outlets for their skills as welders, carpenters and plumbers at the ship-building yard of Henry Robb, which also played a major role during the hostilities. Despite the fact that Leith has a history of ship-building stretching back over 500 years, with Ramage and Ferguson, S. and H. Morton and Menzies among the famous names, Robb's found it increasingly difficult to obtain orders during the post-war years. In 1968, in a bid to strengthen its business, the yard merged with the Caledonian Shipbuilding Company of Dundee and, in 1977, the combined companies were in turn incorporated into the unsuccessful British Shipbuilders. Robb's regained its freedom in 1982 and succeeded in getting an order for a British Rail Sealink passenger car ferry. Named the *St Helen*, she was launched in September of the following year, sadly the very last vessel to be built at Leith.

Amongst the orders, which helped keep Henry Robb alive during its final years, were those from one of Leith's best-known shipping companies, Currie Line Ltd. The company traced its origin back to 1836 and took its name from James Currie, whose brother Donald was responsible for the famous Castle Line, whose Royal Mail Steamers carried the mail and passengers to South Africa every week for over a century. Currie ships were often chartered to provide additional tonnage on the Cape Town route. In 1969 Currie Line Ltd was taken over by Anchor Line, but the familiar name still survives in Leith as it acts as port agent for other companies' vessels.

Three years later, in 1972, Anchor Line also took another well-known firm of ship owners, George Gibson and Company in tow. Gibson Line was founded even earlier than the Currie Line, first coming into business in 1820. Exactly a century later in 1920 it merged with Glasgow shipowner, James Rankine, to form the Gibson Rankine Line. Gibson's had the charming custom of choosing names connected with Sir Walter Scott for all of its vessels, following the launch of the *Abbotsford* in 1870, and continued this practice for over 100 years right into the 1970s, with its gas tankers *Teviot* and *Traquair*.

Another of Leith's famous shipowners who loyally chose distinctive Scottish names for its vessels was the Ben Line. The first of its ships with the prefix Ben was the *Bencleugh* in 1853 and the tradition was maintained for 140 years until the company pulled out of shipping in 1993. Ben Line became particularly famous on its routes to the Far East.

No list of Leith shipowners could be complete without mention of Christian Salvesen, but when the young Norwegian first came to Scotland in the 1840s it was to work in his uncle's shipping agency in Grangemouth. He moved to Leith in 1853 and became a British citizen in 1859. By the beginning of the 20th century, Salvesen owned one of the largest fleets in Scotland, with over 30 vessels, and expanded the business still further by sending a whaling expedition to Antarctica. By 1909, Salvesen had established a base in the icy wastes of South Georgia, which it called Leith Harbour. During the First World War, Salvesen was the first Leith shipping company to loose a ship to enemy action, when the *Glitra* was sunk in the North Sea by an enemy U-boat. Up until this time the company's funnel design was red, white and black, but this was deemed too similar to the German flag and so it was changed to red, white and blue, a distinctive colour scheme which in the post-war years became famous around the world.

Again during the Second World War, Salvesen suffered losses. One of the saddest was that of the oil tanker *Salvestra*. Originally built to carry whale oil home from the Antarctic, at the beginning of the hostilities she was diverted to the USA to bring back a much-needed cargo of petrol. On 27 July 1940, *Salvestra*, having sailed over 3,500 miles, was within sight of her home port, when 2.8 miles east of Inchkeith, she hit a mine. The large 500-foot long and 62-foot wide vessel exploded and sank within minutes. Fuel from her tanks washed ashore on both sides of the Forth, but all details of her tragic loss were hushed up by the wartime censors. *Salvestra's* name is a reminder of the company's policy of giving many of their vessels titles beginning with *Sal*, with the exception of its whaling fleet, whose ships usually had names starting with *Southern*. Best remembered is probably its last factory ship, *Southern Harvester*, which continued in service until Salvesen's withdrawal from whaling in 1963. While there is now great repugnance at the idea of whaling, the bravery of the Salvesen seamen and harpooners should be remembered and it should not be forgotten that whale oil supplies played a role in both World Wars and that in the late 1940s, whale steaks were a welcome addition to the Scottish menu during the rigours of post-war rationing. A more pleasant legacy of Salvesen's long links with whaling is Edinburgh Zoo's popular penguin parade, because it owes the origin of its world-famous penguin colony to the birds brought home aboard *Southern Harvester* and her sister ships at the end of each long Antarctic voyage. The popular version of the story is that the penguins were actually brought home by the Salvesen crew members as pets, but when they took them home their wives soon protested that they were not taking up residence in the family bathrooms, and so they were soon gifted to the zoo.

Certainly, the birds from the Antarctic have adapted so well to the Scottish climate and bred so happily, that Edinburgh Zoo has now made penguins an established Scottish export, supplying the requirements of other zoos and theme parks around the world. This includes the spectacular exhibit at Sea World in San Diego, USA, where the penguins are protected from the Californian sunshine by being housed in a warehouse-sized refrigerated building.

Leith Docks today takes in an extensive area, right along the coast from Newhaven Harbour past Middle Craig and on beyond East Craig. The docks comprise a total area of almost 260 hectares, including both areas of water and the surrounding land. The landward areas include extensive quays, warehouses and other outdoor storage areas, an oil depot, two pipe-coating plants carrying out work for the North Sea oil industry, an oil depot, lorry parks and a rail goods yard. The actual docks consist of the Edinburgh Dock, the Albert Dock, the Imperial Dock, the Victoria Dock, the Harbour and the extensive western Harbour. Together they make up an impressive stretch of water covering 150 hectares. There are also three dry docks for ship repairs, two owned by Forth Ports Plc and the other, the Edinburgh Dry Dock, which is privately owned.

The entrance from the Firth of Forth to the docks complex is through a 259-metre long and 31.6-metre wide lock. It can cope with vessels up to 210 metres long and with a beam of up to 30 metres.

Up until the end of 1998, one of the most frequent users of the entrance lock was the quaintly named *Gardyloo*, which sailed out and in again most days from Monday to Friday to dump her 2,000 tons of cargo three hours sailing time out from Leith at the mouth of the Firth. The *Gardyloo* took her name from the traditional cry which in medieval times echoed along the length of Edinburgh's Royal Mile every night at 10 pm, when the striking of the faceless clock in the crown steeple of the High Kirk of St Giles signalled that the auld town's inhabitants could throw up their windows and throw down the contents of their chamber pots into the street and the 1990s *Gardyloo's* cargo consisted of similar raw sewage. The shout, *Gardyloo*, was a corruption of the French, *Gardez l'eau!*, meaning, 'Look-out, here comes the water!' It was, of course, very dirty water and in the Middle Ages passers-by in Castle Hill, the

Lawnmarket, the High Street, the Canongate and Abbey Strand — the five streets which make up the Royal Mile — had to be fast to shout, 'Haud yer hand', if they did not want to receive a sewage shampoo. Now the European Community has indicated it is issuing a similar warning and that from the end of 1998, new regulations will have the same effect on the *Gardyloo's* dumping operation in the Forth. This will leave the *Gardyloo's* owners, East of Scotland Water, with a considerable problem about how to find an acceptable way in which to dispose of 'The Flowers of Edinburgh', as the waste used to be euphemistically described and controversy rages about whether it is better to spread it on the farm fields of Fife, than to disperse it in the Forth estuary off its shores. One thing is certain, and that is that the new EC sewage disposal rules banning dumping in the sea will end Edinburgh ratepayers' free trips down the river, which the *Gardyloo* offered as a daily bonus on all of her sailings, her galley even providing breakfast and lunch, if the thought of her cargo did not rob her passengers of their appetites.

The *Gardyloo* herself was never constipated, as her regular operation was facilitated by the fact that the entrance lock to Leith Docks is available for use, subject to weather conditions, round the clock, unlike in earlier times when it could only be opened for a limited time each side of the twice daily high tides on the river. The only days on which the entrance lock is never opened are at Christmas and New Year, when it is closed except for emergencies.

Mention of Christmas and New Year holidays is a reminder of the well-known old tongue twister, 'The Leith Police dismisses us', said to have been used in the days before breathalysers to trap drunk drivers. That phrase is said to have done more than anything else to put Leith on the map, but as described here it definitely has far greater claims to fame. Now, however, it is time to move on further along Edinburgh's city coastline.

From Leith, it is possible to hug the coast by taking Seafield Road, but it is disappointingly uninteresting as it sweeps round past car salerooms and do-it-yourself warehouses on the landward side. Drive on, however, because at the end of it there is a true holiday treat in store at Portobello, which for over 200 years has been Edinburgh's real seaside.

Portobello sounds as if it should really be situated in far warmer climes on one of the Spanish Costas and indeed the name does come from Spanish-speaking Central America. For, according to tradition, Portobello takes its title from the name of the first thatched-roof cottage built in 1742 on this stretch of the south shore of the Forth known until then as Figgate Whins. It was built by an old sea-dog after he retired from serving in the Royal Navy under Admiral Vernon, during one of whose campaigns in 1730 he had helped to capture the town of Puerto Bello on the south-east coast of the Isthmus of Panama. The cottage became a hostelry where travellers stopped for drinks on their journeys from Edinburgh to Musselburgh, until it was demolished in 1862. Meanwhile, in 1765, a brick and tile works was opened and Portobello developed into a small village to house its workers, but it was to its glorious long sandy beach that it really owed its growth. For when the 19th-century health craze for sea bathing reached Scotland, it was ideally situated within easy reach of Edinburgh. Soon, the first bathing machines appeared. These tall, brightly painted wooden huts on wheels allowed the ladies and gentlemen of the period to undress in privacy, before the bathing box was towed down into the water into which they could then descend in their all-enveloping bathing costumes, the men in knitted one-pieces which came right up to their necks and down to their knees and the ladies in voluminous bloomers even more modestly covered in knee-length matching skirts. Thus clad, they could then climb down a short ladder straight into the sea and discreetly immerse themselves with the least possible risk of being seen by prying eyes.

By the middle of Queen Victoria's long reign, however, it did become the thing to be seen beside the sea and by this time Portobello boasted a pier, jutting out into the Forth in the style of the very best of English resorts such as Eastbourne and Brighton and several Portobello place-names even have Brighton in their titles. Designed by Sir Thomas Bouch of ill-fated Tay Railway Bridge fame, the pier was officially opened in 1871. Built of iron, it stretched for 1,250 feet, almost three-quarters of a mile out into the Firth and cost £7,000 to erect. The length which it stretched out to sea meant that the pleasure steamers of the Galloway Saloon Steam Packet Company could call at practically all states of the tide and offer holiday-makers trips both up and down the river. The company was founded around 1850 by Captain John Galloway and at first he operated his excursions using two small former tug boats, but by the time his son, Mr M.P. Galloway, became manager, the line had what were at the time described as:

> five fine saloon steamers. These fast and commodious steamers of handsome appointment sail up and down the Firth of Forth at stated times, touching at many of the most historic and interesting riverside and coastal places in this part of Scotland. Each trip is one of thorough enjoyment, whether up the river or down the Firth and the popularity of the service increases year by year.

The Galloway steamers were headquartered nearby at Leith and made frequent calls at Portobello, but while the steamers' arrivals and departures kept the long pier busy, many of those who walked its length simply did so for the pleasure of walking out over the water and, of course, being seen to be rich enough to afford to do so because strolling upon its wooden decks cost an entrance fee, which kept 'the common riff raff safely away.' One of those who paid his penny and promenaded all the way to the end of the Portobello pier, wrote as follows about the experience:

> The view from the end of the pier is one of great interest and beauty; in front and to each side the blue waters of the noble estuary, broken to the north by the island the lighthouse of Inchkeith, beyond which wind and curve the town studded shores of Fife; to the right North Berwick Law and a peep of the lonely Bass, with, nearer at hand, the bay and links of Aberlady, Prestonpans, Musselburgh and Inveresk, with its conspicuous church spire; to the left Arthur's Seat and the glancing sheen of Edina's domes and spires; and to the south and behind, the Niddrie Woods, Craigmillar Castle and the hills of Pentland and Moorfoot.

The Portobello Pier had outdoor seating accommodation for 2,000 visitors and at the shore end there was also what was described as 'a saloon for concerts and variety entertainments', a reminder of course that Portobello was the birthplace of that most famous of Scottish singers and comedians, Sir Harry Lauder. A plaque on a wall in Bridge Street marks where he was born and occasional concerts in Portobello Town Hall recall his songs.

For those who could not afford the admittance charge to the pier, which lasted until it was finally demolished in 1917, there was always Portobello Esplanade upon which to stroll. A Victorian guidebook extols its virtues describing it as:

A most splendid marine promenade over one mile in length, overlooking a noble expanse of smooth sandy beach. About midlength on the parade is a handsome drinking fountain and on the beach, which affords at all times the greatest facility and safety for bathers there is ample provision for bathing coaches and a commodious suite of salt water baths. The residential accommodation is varied and embraces two good hotels, numerous vital boarding houses and a few larger mansions suitable for first class families. A Town Hall was erected in 1862-63 by a limited liability company at a cost of £3,000 and this with the new Municipal Buildings, both in the High Street, constitutes the most important of Portobello's public buildings.

Even by this time in the 1890s, however, guidebooks were commenting:

In spite of its natural advantages and the great promise it once held out of becoming a really fashionable and high class watering place, the taint of industry militates against its improving in this respect. Its contiguity to Edinburgh makes it a favourite resort of the holiday and Saturday afternoon, 'tripper' and on fine summer days the beach presents a very animated appearance.

Both trains and tramcars linked Portobello to the centre of the capital and made it very easy for the crowds of day-trippers to reach its sands. Later, in the 1920s and 30s, its huge and very popular open-air swimming pool with its numberless art deco clock overlooking the bathers and its marine gardens ballroom kept holiday-makers equally happy by night.

The industry to which the tourist guidebooks referred as retracting from Portobello's prospects as a holiday resort included works manufacturing bottles, bricks, paper and tiles, but the most famous of Portobello's factories was its well-known potteries. The first person to discover clay at Portobello was William Jamieson, who opened the first brickworks around the year 1760. He exploited the fire clay deposits below his own estate, but as more kinds of clay were discovered locally, the brickworks were joined by potteries. The most famous pottery was that of A.W. Buchan and Co. Ltd, which began operations in 1867. It continued in operation for over a century until 1972 and two of its brick-built bottle kilns have been preserved and still stand near the shore on its site in Pipe Street. Most famous of Buchan's products was its pale blue, green and purple Thistle Ware and, although the

Portobello pottery closed over quarter of a century ago, this is still produced in a more modern works in Crieff, to which the business was transferred.

Moving on along the coast again, there was more industry in Joppa. 'A smoky, malodorous place, consisting of a group of sooty buildings situated on the sea-shore half way between Portobello and Musselburgh', is how William Chambers, the future Lord Provost of Edinburgh and owner of the famous publishing firm, described it, when he moved to live there as a boy, when his father was appointed manager of the salt-works. Salt had been produced at Joppa since 1631 using locally mined coal to evaporate the river water and some of the salters' cottages and miners' houses still stand. Brickworks and quarries added to Joppa's industrial aspect, but all except the salt-works on the shore closed down and, in Victorian times, Joppa became the up-market end of Portobello as far as holiday-makers were concerned. The coming of the railway with fast, regular and reliable cheap train services to Edinburgh also made it increasingly popular as a residential suburb and several fine villas and, later, well-built stone tenements were built to house these early commuters. Despite this increased respectability, the old salt-works close by continued production until 1953. Having survived for over three centuries, they were sadly demolished a few years later, thus robbing us of the chance to preserve one of the last examples of this historic Forth industry.

CHAPTER 5

FOR THE NEXT STOP'S KIRKCADDY

The Boy in the Train

Whit wey does the engine say Toot-toot?
Is it feart to gang in the tunnel?
Whit wey is the furnace no pit oot
When the rain gangs doon the funnel?
What'll I hae for my tea the nicht ?
A herrin', or maybe a haddie?
Has Gran'ma gotten electric licht?
Is the next stop Kirkcaddy?

There's a hoodie-craw on yon turnip-raw
An' sea-gulls! — sax or seeven.
I'll no fa' oot o' the windae, Maw,
It's sneckit, as sure as I'm leevin'.
We're into the tunnel! we're a' in the dark!
But dinna be frichtit, Daddy,
We'll sune be comin' to Beveridge Park,
And the next stop's Kirkcaddy

Is yon the mune I see in the sky?
It's awfu' wee an' curly.
See! there's a coo and a cauf ootbye,
An' a lassie pu'in' a hurly!
He's chackit the tickets and gien them back,
Sae gie me my ain yin, Daddy.
Lift doon the bag frae the luggage rack,
For the next stop's Kirkcaddy!

There's a gey wheen boats at the harbour mou,'
And eh! dae ye: see the cruisers?
The cinnamon drop I was sookin' the noo
Has tummelt an' stuck tae ma troosers...
I'll sune be ringin' ma Gran'ma's bell,
She'll cry, 'Come ben, my laddie',
For I ken mysel' by the queer-like smell
That the next stop's Kirkcaddy!

Mabel C. Smith

The 'queer like smell', which Mabel C. Smith's well-kent and oft recited poem made famous, was, of course that of Kirkcaldy's linoleum-making industry. For long, linoleum manufacturing was the Fife town's largest employer and it still makes floor coverings to this day, but to trace the history of the industry, which dates back to 1847, it is best to visit the local museum. It is very conveniently situated right next to the town's railway station, which has direct trains from Edinburgh and Dundee. In the museum can be seen examples of the patterns of linoleum, which were the very latest home-furnishing fashions in bygone years, and the processes, which produced them and made Nairn's the largest and most successful factory of its kind in the world, are clearly explained. In a way this is only fitting, as the impressive grey-stone museum, the library next door and the art gallery above were all given to Kirkcaldy by the firm's owner John Nairn as a war memorial to his workers and all the other local men who had been slain during the First World War hostilities.

Another product for which Kirkcaldy is also justly famed is its Wemyss Ware, the colourful pottery made locally by the Fife pottery of Robert Heron and Son in Gallatoun from 1889 to 1930. The walls of the museum tea-room are lined with splendidly colourful samples from vivid red and green cabbage rose decorated vases to supercilious long-necked 'wally' cats. The word 'wally' now has a somewhat derogatory meaning to it, but this does not apply to the Kirkcaldy cats, as in the past in Scotland it simply meant pottery. Indeed, in Glasgow it was considered frightfully posh to live in a tenement which had a 'wally' close, that is a downstairs entrance hall whose walls were lined with pristine white china tiles. Not quite so up market, of course, was the use of the term 'wallies' as a familiar description for artificial dentures! The Wemyss 'wally' cats were part of a whole menagerie of 'wally' creatures including beasts, birds and even fish produced by several Scottish potteries, of which the best known were the Bo'ness-made 'wally' dugs produced in a pottery on the shores of the Forth further up river at Bridgeness. The Kirkcaldy kittens were, however, much more refined, from their glossy coats to their curious eyes, which seem to stare back and indeed follow visitors as they examine the museum's collection. Like all chimney-piece ornaments, as the 'wally' animals are known by collectors, the

113

Wemyss cats come in pairs, one looking right and the other left, as they are intended for display at either end of fireplace mantleshelves, and it is said they have such a high gloss finish to make it easy for house-proud housewives to wipe off coal dust which rose from the open coal fire crackling in the hearth below.

Similar memories of familiar features of Scotland's past are conjured up by items in many of the paintings in the spacious art gallery, a very practical and well-used living memorial, which linoleum manufacturer John Nairn provided for his town. People in other Scottish towns should envy it compared to their stone obelisks and other statues, which they only visit once a year at the eleventh hour of the eleventh day of the eleventh month. The art gallery, which Nairn gifted to Kirkcaldy and which is now cared for by Fife Council, must indeed rate as one of the best provincial galleries in Britain, with a collection to match, including works by Anne Redpath, S.J. Peploe and the other Scottish colourists including Cadell, Ferguson and Hunter, but for a book about the shores of the Firth of Forth the whole room devoted to William McTaggart must take priority. The sweep and freshness of his seascapes bring the taste of the tang of salt sea air right into the gallery and every visitor will no doubt select a favourite piece from, *The White Surf* to *The Wave* or the plaintive *Away O'er the Sea*, depicting the mother with her two wee lassies who have been left on the shore. But surely *The Storm* is a special masterpiece, with its bairns nestled safely in the cliff-top grass anxiously watching the dangerous drama of the attempts to rescue those on the stricken shipwrecked vessel in the wave-lashed seas below. Children's relationship to nature is an essential element in all of McTaggart's works and the accompanying notes in the Kirkcaldy Art Museum suggest that the boys and girls in the pictures are painted in such a way that they merge with the landscape, or more accurately in most instances, the seascape, so that they almost become part of it as if they are of the same substance or essence, both possessing a kind of natural innocence, which McTaggart valued above all else. This innocence certainly shines out of his early piece, *Going to Sea*, which shows three laddies listening eagerly to the tales of a sailor about his distant voyages and adventures in far-flung foreign lands, as so many wee boys must surely have done in places along the Fife shore in years past.

Even today the Forth does apparently still inspire some local young folk, for in startling contrast to the McTaggarts on the walls, Kirkcaldy's curator Dallas Mechan has daringly chosen to display Martin Rayner's 1991 strikingly modern three-dimensional piece, *The Sea Marker*, right in the centre of the room. Inspired by one of the many intriguingly named buoys such as The Hen and Chickens, which bob about out in the Forth, *The Sea Marker* imaginatively and amusingly captures many aspects of the life and legend of the river from its capstan top to its bare-bottomed, or rather bare-tailed, mermaids with, in between, in an intriguing mixture of carved and painted wood, copper and even epoxy resin, a lively catch of fish and folk, like the whaler with his harpoon poised. Notice that the wee fishing boats are all accurately Kirkcaldy registered. In the middle of the next room is displayed another of Rayner's subsequent works, his 1992 *Silver Darling*, which was commissioned by the Kirkcaldy Gallery. Appropriately, the sea box which is an integral part of it is being used to collect cash to help with the restoration of several of its other works of art just as sea boxes in Forth towns have hoarded money for deserving causes for many centuries. The ship-shaped *Silver Darling* appeals specially to children and older visitors who have not forgotten what it is like to feel young and, in a way, captures much of the feeling of fun which this anything but dry and dusty gallery and museum inspires. An especially pleasant touch is its custom of each season inviting a different member of staff, from the cleaners and attendants to the exhibition organisers, to select and highlight a particular piece from its collection. One recent choice was an oil painting entitled *The Smugglers* which was picked by Chargehand Attendant Derek Nelson, who went on to explain his choice by recalling his childhood trips on his father's fishing boat and his pride in being the only one of his primary classmates who survived a school ship cruise across a stormy North Sea, without being seasick, because of the salt water which he had inherited in his veins!

Downstairs, the museum has an equally warm atmosphere and a very welcoming 'Please DO Touch' sign at the entrance. Its exhibits illustrate well many other aspects of the town's history, from the pains of schooldays, with a locally produced lithe leather 'Lochgelly' tawse which used to be described as Fife's best-known export, still hung at the ready, to the enjoyment of its famous spring funfair, which is the largest street fair in the whole of

Europe. The Links Market, which can trace its continuing descent all the way down from a charter granted by King Edward I giving Kirkcaldy the right to hold an annual market every Easter, takes place, as the name suggests, right on the shores of the Forth and it is there each year that Scotland's show families bring all their sideshows and rides out of winter storage and set them up to begin the new season, just as their ancestors have done for generations. It is, in fact, official policy to give preferential treatment in the allocation of sites to these long-established show people and the Convener of Fife Council, which is now the local government authority with responsibility for Kirkcaldy, still dutifully turns out to welcome them officially just as the Provost, magistrates, councillors and town officials always did down through the ages, giving an idea of how important the Links Market has been and still is to the burgh's economy. Today the rides are larger, more garishly neon-lit and terrifying in true white-knuckle fashion than ever before, but in many other ways all the fun of the fair has not altered, from the excuse to eat junk fast food to the chance to enjoy a quick kiss and cuddle on the waltzers or the jungle ride.

The right to hold an annual April market in Kirkcaldy was re-confirmed by the Scottish Parliament to Sir Andrew Ramsay in 1672. In those days, the area occupied by the market was from 'John Louden's Wynd to East Bridge; from Linktown Market on Links Street and from Kirkcaldy boundary to Bridgeton; and Pathhead Market to Mid Street'. Nowadays, Kirkcaldy's yearly Links Market is equally strung out all the way from Charlotte Street right to the south end of the Esplanade near to Bridge Street. The Links Market is the longest in the country, a reminder that Kirkcaldy's nickname is indeed 'The Lang Toon'. Taking in Linktown, Invertiel, Pathhead, Sinclairtown and Gallowtown, Kirkcaldy stretches for well over four miles.

Today its harbour at the east end of the Esplanade has been officially closed to commercial traffic since its dock gates were damaged several years ago and proved too costly to repair, but it was very different in earlier centuries when it bustled with trade. In 1334, Kirkcaldy was granted by King David II to the monastery of Dunfermline and for over a century was subject to its regality. Then, in 1450, it was created a royal burgh with its own right to levy harbour customs. Its trade flourished with exports of coal, salt and fish and by the 17th century it had a fleet of over 100 ships registered at its port. In 1644, Kirkcaldy's fortunes seemed set to flourish further when King Charles I re-affirmed its royal status and declared it a free port, but his blessing proved a poisoned chalice because in the Civil War which followed it placed the town on the wrong side. Over 90 of its vessels were either attacked and sunk at sea by the Parliamentarian Roundheads or were captured by them and the town suffered a further reverse when the king was executed and Oliver Cromwell's troops invaded Scotland. Cromwell's General Monk captured Dundee and with it the warehouse in the city where £5,000 worth of Kirkcaldy's possessions had been stored for supposedly safe keeping during the hostilities.

After the Act of Union, uniting the Parliaments of Scotland and England in 1707, Kirkcaldy benefited from the improved trading conditions and linen manufacturing was established in the town. In 1739, an annual market was established for the sale of linen cloth and the local magistrates did everything possible to encourage the trade. By 1743, 300,000 yards of linen were stamped as duty having been paid at Kirkcaldy, including some produced in the neighbouring villages of Leslie, Dysart and Abbotshall. It was mostly described as coarse ticking, but some of the linen was fine enough to be made into handkerchiefs. Most of the linen was exported through the harbour to markets as far away as the American colonies and the West Indies, but the trade was crippled by the war with France which broke out in 1756 and which was later called the Seven Years War. As a result of attacks by French naval vessels, Kirkcaldy's fleet of merchant vessels was reduced to only one 50-ton coaster and two little ferry boats and the town's linen looms were at a standstill. When the hostilities ended in 1763, however, a local entrepreneur, James Fergus, determined to produce linen of a fine enough quality to sell on the British home market. He succeeded in spinning a fabric of first-class quality and by the end of the 18th century one million yards of this finer cloth was being produced annually by Kirkcaldy's linen mills. By 1818, this quantity had doubled and over 5,000 local men and women were employed in the trade. In 1821 the country's first power-loom factory was established in the town and it was Kirkcaldy industrialist James Aytoun who improved the machinery used to spin the flax and adapted it to produce linen yarn. One well-known Kirkcaldy family involved in the industry were the Blyths, most famous of whose descendants is well-known, right-wing Conservative politician Michael Portillo who used to spend child-hood holidays here with his maternal grandparents and who, in 1997, made a sentimental journey back to the town.

About one third of the flax used by the Kirkcaldy linen mills was grown in Scotland., but the rest had to be imported, thus providing plenty of trade for the harbour. Most of the imported flax came from Riga in the Baltic and a branch of the North British Railway was constructed to transport it from the quayside to the local mills. In Victorian times local dye works connected with the linen trade, brass foundries, breweries, potteries and corn and meal mills in addition to the floorcovering and linoleum works, all contributed to Kirkcaldy's growing prosperity.

Such well-managed prosperity would no doubt have delighted Kirkcaldy's most famous son, the world-renowned economist, Adam Smith, author of *The Wealth of Nations*, in which he suggests that the way to success is for each place to concentrate on what it does best. Smith was born in the town in 1723 and was educated at Kirkcaldy Grammar School, where he received the sound grounding which stood him in good stead when he went on to study, first at the University of Glasgow and later at Baliol College, Oxford. He lies buried in the graveyard of the Kirk of the Canongate in Edinburgh's Royal Mile to which many students of economics, especially from Japan, still make pilgrimages. He is, however, also commemorated in his home town with the name of the Adam Smith Theatre.

Someone whose story might well be dramatised there is another of Kirkcaldy's sons, Michael Scott, who lived in the town in the 13th century. He was an early philosopher, physician and scientist, but because of his experiments the townsfolk were convinced that he was a wizard and possibly even in league with the Devil. Scott was born at Balwearie Tower and, despite the suspicions of the locals, in those days before Scotland had any seats of further learning, he went on to study at the universities of Oxford, Paris, Padua in Italy and Toledo in Spain. He became a fluent linguist and his brilliance was recognised by Kaiser Frederick II, who appointed him as his royal court astrologer. Very appropriately, the colourful story of Scott, the reputed wizard, was immortalised by another famous member of the Scott family, Sir Walter, in his poem *The Lay of the Last Minstrel*.

Kirkcaldy's most famous son was, however, undoubtedly, Robert Adam, the architect, who was born there in 1728 and whose stylish Georgian designs range from the massively magnificent palace block on the north side of Edinburgh's Charlotte Square, where the Secretary of State for Scotland and the Moderator of the Church Scotland both have spacious apartments and where the National Trust for Scotland's Georgian House allows curious visitors a glimpse of 18th-century high society living, to Scotland's finest stately home, Hopetoun House, the residence of the Marquis of Linlithgow, which overlooks the Forth from its hill-top site between South Queensferry and Blackness Castle. Adam died in 1792 and was honoured by being buried in Westminster Abbey, but his work was continued by his two sons.

Other famous residents of Kirkcaldy included Thomas Carlyle, who taught mathematics at the town's Grammar School from 1816 to 1819 and the famous churchman Edward Irving, who also lived there at the same period. The two men became close friends and loved to talk as they walked along the foreshore of the Firth. Their voyage by rowing boat out to Inchkeith is described in the chapter on the island. After he had become famous, Irving returned in 1828 to Kirkcaldy to preach and so large a congregation crowded into the Parish Church that the gallery collapsed, killing 28 of the worshippers.

Today Kirkcaldy is a busy shopping centre, not just for its own townsfolk, but for those from Glenrothes New Town to the north, the former coal-mining towns of West Fife and the small rural communities and fishing ports of the East Neuk, who come to enjoy the facilities of the Mercat Shopping Mall. Now Forth Ports Plc has recognised the possibilities which this offers for the redevelopment of its harbour area, lying, as in many old port towns, immediately adjacent to the town centre. Its imaginative redevelopment proposals envisage the filling in of the inner dock, which was originally opened in 1907, and major environmental improvements to the outer harbour, which was created in 1859, offering great potential for the building of new homes with spectacular views out over the Firth. The development also aims to revitalise the whole area by including in it activities to enhance the harbour as a centre for leisure. With its combination of houses, quayside shops, a large car park and recreational facilities, including a marina for small dinghies and other pleasure craft, a boat clubhouse for their owners and a heritage centre for visitors, the plan for the old harbour site could well form a focal point for the northern end of the promenade. With outline planning permission already granted for this interesting proposal, it may not be long before the harbour regains the importance which it once enjoyed in Kirkcaldy.

From the harbour site it is about two miles along the shore to Dysart. Today it is a quiet little residential backwater with many of its quaint homes protected by the National Trust for Scotland under its Little Houses Scheme. Of particular interest is 17th-century Pan Ha', whose name is a reminder of the salt industry which used to flourish there. Dysart's harbour once had a good commercial trade in both salt and coal and could accommodate vessels with a draught of up to 18 feet. The harbour also used to export considerable quantities of textiles ranging from linen, some of which was manufactured at the village's own mill, to woollens and tweeds produced in other towns in Fife. Dysart is a very picturesque little place and it also has the claim to fame of being the birth-place of John McDougal Stewart, who in 1861 and the following year became the first man to cross Australia from the south of that vast continent to the north. His birth-place is now a museum tracing the Fife explorer's life and his famous trek right across Australia's barren and inhospitable Central Desert. The museum is open on weekdays from June to August.

Visitors to Dysart come now just for an hour or two, but in Victorian times the family of John Buchan, the distinguished Scottish author and diplomat, took a house overlooking the shore for the whole of the summer season. In her autobiography, his sister Anna recalls that it would have been fine if it had been clean, but that nevertheless the children of the family fell in love with it because of its resident cat called Gentle Annie, and the discovery under one of the beds of a broody, clucking hen desperate to hatch a clutch of eggs. The area was already well known to the Buchan children, because their father, the Revd John Buchan, had earlier been minister of the church up the brae about three miles away at Pathhead. There, they had lived in the manse for 12 years from 1876 to 1888, before moving to Glasgow.

A highlight of that summer season at Dysart for the young Buchans was the opportunity which it gave to explore the nearby ruins of Ravenscraig Castle, which occupy a steep cliff-top site overlooking the Firth. The castle was constructed in 1460 by King James II as one of Scotland's earliest artillery forts, to defend the area against attacks by the English navy and also from being plundered by the pirates, who in those days sometimes harried other merchant shipping in the mouth of the river. It was later besieged during the Republican period in the 1650s by the Lord High Protector, Oliver Cromwell's soldiers. It gained literary fame when described as Ravensheugh by Sir Walter Scott in his *Lay of the Last Minstrel*. Ravenscraig is open to visitors throughout the year and, apart from its two round towers, is accessible to those who are physically challenged. The west tower was for a time the royal residence of King James II's widow. An interesting feature is it outward sloping wall head which is unique in Scotland.

As far as John Buchan's holiday in Dysart is concerned, it is interesting to ponder whether the village is the one which inspired the setting for the opening chapter of his now much neglected African adventure novel *Prester John*, which he wrote in 1910. Some of the author's devotees suggest that Buchan had Crail in mind, but Dysart has in many ways a similar location with hills rising behind it. Could it have been its rocky shore to which Buchan has his young hero steal away to listen avidly to the evangelical black preacher, only to be soundly leathered by his father upon his return, but nevertheless to set him off on his great South African safari?

From Dysart the coast runs north-east to West Wemyss, Coal Town of Wemyss and East Weymss. The unusual place-name found in the titles of all three of these adjacent villages is derived from the Gaelic *Uiam*, which progressed through the Old English, *Weim* to *Weem* and eventually into its present form of Wemyss, which means a cave and it is indeed not just one cave but a series of them which gives particular interest to the shore at this point on the Firth.

The Wemyss caves were originally formed by the action of the sea swirling into crevices in the sandstone cliffs. Between 4,000 and 3,000 BC it is believed that there was some kind of earth tremor, which resulted in the land rising. Thereafter the sea again ate into the sandstone forming a second series of caves. Again, the land appears to have risen, because today the caves are all above high-water mark. Archaeologists claim that symbols carved on the walls of the caves show that they have provided shelter for people since at least the Neolithic or Bronze Ages, between 3,500 and 1,000 BC. The oldest symbols are cup-like markings in the Court Cave. Little is known about their meaning, but more can be deduced from other markings, which are believed to date from AD 400 to 900 and are thought to be of both Pictish and Viking origin. The symbols include crude representations of animals and birds and of domestic objects such as cauldrons and combs, but most interesting are the tridents and ship in Jonathon's Cave and the carving of the Viking God of War, Thor, in the Court Cave.

With the caves' situation on the shores of the Firth of Forth, the representation of a ship is particularly fascinating as it provides a glimpse of the kind of vessel which sailed these waters some time between the Bronze Age and Pictish times. It shows a clinker-built sailing ship of a similar design to that used for fishing boats right through to the 19th century. The trident markings, which also occur in Jonathon's Cave, may also have a connection with ships and the sea as it has been suggested that they may be marks made by medieval merchants.

It is in the nearby Court Cave that these great adventurers, the Vikings, are believed to have left their mark, with markings depicting the greatest God Thor and, as befits a deity who made the thunder roar as he forged his massive weapons, his sacred hammer is also shown. Some of the other markings on the walls of the cave may also be of Viking origin, but it is not by these Norse warriors that it is said to be haunted, but by the ghost of Mary Sibbald, the daughter of a wealthy laird who had his mansion home in the west of Fife. Young Mary was a most attractive fair-haired, blue-eyed young lady and her father planned a suitable match for his lovely daughter, but to his fury she fell in love with a gypsy, who persuaded her to desert her comfortable home and run away with him. Together they travelled east through Fife until they caught up with the rest of his Romany band at East Wemyss. There, Mary became involved in an incident involving the theft of some fruit. She was arrested and soon brought to trial before the Baron Baillie of East Wemyss, who held court in the cave, thus giving it its name. At her trial, Mary pled that she was innocent and that the fruit had been stolen by one of the other gypsy women called Jean Lindsay. The Baron Baillie nonetheless found her guilty and, despite her obvious fine breeding and good up-bringing, resolved to teach the young runaway a lesson for mixing with the gypsies, by sentencing her to be punished with a sound flogging. Scottish law laid down that she must be stripped to the waist so that the thongs of the long leather lash could leave their mark on her bare back. As the big bell in the roof of the Court Cave was tolled to tell the villagers of Wemyss to come to witness the public whipping, which was about to be administered, Mary wept and pleaded to be spared this public humiliation, but the East Wemyss executioner showed no mercy and ripped off her bodice so that she could be chastised as decreed.

During the weeks which followed, so the story goes, the livid scarlet weals left by the thongs across her pale white back did slowly heal, but the hurt which the embarrassment had caused her soul did not and within the year she died of a broken heart. The story, however, did not end there because it is claimed that Mary came back to haunt the gypsies. In the end, terrified by this ghostly apparition, Jean Lindsay the gypsy girl confessed that she was indeed the real culprit, but poor distraught Mary still returned to haunt the Court Cave, where she had been so cruelly scourged and humiliated.

High above the Court Cave on the cliff-top stands the ruins of Macduff's Castle and Mary's ghost is also said to haunt it. Usually she is sighted running through the grounds wearing a billowing white dress, but she has also been reported as appearing staring out of a window in the East Tower, to which there is now no way of gaining access. Interestingly, however, no matter where Mary's ghostly figure is claimed to be seen, she is always described as being fully clad, having regained the dignity which was stripped from her before her punishment in the Court Cave all these centuries ago.

Sometimes the story of Mary and her haunting of the Court Cave becomes entwined with another romantic story of no less a person than King James V. The Stewart monarch was well known for his liking for wandering the length and breadth of his kingdom, disguised, as mentioned earlier in the chapter about Cramond, as a poor commoner called the Gude Man of Ballangeich, so that he might hear what his subjects truly thought about him and life in Scotland under him. One night, shortly after the death of Mary Sibbald, King Jamie is said to have come to the cave and enjoyed drinking with the gypsies around the camp-fire. As the hour grew late and the ale and the wine flowed freely, the gypsies began to quarrel and one accused Jean Lindsay of having given false evidence against Mary and of herself being guilty of the theft of the fruit. As the words, 'You were the thief', echoed around the walls of the cave, a woman dressed in white and with fair hair and soft blue eyes is said to have appeared before the king. Startled and shaken by what he had just seen, King Jamie is said to have taken a hurried leave of his gypsy hosts and made his way up to Macduff Castle, where he confronted the owner Lord Colville about the public scourging and subsequent death of Mary. Colville duly summoned his Baron Baillie to explain about Mary Sibbald's alleged theft of the fruit, her trial in the Court Cave and her bare-backed punishment with the lash and as the King described the ghost with her white dress, blonde hair and pale blue eyes, he fell on his knees and confessed that ever since he had ordered the flogging, he had been haunted by the look in these same eyes as Mary pled her innocence.

Yet another version of the story of the Court Cave separates the story of the king and insists that his visit to the gypsies almost cost him his life. Again King Jamie, dressed as the Gude Man of Ballengeich, is described as arriving at the cave on the shore of the Forth after dark and enjoying a drinking session with the gypsies around their roaring camp-fire. As the evening wore on, Jamie became very attracted to one of the raven-haired gypsy girls who responded to his advances. This infuriated the gypsy chief because she was also his favourite. In his temper, the chief grabbed the girl and smacked her across her cheek. As she cried, to try to pacify him, His Majesty produced a gold coin from his purse, but this had the opposite effect and as the chief drew his dagger to stab him, the King only saved his life by revealing his true identity.

After all these tales to do with the Court Cave, the other caves may seem dull by comparison, but are all worth exploring. The East and West Doocot Caves take their names from the fact that in the 17th century they were used as pigeon lofts, not for racing pigeons, but for birds to supplement the diet of the local laird and his family with fresh food during the winter months, when fresh beef and mutton was impossible to obtain. At one time four caves were used for this purpose and there was also a dovecote on the shore of the Firth. The pigeons which they housed were so valuable that they were included in her dowry when the laird's daughter was married. Thousands of pigeons lived in the caves and at the back can be found the pigeon holes, which were carved into the walls to provide nesting spots for the birds. One of the original four caves used as dovecotes came to an untimely end during the First World War, when an army gun emplacement was built above it. When the gun was fired the cave collapsed.

Jonathon's Cave takes its name from the poor man, who with his family lived in it for many years. Later, in Victorian times, Jonathon's cave was used as a nail-making workshop. The nails which it produced were used by local boat builders. Unfortunately, the other of the Wemyss caves which housed an industry, the Glass Cave, can no longer be visited. Situated to the west of East Wemyss, this large 200-foot long, 100-foot wide and 30-foot high cave was used to house one of the country's oldest glass-making works. It was established in 1618 by Sir George Hay, who was Lord Clerk Register and later became Lord Kinnoul. Its strange setting in the cave was specially chosen because it was immediately adjacent to the shore with its readily available supply of sand with cheap supplies of coal available nearby. The East Wemyss glassworks was, however, apparently not a great success, because in 1619 the Scottish Privy Council reported to King James VI, who was in an impecunious state in London, that he could not raise any money by taxing it, as its total income for the year did not cover its running expenses for one month. This may, however, have been a little bit of an exaggeration because despite its reported losses, glass-making continued in the East Wemyss Cave throughout the 17th century and, in 1698, Earl David of Wemyss managed to persuade the Scottish Parliament meeting in Edinburgh to pass an Act granting him the monopoly to make certain items of fine glassware. In 1730, however, the cave glassworks went bankrupt and soon afterwards fell into disrepair. Throughout the 19th century the ruined works continued to be a popular attraction for Victorian holiday-makers, but the subsequent sinking of the shaft of the Michael Colliery just to the east of the cave affected it and eventually caused its collapse.

Finally, there is the Well Cave, so-called because it once apparently contained a well of fresh water, which was so pure that it was believed to have great curative powers for many diseases, especially jaundice. When Christianity came to the area, the well was dedicated to St Margaret. It was to the Well Cave that the people of East Wemyss used to make a torchlight procession on the first Monday of the New Year for the Hansel celebrations. Proceedings began with the singing of psalms and hymns around the well, after which the villagers enjoyed glasses of wine and cakes. Finally, before leaving, each of the villagers drank from the water of the well, which was said to guarantee them health and happiness throughout the coming year. There is also a legend that a fairy piper used to play in the Well Cave and this ties in with another of the many stories that a piper entered the Court Cave playing his pipes but never re-emerged. Yet another story claims that a secret underground passage connects the Well Cave to the castle high above and it is therefore sometimes known as the Castle Cave.

Standing 40 feet above the waters of the Firth, the castle also has two names, Kennoway Castle and Macduff's Castle. It is, however, as the latter that it is most popularly known, because it is claimed that the lands it guarded formed part of the estate of the famous Thane of Fife, who William Shakespeare immortalised in his 'Scottish Play'. The two red sandstone towers which remain, are however mainly of 16th-century origin, at which time it was the home of the Wemyss family. The castle remained inhabitable for around another century, but the second Earl of Wemyss moved the family seat to Wemyss Castle near West Wemyss.

Wemyss Castle dates from the 1400s and it was there that Mary, Queen of Scots was first introduced to her cousin and future second husband Henry, Lord Darnley, in February 1565. The castle has another royal connection because King Charles II was a guest there in July 1650, not long after his father's execution and again later during the period of Oliver Cromwell's Republic, in July 1657, three years before he was restored to the throne. Another interesting link with the events which shaped the country's history is that Sir David Wemyss was one of the two Scottish Ambassadors, who along with Sir Michael Scott of Balwearie fame travelled in 1290 to the Norwegian royal court to bring the ill-fated Little Maid of Norway across the North Sea to Scotland. The story of their storm-tossed voyage is vividly dramatised in *The Ballad of Sir Patrick Spens*, which every Scottish pupil used to be taught, but the castle's own particular link with this incident is that it became home to the large Viking silver bowl, which King Eric of Norway presented to mark the occasion. In the castle gardens there are also the impressive ruins of a typically 16th-century mansion and the Wemyss family burial grounds.

The Wemyss family owed its considerable wealth to its involvement in the development of the coal-mining industry, owning collieries as far away as Lochgelly to the west of Kirkcaldy as well as many pits nearer their castle home. They founded Coaltown of Wemyss to provide accommodation for their miners and were involved in 1872 in the construction of a small dock at a cost of £10,000 at West Wemyss to supplement the existing harbour and make it easier to ship out their cargoes of coal. Their enterprise was, however, soon challenged by the construction of a larger better equipped dock just along the coast at Methil. Six hundred feet long by 300 feet wide and with an entrance width of 50 feet and with a depth of water of 23 feet, it was opened in 1875 and as it could cater for colliers of up to 3,000 tons and was equipped with the latest hydraulic lifts and coal hoists described at the time as being 'of the most modern and powerful type', it soon captured most of the trade from West Wemyss. The dock at West Wemyss has long been filled in, but a sense of how much more important this wee place once was in the days when it was a Burgh of Barony may still be gauged from its fine 18th-century tolbooth, whose clock still chimes out from its tower overlooking the main street.

Methil dock is still open and operated by Forth Ports Plc, handling mainly cargoes of imported Baltic timber and other materials for Fife Council's own direct labour department. Methil's other lifeline has been the North Sea oil and gas industry for which the local Kavaerna yard has supplied equipment, but in February 1998 the Norwegian company made 300 of its workforce redundant. Methil's trade now is sadly only a fraction of the three million tons of coal which it exported each year at the beginning of the 20th century, when it was the busiest coal port in Scotland. Methil remained an important East coast port throughout both World Wars, so much so that during the Second World War it attracted the attention of German spies, perhaps equally interested in the fact that all of Britain's North Sea convoys formed up just off its shore. Stories of Methil's 300-year history as a coal exporting port since the second Earl of Wemyss opened its first harbour in 1662 and of the Wellesley and the other pits which supplied it are brought to life in the Heritage Centre, which now occupies the 1930s post office building in Lower Methil's High Street.

In its day, the Wellesley was one of the largest collieries in Scotland, its workings covering an area underground of 25 square miles, criss-crossed at different levels by 90 miles of roads and workings, a third of them connected with steel haulage cables, which hauled the tubs of coal to the foot of the 1,500-foot deep shaft, up which they were raised to the surface in under a minute. Many of the workings at the Wellesley dipped deep under the bed of the Firth and pumps had to work around the clock to battle with the flood water from the river. Names for the workings, like the Dip Mine and the Basin Dook, were a constant reminder to the miners of just how dangerously deep under the Forth they worked, but still there was sadness when the last shift 'loused' in 1967 and the Wellesley was closed. With its pumps switched off and silent, the waters of the Forth soon swirled in, flooding its labyrinth of underground workings. For a few years the Wellesley's modern washing plant continued to process coal from other collieries in East Fife, but soon these supplies dwindled as, one by one, the pits closed and Scotland's coal industry was allowed to decline, unable to compete with cheap foreign imports from open cast workings in places as far away as South Africa and Australia.

One Methil man who sailed the waters of the world was captain George Moodie, who gained fame as master of the tea clipper *Cutty Sark*.

For a time Methil's neighbour to the west, Buckhaven, also benefited from the construction of some of the oil rigs, whose huge legs straddled the shore like a steel giant out of Swift's *Guiliver's Travels*, and a rig is still sometimes towed into the bay for repair, but on the whole the local economy is again depressed and most local interest focuses around the fortunes of East Fife Football Club, which at least guarantees the district a mention on the Saturday afternoon sports results.

Methil has always been a workaday place of pits and pints, football and fish suppers, the dogs and drams in the pubs, but its near neighbour, Leven, always seems to have had greater pretensions. For, although separated from Methil only by the Bawbee Bridge, Leven marks the end of Fife's coal-mining coast and the beginning of the Kingdom's real seaside. For a time in the 1920s and 30s, indeed Leven enjoyed a popularity with Glasgow holiday-makers, who arrived by train, but today although Leven still has a caravan site, most visitors in this car-owning age prefer to drive on further to discover the charms of that corner of Fife known picturesquely as the East Neuk. Before leaving Leven's years as a holiday resort, if the pun may be excused, it is worth remembering that its sands once boasted their own Pierrot troupe to entertain the summer crowds and that the area still has an interesting little professional theatre. It is housed in Buckhaven's former St Andrews Church, about which itself there was quite a drama back in Victorian times. For St Andrews Church, which was designed by well-known Scottish architect William Burn, was originally erected in St Andrews in 1825, but in 1869 was carefully dismantled stone by stone and then re-erected along the coast in Buckhaven, or Buckhind, as its inhabitants still prefer to call it.

Another Buckhaven curiosity is that it was at its junior secondary school that progressive Scottish educationalist R.F. MacKenzie pioneered many of his ideas, somewhat to the bewilderment of local parents. MacKenzie's notions about setting children free and his absence of discipline brought about a flurry of interest from the Scottish press, while the Buckhaven bairns were happy to enjoy the many trips which he arranged for them to the country-side. Later, when he moved north to Aberdeen's Summerhill Academy, he tried to take these liberating moves still further, leading to his controversial dismissal. Another well-known name connected with the area is that of Scottish folk singer Jean Redpath, who was born in Leven.

Leven takes its name from the river which flows south-east from Loch Leven near Kinross, to emerge into the Firth of Forth at this point. Sixteen miles long, its waters were at one time described as 'pure and limpid', but the paper mills and other industries which were attracted by this source of supply in Victorian times changed all that. Nearer Leven, the coal industry which also flourished near its banks detracted still further from the attractiveness of this Forth tributary.

Originally, the only harbour at Leven was provided by a small inlet at the mouth of the river, but this was difficult to access and even under favourable conditions was navigable only by small sailing ships of up to 300 tons. In 1876, therefore, a Harbour Act was passed through Parliament, which empowered the digging of a proper dock and the building of a river wall and stone quays with railway sidings. These works were completed in 1880 at a cost of £40,000. They provided Leven with a dock 500 feet long and 250 feet wide and with a depth of 16 feet of water, which was capable of handling ships of up to 800 tons. Its imports and exports reflected the local industries around Leven with flax and tow for the local hemp and rope works and linen-weaving factories, pig iron for the foundries and barley for the Fife distilleries, Leven still having strong connections with the whisky trade to this day. For a time, Leven Docks also exported coal, but the superior facilities for handling coal at Methil only a mile along the coast led to a marked decline in trade and the eventual closure of the port.

Today Levenmouth, as it has become known in local government speak, is a somewhat depressed area with high unemployment, but Fife Council community services have spent money on an indoor sports centre and swimming pool complete with a 75-foot long water flume, on a site overlooking the river. The pool is described as:

> Free form with a sloping beach area, water geysers, fountains, whirlpool, jets and cannons, whilst incorporating a 25 metre area which provides an ideal facility for all types of water sport including competitive swimming. The wave machine makes six different patterns.

The complex also offers a fitness room packed full of torture chamber-like weight machines, an equally horrendous, wooden, electrically heated sauna, sun beds, described as 'ergoline' and a vast breeze-block-built sports hall. The sports complex is no doubt a blessing on a winter's day, but thankfully, a few hardy souls still walk along the shore to the north-east of the river mouth, where Leven's traditional attractions of windswept shore, paddling pool, putting green and golf courses can still be enjoyed, not to mention the natural beach with its equally natural wave maker, although it cannot be guaranteed to produce half a dozen different patterns. While the indoor centre boasts 'Birthday parties catered for all ages', at a price, picnics on the sands are still delightfully free and of course, Leven still possesses its other beautiful natural attraction, Letham Glen with its tree-lined walks, nature trail and pets' corner.

From the entrance to the glen, the main road leads north-east past several 1920s or 30s art deco style villas to Lundin Links. Lundin Links has always had the reputation for being an up-market residential douce wee place with its rows of substantial grey sandstone homes with their solid, equally grey slate roofs lining the main road and its fine golf courses and well-maintained tennis courts to cater for the residents' leisure pursuits.

A couple of miles further on, Upper Largo has a similar refined feel to it, with its hotel and tea-room and, again, its pleasant stone-built homes, many with fine views out over the Firth. For even more spectacular views, make a short detour inland at this point and climb Largo Law or little Norries Law. At the foot of Norries Law lies the home of Sir John Gilmour, over whose fields the Balcormo Point-to-Point takes place each spring. Held usually on the last Saturday in April, this is an event where the country meets the town, as folk from all walks of life, from all over Fife and beyond, congregate for an exciting afternoon of racing. Point-to-point takes its name from the time when enthusiastic amateur riders challenged each other to discover whose horse was the fastest, riding from one church spire to another across open countryside, jumping any fences and hedges which intervened on the way, and to the present day these races, held on this hillside course above the Forth, still capture much of this zestful, colourful, outdoor fun. The bookies are there to take bets, but just as important for an enjoyable day out in the fresh air as whether a bet comes up or not, is the success of the many tailgate parties in the temporary carparks set up in the adjoining fields and the chance to meet and chat to old friends. Balcormo Races are not the setting for Ascot hats and Royal Enclosure fashions. Rather they are the place for sheepskins, warm fleeces and well-filled hip flasks, because as the tide comes in up the Firth the wind is sure to follow, but as it does, breathe deeply, for this is truly the freedom of Fife.

One of Fife's most famous sons, Sir Andrew Wood, probably hailed from these parts and certainly held lands at Largo. He was one of the best sailors which the Forth ever knew and his 15th-century exploits as captain of his two ships the *Yellow Carvel* and the *Flower* have become almost legendary, thanks to being recorded for posterity by Robert Lindsay of Pitscottie near Cupar in his *Historie and Chronicles of Scotland*. For, as well as undertaking peaceful and very prosperous trading voyages as a merchant in his two vessels, Sir Andrew was always willing to lend them to support his monarch, King James III, in times of strife against the auld enemy, the English, which were pretty frequent in his day. In particular, he played a leading role in supporting the king's cause before the Battle of Sauchieburn in 1488, by ferrying both troops and supplies, but despite his efforts, the fight was lost and James was treacherously murdered. Despite James

IV having been to a greater or lesser extent implicated in this deed, a fact which he recognised by forever more doing penance by wearing a chafing iron chain around his waist, Sir Andrew gave his allegiance to the new young monarch and appears to have been appointed commander of the incipient Scottish navy. To begin with, Sir Andrew continued to use his own vessels for these purposes and achieved a great victory for Scotland by succeeding in capturing three English vessels under the command of Stephen Bull, with which he sailed triumphantly into the Forth. For this, James IV rewarded the Fife captain with a knighthood and appointed him in charge of the port of Dunbar. According to Lindsay of Pitscottie, Wood then also went on to become the proud commander of the king's pride and joy, *The Great Michael*, although this cannot be proved. However, Sir Andrew's other naval exploits have been sufficient to earn him the nickname of 'The Scottish Nelson'.

It is, however, as birth-place of a much more disreputable sailor that Largo is famed, as revealed in Chapter 7.

CHAPTER 6
MUSSELBURGH PIE

Musselburgh is a town which nowadays almost seems to have turned its back upon the Firth, but there's no denying the origin of its name. It is derived from the rich mussel beds which used to lie just off the shore at this point, the harvesting of which used to provide the town with its main source of income. Mussels were indeed at one time so plentiful and so cheap when they were landed here that local folk often added them to their steak pies. This they did not as an added luxury touch to the traditional recipe, but as what is known in the catering trade as an 'extender'. In other words, the addition of the tasty little shellfish was a cheap way of eking out the much costlier meat content of the dish, just as in other inland places in Scotland this same money-saving exercise was achieved by chucking in some mushrooms or maybe even sausages to make the steak go a wee bit further. In Scotland, steak pies have always been synonymous with something special and are still served on special family occasions, whether happy ones, such as on New Year's Day or sad, such as meals for mourners after funerals. Now, however, Musselburgh pie only seems to feature as an expensive item on Taste of Scotland menus, which is a pity because it is so simple to add this extra ingredient to turn an ordinary pie into something really special.

An approach in 1997 by a shellfish producer in East Anglia to collect mussels from the waters off Musselburgh and guarantee their edibility by taking them south to the clean waters of the Norfolk Broads for two weeks, before marketing them, was rejected, but as pollution in the Forth lessens there are hopes that in the future local mussels will be back on the menu. In the meantime, however, local inhabitants don't have to make do with the symbolic mussels which grace the burgh's coat of arms as a reminder of the once rich shellfish harvest from the Forth. They can obtain plentiful supplies of the real thing, gathered in other Scottish waters, but sold right on their doorsteps, by the town's famous fishmongers Clark Brothers, whose brightly painted premises with a model of a Leith-registered fishing boat above the entrance stands directly opposite the old harbour at Fisherrow. In these days when the only fish too many shoppers see are the plastic-wrapped, supermarket variety, Clark Brothers' spotlessly fresh little shop is a delightfully delicious reminder of the good fishmongers' shops which used to be a feature of the High Street or Main Street of every Scottish town. Details of the pick of the day's catch are chalked on a board by the door, but the Clarks and their knowledgeable staff are also always willing to advise on the best buys and the ways to cook their king and queen scallops, fresh crabs and vast array of other shellfish, herring, white fish, trout and salmon. As well as selling this wide range, Clarks also cure their own fish. Amongst the white fish it is interesting to see plump, fleshy monkfish tails which, chunked up and breaded, used to masquerade in less scrupulous restaurants as cheap imitation scampi, but which are now much in demand in their own right and selling at prices dearer than sole and almost double that of haddock.

Directly opposite the fishmongers' stands the Quay, a modern leisure recreation centre with function suites and the Harbour Restaurant. Despite its name, the Harbour disappoints, because although its kitchen is only yards from all the riches available from Clark's, its menu is boringly routine, offering little more in the way of seafood than prawn cocktail and haddock and chips. Its idea of the heights of Scottish cuisine are steaks and haggis-stuffed chicken with never a taste of Musselburgh pie.

Sadly, the old Fisherrow Harbour, which the ugly Quay complex now dominates, is equally disappointing, especially when the tide is out and its muddy bottom is exposed for all to see. In its literature, Fisherrow Yacht Club, which has its clubhouse opposite in New Street, describes the harbour as 'unpretentious' and that is a fair summing up. Compared to the harbours across the Firth in Fife, Fisherrow lacks atmosphere, colour and charm. The only old building is the two-storey high, stone-built, pantile-roofed Harbour Master's Office and even it has an air of neglect, the 'urgent' notices to mariners in its window dating from the 1980s.

A century ago a Victorian description of it also makes it sound as if it had really missed the boat even then. It reads:

Whatever importance attaches to Musselburgh as a seaport and fishing station — and it is not very great in either respect — it owes to its suburb of Fisherrow. The harbour here is small and consists of a tidal basin, enclosed by two substantial stone piers. Situated on the inner edge of a wide expanse of sandy beach, it is shallow even in the most favourable circumstances and quite useless even for small craft when the tide is out. The population share in great measure the exclusiveness and peculiarities of the fisherfolk of Newhaven, the women of each place affecting the same style of dress, well known in the streets of Edinburgh and neighbourhood. Altogether in round numbers, the fishing boats belonging to the port number about fifty, forty of which are of first class order, and the industry gives employment to between 200 and 300 fishermen, besides women and children. The largest industries are the manufacture of paper and of fishing nets. The factory, which produces the nets is one of the biggest in the country. It employs 700 hands, many of them women.

Nowadays, all traces of the fishing industry have gone and its fishing boats have been replaced by a fleet of modern pleasure craft, mostly owned by members of the yacht club, whose white-hulled safety boat lies alongside one of the quays. Fisherrow Harbour is also the home of Musselburgh Water Ski Club, which has its hutted headquarters nearby along the promenade. Moving further east, the next feature of interest is another of the Forth's tributaries, the River Esk, which flows into the Firth at this point on the south shore. Musselburgh was at one time known as Eskmouth and it was the original bridge over the Esk which contributed to the burgh's growth, as it brought the passing trade to the town of all those travelling from Edinburgh down the East Coast to London and the South. The solid, old, three-arched stone bridge, which is high and narrow in the middle, was built in the early 16th century and replaced by the newer five-arched one a short distance downstream in 1807. Designed by the famous architect and engineer, Sir John Rennie, it was widened to cope with the early growth in modern traffic way back in 1924 and today still makes an impressive entrance to 'The Honest Toun', as Musselburgh is often known.

The nickname of 'The Honest Toun' is said to have been earned by Musselburgh's townsfolk, when they refused any payment for the way in which they had honoured the body of King Robert I's nephew, the Earl of Moray, when he died there in 1332. It is a title still remembered, particularly each summer when the local folk turn out to perform the ancient ceremony of riding the marches, which is the traditional Scottish version of beating the bounds.

Swans and ducks provide the only action on the River Esk, but once the old bridge which spans it at Musselburgh was part of the busy main route between Scotland and England. Arthur Down.

Musselburgh has a lot of traditions to remember because it is really steeped in history. These lands which were part of the Parish of Inveresk, in other words the parish at the mouth of the River Esk, were originally granted by King David I to the monks of Dunfermline Abbey. It was created a Burgh of Regality in 1562 and was further honoured as a Royal Burgh by King Charles I in 1632, but this was immediately challenged by the Lord Provost and Bailies of Edinburgh, who saw it as a threat, and the city won its appeal.

An impression of how important Musselburgh was in past ages may still be gained, however, from the impressive, old, thick stone-walled Tolbooth, which still dominates the busy High Street scene. The Tolbooth was a kind of combined seat of administration, courtroom and jail, and the market cross, where important announcements were made and punishments inflicted, still stands nearby on the north side of the street. The Tolbooth was erected in 1590, but the stones from which it was built are older than that as they were plundered from the former chapel of Our Lady of Loretto, which dated from the previous century, but which was officially vandalised by the Lords of the Congregation, helped by the local population, at the time of the Reformation. Before then, in Catholic times, the chapel was a popular place of pilgrimage, especially for expectant mothers, as Our Lady of Loretto was believed to be able to guarantee the safe delivery of their babies.

The name Loretto is still remembered in modern Musselburgh as the title of the town's famous, English-style, public school, whose spacious grounds and playing fields may be glimpsed at the end of the High Street, a slight bump in which is also a reminder that the school has its own private tunnel underneath. The school has a fine chapel, but most famous of Loretto's buildings is Pinkie House to the east of the High Street. It was acquired by the school in 1951 and now serves as one of its boarding houses, but dates back all the way to the 16th century, when it originated as a tower house belonging to the Abbot of Dunfermline. After the Reformation it became the property of Alexander Seton, who later became Earl of Dunfermline and he added its most distinguished feature, the Painted Gallery, with its tempera decoration. It was there, in 1547, that the injured from the Battle of Pinkie, which was fought nearby and in which the Scots were defeated by the invading English, had their wounds treated.

Today, the only wounds received by the boys of Loretto are those inflicted in battles on the rugby field and, indeed, the school's pupils have always been reckoned to be a particularly healthy lot, thanks to the progressive outdoor educational ideas of its pioneering Victorian headmaster, Hely Hutchison Almond. He believed that even as they slept boys should receive plenty of good fresh air and insisted that all dormitory windows be kept open not just during the day, but throughout the night, no matter how chill the east wind blowing in off the Forth. By day, he also believed in the health-giving powers of sea bathing and as part of his rigorous programme of physical education, which was way before its time, he launched three wooden rafts on the river. Two were anchored 30 yards off Musselburgh Links and the other further out in the river and the boys had to swim out to them daily. To encourage his pupils to learn to dive he installed broad wooden rails around the rafts.

While the scholars of Loretto in earlier years swam off the Links, it was on these grassy flat lands themselves that the townsfolk enjoyed their sport, starting with no less a personage than King James IV. For it was on Musselburgh Links in the year 1504 that His Majesty is claimed to have first played the then new sport of 'gowff'. Whether golf was a native Scottish invention or, heresy of heresies, imported across the North Sea from the Netherlands, with which traders from these parts had such frequent dealings, has long been debated, but what is certain is that, ever since, Scots have enjoyed many, many hours chasing wee white balls over the green turf which forms some of the finest links courses anywhere in the world. In 1836, Musselburgh Links became the home of the Honourable Company of Edinburgh Golfers and with their hickory-shafted wooden clubs and early stitched leather balls stuffed with feathers, later replaced with cheaper ones made of rubbery gutta-percha, they played over them throughout Victorian times until 1891, when they moved to the now much more famous Muirfield. Golf clubs and golf balls used to be made in Musselburgh. There is still a 9-hole course within Musselburgh Race Course. Horse racing at Musselburgh dates back to 1816.

Another favourite institution still to the fore in Musselburgh is Luca's celebrated High Street ice-cream shop and cafe, claimed by many to make the finest genuine Italian dairy ices on the whole of the East Coast. This is quite a boast, for immigrant Italian families during the early years of the 1900s opened ice-cream parlours in most Scottish towns, especially at the seaside, where vanilla cones, 'sliders' and, in these much less politically correct days, 'Black Men', ice-cream deliciously sandwiched between chocolate-coated nougat wafers, became as synonymous with summer holidays as the steak pies mentioned earlier were with family occasions. In the Forth Valley alone there were the famous Fortes of Alloa, who went on to fame as owners of Trust House Forte Hotels, the Serafinis of Falkirk, the Corvis of Bo'ness and the Nardinis of Queensferry, but many connoisseurs rate Luca's ices as supreme. In the 1950s, when the relaxation of petrol rationing after the Second World War again made possible organised coach outings, many made detours specially to sample the delights of Luca's. During the craze for so-called evening mystery tours, after many twists and turns en route, the secret destination often eventually turned out to be Musselburgh and whole busloads of passengers used to crowd into the little High Street cafe, or if it was already filled to capacity, stood happily on the pavement outside proving for all to see that 'Luca's ices were often licked, but never beaten!'

From Musselburgh, with its Brunton Theatre, its cafes and restaurants, its racecourse, other sports facilities and its fine public school, it is just a short journey east along the shore of the Firth to much more workaday Prestonpans. The Pans, as it is referred to locally, takes its name from the once prosperous saltpans, which once flourished here thanks to the combined availability of cheap coal to boil the never-ending supply of gallons of water from the Firth. Once evaporated, the water left behind its silver prize of sparkling salt, a commodity so necessary for life that the Scottish Parliament taxed it just as today the government gains its income from those other necessities of life, petrol and whisky.

The only problem with salt production at Prestonpans, as at all other saltworks on the Forth, was that even in the Middle Ages the river water was far from clean. To try to purify it, therefore, the water was first transferred into large, deep ponds called reservoirs where the silt had to have a chance to settle, before it was finally moved into the pans for processing. It was the task of the women of the Pans and their children to ensure the supply of water and this they did using what were known as wand pumps. These were great wooden contraptions like muckle big see-saws, except that on one end of the plank, instead of a seat for a wee bairn there was a large wooden basin. This was dipped under the surface of the river at high tide and once it was brim-full of water, the women and their weans leant all their weight on the other end to raise it high in the air, before birling it round until it was over the shore and couping its contents into one of the reservoirs.

The whole process was then repeated several days later to transfer the water into the actual saltpan, which consisted of a large, shallow, oblong-shaped iron container, approximately seven metres long by four metres wide, which was raised on short stone pillars so that fires could be lit beneath its entire area. The fires were fuelled with what was known as panwood, which, despite its name, was actually the poorest quality coal from the local pits. This dross was not fit for export or even sale on the home market, but the pans provided a use for this otherwise unsellable product.

Despite the prior use of the reservoir, the water in the pan still always contained impurities and so, to rid it of these as it began to simmer, a bucket of ox or sheep blood, obtained from the local slaughter-house, was always tipped into it. As the water then came to the boil the albumen in the blood thickened and congealed, thus forming a scum, like that which comes to the top when making home-made jam. With it all the impurities in the bubbling solution were brought to the surface and it was then the job of the womenfolk to carefully remove it. This they did by stretching out over the steaming pan and scraping off the blood clotted scum with specially made wooden rakes, as these did not conduct the heat and burn the women's hands as using iron ones would have done.

When the clear solution left behind eventually evaporated, the salt workers also used wooden spades to remove the salt crystals left behind on the sides and bottom of the pan so as not to damage the ironwork and a set of these wooden implements, including one of the wooden boxes in which the salt was transported, is preserved at the Royal Scottish Museum in Edinburgh's Chambers Street. To produce six tons of salt it took 100 tons of coal. The fires beneath the saltpans on the shores of the Firth at Prestonpans were never allowed to go out and the ruddy glow from them was often used as a primitive form of lighthouse by the skippers of the little sailing ships which docked at the town's small harbour to export its products to the continent, and especially to the Scandinavian countries which in general lacked their own supplies of coal and thus, in turn, could not produce their own salt.

The only time of the week when the fires below the pans at Prestonpans and all the other saltworks along the length of the Forth from Kincardine, or Newpans as it was originally called upstream, to St Monans down river, were damped down was on Saturday evenings. This was because all the local kirk sessions religiously forbade the production of any salt on Sundays so that the salt workers and their families could all faithfully attend church. Even this delay, however, was turned to advantage by the crafty salt masters, because the slower rate of evaporation of the water in the pan resulted in larger grains of salt being formed and these were carefully gathered on Monday mornings to be marketed as a costlier delicacy known appropriately as Sabbath Salt, when it graced the tables of the wealthier classes. It is interesting to note that large-grained sea salt is again available from delicatessen stores as a saltier alternative to the usual fine white rock salt and that Scotland's own Highlander Crisps, produced in West Lothian, has introduced a sea-salt variety to its range of flavours.

Perversely, it was the introduction onto the market of cheaper rock salt from Cheshire in England and Saxony in Germany, which helped to destroy demand for salt from the Forth. The arrival of this rival product came shortly after the Agrarian Revolution in the middle of the 18th century had already reduced the general demand for salt. This came about because before the Agrarian Revolution there was no winter fodder available to feed the cows and sheep and therefore, apart from breeding animals, these beasts had to be slaughtered in the autumn and their meat salted away to provide food supplies until the following spring. This was done by either dry salting, that is by sprinkling salt between each layer of beef or mutton or perhaps slightly more preferably by bottling the meat in brine. After the agricultural improvers of the 1700s introduced turnips, mangolds or mangels as winter feeding for the cattle and sheep these distasteful practices were no longer necessary, but this improvement in Scotland's diet was achieved at the expense of the Forth salt industry.

For a time the Scottish salt manufacturers tried to fight back by themselves importing small quantities of rock salt to mix with their own product to improve its quality, but as Victorian palates became more genteel demand for the stronger-flavoured Scottish sea salt continued to decline. Production at all the saltpans along both shores of the Forth decreased. In 1890, the fire at the last of the 13 pans at Bo'ness, which had been the largest rival to Prestonpans and which had given the town place-names such as Grangepans and Panbrae Road, was extinguished.

Down river, however, production of salt continued into the 20th century at both Joppa and Prestonpans but after 1900 sea salt was only used for non-edible purposes. These included medicinal uses ranging from throat gargles to salt for footbaths, but it was mainly demand from Scottish local authority transport departments for salt to mix with grit to spread on icy and snow-covered roads throughout the country which kept the East Lothian pans in business, the last salt being produced at Prestonpans during the 1950s.

Prestonpans' other major heavy industry, coal-mining, has also died out, the town's Preston Grange Colliery, whose workings used to run out under the bed of the Forth, having closed in 1963. Its surface workings are now open to visitors as part of the Scottish Mining Museum, whose main premises are a few miles inland at the Lady Victoria Colliery, Newtongrange, Midlothian. Here on the coast, the museum's main exhibit is the former pit's massive beam engine, used in the past to pump river floodwater from its

The winding gear still stands at Preston Grange Colliery on the coast to the west of Prestonpans, but its wheels have long stopped turning and the site is now part of the Scottish Mining Museum, whose headquarters is a few miles further inland at Newtongrange. Every pit had its own distinctive winding gear to take the miners up and down the shaft to and from their work and to bring the coal they hewed to the surface. To those involved in the coal industry the winding gear was very much each colliery's individual signature. Arthur Down.

underground workings It is now unique in Scotland. More common is the former pit's winding wheel, similar ones being a familiar sight at collieries across Central Scotland. Its wheel used to turn throughout each shift to bring the loads of coal to the surface, where they were loaded onto railway waggons, few of which also remain on the site beside the main coastal road.

Across the road is a strange dome-shaped structure, which capped one of Preston Grange's ventilation shafts. It was originally much closer to the shore of the Firth, much of the flat grass-covered land which now separates it from the water having since been reclaimed from the river. Now it forms a pleasant coastal walk into Prestonpans, whose sea front, for a wee place with such a down-to-earth, hardworking background, exhibits unexpected cultural depths. For there, overlooking the river, may be found a display of modern sculptures by Leslie Frank Chorley. A plaque informs the curious that Chorley died in 1968, but not why his

This unusual structure on the grassy shore just west of Prestonpans is not a Second World War pill box defence as many passing motorists think. It is the top of a ventilation shaft which provided fresh air for the miners of Preston Grange Colliery, whose underground workings ran out under the bed of the Forth. The shaft was originally closer to the water's edge, before land reclamation took place. There is a coastal path from this point, which provides a pleasant stroll into Prestonpans. Arthur Down.

interesting works decorate the little esplanade at Prestonpans. Nor is that the only mystery, for ranged on either side of his sculptures are two tributes to the poet Robert Burns. One is a substantial stone-built shelter and the other more recent addition is a monument with inscriptions from the bard's most famous works, erected to mark the bi-centenary of his death in 1996. This was an anniversary which to its shame, much of the rest of Scotland chose quietly to ignore, so all the more credit to Prestonpans Burns Club for its enthusiasm and these interesting additions to the local coastal scene.

Burns, of course, wrote 'Scots wha hae wi' Wallace bled, Scots wham Bruce has oft times led', but despite his known Jacobite sympathies does not appear to have put pen to paper to commemorate their famous victory at the Battle of Prestonpans on 21 September 1745. Sadly, the site of the battlefield is equally

The three forms making up this striking 1968 sculpture by Leslie Frank Chorley on the sea wall in the centre of Prestonpans represent the sea, the coal mining industry and salt panning, which all contributed much to the history of this interesting little East Lothian burgh. Arthur Down.

neglected and visitors have to be content with a quick glance as they drive past on the main road which bypasses the town. Perhaps some day there will be a visitor centre to do justice to this daring dawn raid, which caught the government troops so entirely by surprise and which gave the Jacobites such a welcome morale boost. The Jacobite victory at Prestonpans is for the present best remembered by the words of the well-known Jacobite satirical song, 'Hey Johnnie Cope are ye waking yet.' Cope had sailed up the East Coast from London and then travelled on to where his soldiers were encamped on flat ground near the river in his heavy campaign coach. Perhaps, if a battlefield interpretation centre is eventually opened on the site, it may tell the little-known story of a strange find which the Jacobites made in the depths of the abandoned coach.

As after any battle in those days, the victors gathered together as much booty as they could find, including the government troops' abandoned cannon and their campaign chest containing £4,000, which Cope had left for safe keeping in Cockenzie House, where he had spent the night and which he was forced to leave

With its iron window grids and door this sturdy, stone-built structure may look like the local jail, but is actually a shelter erected on the seafront at Prestonpans by the enthusiastic local Burns Club and dedicated to the memory of the poet. Arthur Down.

behind as he fled in haste. To add even further to the general's deep embarrassment, soon all of his personal possessions were dragged from his coach and shared out by the eager Highlanders, but there remained several mysterious long rolls of a rather soft brown-coloured substance, the likes of which the clansmen had never before seen. One by one, the brown rolls were carefully passed from man to man, until one of the clan chiefs looked at them most knowledgeably and declared that they were undoubtedly one of Cope's medicines and were, in fact, a most expensive ointment. Soon, tiny quantities of Johnnie Cope's Salve, as it became known, were fetching high prices among the members of Edinburgh's high society, who flocked to pay tribute to Prince Charles Edward Stewart, who had taken up residence at Holyrood Palace.

The miraculous new cure might well have enjoyed a prolonged vogue, had Prince Charlie been content to rule Scotland, but his disastrous march into England and his retreat from Derby and subsequent defeat at Culloden the following year in 1746 brought

Chairman of the Heather and Thistle Society in Houston, Texas, internationally renowned Burns scholar, Dr Arthur Down, studies the verses of A Man's A Man For A' That, *inscribed on this monument erected on the seafront at Prestonpans by the town's Burns Club on 21 July 1996 to mark the bi-centenary of the poet's death.* Arthur Down.

in their wake a large number of young English army officers to the Scottish capital and one of them happened to be shown a little of the precious salve. There was consternation among the Scots when he explained that this was no medical wonder cure, but a new delicacy. They were sceptical when he told them that it was already all the rage in London. However, when he ordered up a kettle full of boiling water and showed them how to make cocoa, the wafting aroma was sufficient to tempt them to agree to try a sip. They liked what they tasted and so, 'hot chocolate, drinking chocolate', as the Cadbury's television commercial used to proclaim, first came to Scotland. Even in England, however, where the first chocolate had been sold in London almost a century before in 1657, it remained an expensive luxury to be enjoyed only by the rich, until the high import duty on cocoa beans was at last greatly reduced in 1853 as part of the government's free trade policy. Chocolate in bars gradually came onto the market, in addition to cocoa as a drink, but it was not for over another 20 years that they became a popular sweet treat when the Swiss manufacturers, Nestle, first marketed sweet milk chocolate in 1876.

While Scots were slow to develop their taste for chocolate, many have long had a liking for alcohol, sometimes sadly drinking it to excess. This was indeed the case amongst some of the salt workers, miners and sailors of Prestonpans and so the town came up with an interesting attempt to solve the problem, evidence of which can still be seen to this day. The solution was found across the North Sea in Sweden, in the Baltic port of Gothenburg. There, Sweden's well-known liberal social reformers had decided that the best way to tackle the problem of drunkenness amongst the town's seafarers was not to ban alcohol, but to make it available to them only under strictly controlled conditions. This they did by establishing a public house run as a co-operative store, where they could make their own strict rules about drinking, free from commercial pressures. The co-operative venture also meant that profits could be reinvested to provide members with sickness benefits and pensions and even help the local community by buying an ambulance and paying for a district nurse. The people of Prestonpans were very impressed and decided to set up a similar venture on this side of the North Sea. They called the pub the Gothenburg and to this day the black-and-white-painted, half-timbered 'Goth' as it is affectionately known still stands, overlooking the Firth, and still serves the people of the Pans.

Prestonpans became a port under a charter granted by the monks of Newbattle in 1526 and during its early years its customs dues were as great as those of Leith burgh. It achieved the status of a burgh of barony as long ago as 1617, when King James VI and I, on his only return visit to Scotland after the Union of the Crowns in 1603, granted a charter to Sir John Hamilton of Preston, the Priest's Farm Town. From then on, however, Prestonpans did not flourish as much as was expected. As ships grew larger, its harbour proved too small and mud-silted to accommodate them. The town itself seemed to lack planning and in Victorian times

The twin chimney stacks of coal-fired Cockenzie Power Station tower over the Firth and are landmarks for over twenty miles around. The length of the glass-fronted generating station separates The Pans from Cockenzie and it would perhaps have been more appropriate if Scottish Power had named it after the former as Prestonpans has always been the much more industrial of the two neighbouring burghs. The covered bridge across the coast road carries the supplies of coal to the generator. Arthur Down.

one visitor described its single street as 'ziz-zag at both ends and crooked in the middle'.

Today, both literally and figuratively, it is overshadowed by the looming grey bulk of the huge Cockenzie power station with its towering chimneys and the massive sprawling mounds of coal which feed its voracious appetite as it supplies power to the Scottish grid. Cockenzie does, however, still have its traditional industry of fishing and several boats still operate from the harbour. Like many harbours on the Firth of Forth, it is best viewed at high tide, for when the water ebbs its oozing black mud flats are cruelly revealed.

As in all parts of Britain, Cockenzie's fishing trade has been adversely affected by a decrease in stock and an increase in regulations, but what remains of it is mainly centred on the neighbouring harbour of Port Seton. This harbour was formally declared open in 1880. It was constructed mainly of concrete and covered an area of almost eight acres with a depth of water at

Nestling directly below the massive power station which puts the burgh on the modern map, old Cockenzie Harbour is still home to many small vessels, but pleasure craft now outnumber the fishing boats, which mainly use the more modern facilities at neighbouring Port Seton. Arthur Down.

high tide of 16 feet. The total cost of its construction was £11,800, of which £2,000 was contributed by Lord Wemyss. A 21¹/₂ foot high cast sea wall was constructed all of 730-feet long, with a cross pier at the end which was nicknamed the Hammer Head. From the west it was protected by a breakwater 450-feet long, 19¹/₂ feet high and just over 12 feet broad. This gave an entrance to Port Seton Harbour of 125 feet in width. In 1885 the middle pier was added at an additional cost of £5,000 and the harbour was further deepened. By 1891, Port Seton boasted a fleet of 40 deep sea boats, each with a crew of seven men and 27 smaller yawls each with a crew of five hands. A contemporary writer noted, 'The fishermen of Port Seton are most industrious and prosecute the herring fishing at distant ports'.

When the crews of the Port Seton boats returned home it was to neat cottages in what was described as 'a model fishing village' and to this day there is a definite sense of community about the place. The fishermen still run their own co-operative store opposite the landward end of the harbour, whose windows are crowded with items ranging from cheaply priced washing-up liquid to expensive items of ship's chandlery. Across the street are several

Port Seton Harbour is still the home port for several fishing boats, and the buildings where their catches are processed can be seen lining the quayside, but increasingly the fishing industry is being concentrated in main centres such as Peterhead and the days of the small ports seem numbered. Arthur Down.

fish shops, where it is possible to buy the freshest of the day's catch and several fish and chip shops which, besides catering for local customers, are also popular with holiday-makers, who still come to the area's coastal caravan and chalet parks, although in nothing like the numbers of Glaswegians who used to look upon this as a far-flung seaside destination in the 1920s and 1930s, long before the coming of jet aircraft and their discovery of cheap package deals to the Spanish Costas.

While today Cockenzie is mainly a rural coastal retreat apart from its power station, it was in past centuries important in the development of Scottish industry. For it was here, on this windswept shore of the Firth, that English industrialist Dr John Roebuck found the solitude which he required to build what became known as the Secret Factory. Roebuck was the son of a prosperous Sheffield cutler. His family were of French Huguenot stock and had come to England to escape religious persecution, but even in this country in the middle of the 18th century, young Roebuck discovered that, as a non-conformist, he was denied entry to England's only two universities at Oxford and Cambridge, as

This colourful tiled mural was erected overlooking the New Harbour at Port Seton in 1990. It is the work of the pupils of Cockenzie Primary School, some of whose fathers are fishermen and was part of a project entitled Community which was co-ordinated by visiting artist Kenny Munro with the support of Headmaster John Roy and his staff. Interestingly the children have chosen the name Hope *for their fishing boat, but falling catches combined with restrictive European Community dictates appear to give little hope that Cockenzie and Port Seton will continue for much longer as fishing ports.* Arthur Down.

they would only admit male students who were communicant members of the Church England.

Roebuck therefore came north to the University of Edinburgh, which was proudly free of any such religious bigotry. There he studied medicine, and later went to the famous Leyden University in the Netherlands where he completed his degree by submitting a learned thesis and was awarded his doctorate. He returned to England where he began to practise as a general practitioner, but found he was too upset by the suffering which he was forced to inflict on patients in those days before the development of either antiseptic or anaesthetic surgery. He therefore decided to quit medicine as a career and turn to his second love which was the study of metals.

It was to develop this new line of business that he returned to Scotland, because he remembered from his student days at Edinburgh how he had loved to find peace and solitude by wandering along the shores of the Forth and decided that would be the ideal place to found a chemical plant where he could quietly work on a pioneering process. To ensure security he ordered 12-foot high stone walls to be built around the whole site and paid armed guards to patrol them every night. Not surprisingly, the local folk of Cockenzie and Prestonpans soon nicknamed the place the Secret Factory. Rumours began to spread that the mysterious English doctor with his strange Yorkshire accent was producing a substance as clear as water, but which burned like fire. Some even declared that he was a warlock in league with the Devil. Far from it, Roebuck was actually a very shrewd businessman, who had discovered the new lead-chamber process for producing cheap sulphuric acid, which was in great demand not just from its traditional users in the jewellery trade, but from many other metal workers, thanks to the growing industrial revolution.

Roebuck's lead-chamber method of producing sulphuric acid remained in use for over two hundred years until the 1970s, but because he had invented it in Scotland he found it impossible to patent it in England and, despite all his security precautions at Cockenzie, a disgruntled employee whom he sacked sold his idea to a firm in Newcastle.

As on several future occasions during his long and varied life, the 'indefatigable Dr Roebuck', as he became known, shrugged off his misfortune and looked around for another opportunity on which to test his ever-fertile brain. During his time at the Secret Factory, he had made the acquaintance of the Cadell family who had their home at Cockenzie House. He found that they had much in common, because they were in the business of importing large quantities of iron and smaller amounts of steel. Just at the time when their business was booming thanks to the demands of the hostilities between Britain and France from 1756 to 1763, which eventually became known as the Seven Years War, they found their supplies cut off because the merchant ships carrying their cargoes from the continent were attacked and destroyed by enemy naval vessels. They decided, therefore, to establish Scotland's first large-scale iron works and Roebuck went into partnership with them.

Up until this time, the tiny quantities of iron produced in Scotland had come from very small rural iron foundries in remote locations, mainly in Argyll, where they were situated in the forests, because large quantities of charcoal, produced by burning wood, were required in the smelting process. The Cadells believed that they had discovered a way to make iron using coal and at first planned to build their new works close to their Cockenzie home, where there were supplies of both coal and ironstone available. It was Dr Roebuck who persuaded them that much more thought was required to ensure that they choose the correct site, which for one thing he felt should be nearer to the Highland forests in case their efforts to try smelting using coal did not succeed. In addition, he laid down that the site for the new factory should be on level ground, with adequate supplies of water and have good access to sea transport, both to ensure supplies of raw materials and to ship out the heavy finished products, which could not have been moved by land because of the atrocious state of Scotland's 18th-century roads. In the end, the Cadells and he decided to site the new works on the shores of a tributary of the Forth to the west of what is now Grangemouth and thus the Carron Iron Works, and not the Cockenzie Iron Works, gained world-wide fame as the producer of the wartime Carronades, the short muzzled cannon, whose greater accuracy ensured British victories against Napoleon, both at the Battle of Trafalgar in 1805 and the Battle of Waterloo in 1815 and, thereafter, of peacetime kitchen cooking ranges.

CHAPTER 7

IN CRUSOE'S FOOTSTEPS

My father being a foreigner of Bremen, I was called Robinson Kreutznaer; but by the usual corruption of words in England, we are now called, nay we call ourselves, and write our name, Crusoe.

Thus Daniel Defoe begins his most famous book, *The Life and Adventures of Robinson Crusoe* and today by coincidence, that original German connection continues, because the curator of the Crusoe Centre in Lower Largo hails originally from Schlesvig Holstein and was educated in the great maritime city of Hamburg on the River Elbe. He is Bob Jurgensen, the ebullient host of Largo's popular Crusoe Hotel, on whose ground floor the centre dedicated to Defoe's hero is situated. There could not be a better setting for the Crusoe Centre, for not only is it within yards of where local sailor Alexander Selkirk, upon whom Defoe based his celebrated fictional character, was born in 1676, but it also stands right on the edge of the harbour, whose waters lap its foundations and whose waves in winter crash excitingly right up to the windows of the Castaway Restaurant on the floor above.

The old whitewashed Crusoe Hotel on Lower Largo's quayside acts as a magnet for Defoe enthusiasts from all over the world and Bob Jurgensen is not only happy to show them his collection of Crusoe curios, but is also delighted to learn from them both about their fictional hero, and even more so about the local man who inspired the book. One guest who stayed at the hotel was the Japanese leader of the recent National Geographic sponsored expedition to Juan Fernandez, where Alexander Selkirk elected of his own volition to be marooned, and the set of coloured photographs, which he donated to the centre, does much to bring to life the story of the real Robinson Crusoe.

Selkirk was the son of Lower Largo's snab, the local shoe and boot maker, but young Alexander would not settle to a trade like his father and as a youth got into several scrapes with the law. His unruly exploits continued into his twenties, until at the age of 27 things became too hot for him in the little Fife village and he ran away to sea. He proved a good and able sailor and gained the

The Crusoe Hotel and Exhibition Centre overlooks the little harbour at Lower Largo. The village was formerly on the Fife Coastal Railway and the now disused viaduct which used to carry the line still stands behind the hotel. Kingdom of Fife Tourist Board.

position of sailing master aboard the privateer *Cinque Ports*, which belonged to the well-known navigator, hydrographer and explorer-turned-buccaneer, William Dampier. In 1704, Selkirk sailed on an expedition aboard the *Cinque Ports* all the way to the South Pacific. Unfortunately, the rebelliousness of his youth followed him into adulthood and he frequently quarrelled with the master of the *Cinque Ports* and even dared challenge his orders to the crew. As the long voyage continued, the animosity between the two men grew, until it came to a head while the Cinque Ports was in the middle of the Pacific Ocean. There was a furious quarrel and the captain threatened that when the *Cinque Ports* returned to port, he would have Selkirk court marshalled. Instead, perhaps in an attempt to call the captain's bluff, Selkirk demanded to be set ashore on the nearest island. The skipper seized the opportunity and thus Selkirk found himself the sole inhabitant of the otherwise, at that time, uninhabited desert island of Juan Fernandez, 800 miles off the distant coast of Chile. Any hopes that Selkirk might have harboured that the *Cinque Ports* might return to pick him up were ill founded and so he found himself marooned. In the end, Selkirk lived his lonely existence for four years and four months, before in the end he was rescued by another privateer, skippered by Captain Woodes Rogers.

Clad in goatskin as Defoe depicted him as Robinson Crusoe, the statue of Alexander Selkirk looks appropriately seaward from its lookout site above the door of the house where he was born. Although old, it is not the original cottage. Kingdom of Fife Tourist Board.

Alexander Selkirk returned to Largo in 1712 and a version of his real-life experiences on Juan Fernandez was printed and published the following year, just at the time when Daniel Defoe was desperately looking for the theme for a novel. Defoe had enjoyed considerable success with his factual journal of his travels through Scotland, written while allegedly spying for the English government in the run-up to the Union of the Parliaments in 1707 during the period that he was editor of Scotland's earliest newspaper the *Edinburgh Courant*. But until that date a theme for a fictional adventure story had eluded him. Selkirk's story of his stay on Juan Fernandez provided him with exactly the colourful tale he was seeking and in 1719 he issued the first copies of *Robinson Crusoe*, which to this day is still one of the world's best-known, classic, adventure yarns. By the time *Robinson Crusoe* appeared, Alexander Selkirk had gone back to sea and succeeded in becoming a lieutenant in the Royal Navy. Sadly, he died only two years later at the age of 45.

We will never know if the men who served under Selkirk ever knew of his celebrated past, but his Fife home village has never forgotten him and just along the shore road from the Crusoe Hotel, an appropriately Crusoe-style statue, with the hero depicted as clad in goat skin, stands above the door of the house which occupies the site of the humbler home where he was born. Before hastening on to see it, however, it is well worth lingering for a meal at the Crusoe Hotel's Castaway Restaurant, because Bob Jurgensen's son has become one of Scotland's top young chefs and, as befits an eating place with such a seafaring setting, its seafood dishes are always a speciality of the menu. The Crusoe's cuisine and the warm hospitality dispensed by Mrs Jurgensen in the hotel's shipshape little bar, won the hotel a special mention on *Breakaway*, the BBC Radio Four holiday programme's coverage of the East Neuk of Fife. It was a recommendation based on personal experience because its presenters chose to stay in the Crusoe's new sea-view bedrooms, with their panoramic views across the Forth, which were added recently with the support of the Scottish Tourist Board.

The Tourist Board's involvement in the East Neuk is very well justified, because this is truly a corner, as the Scottish word 'neuk' indicates, for those who want to escape from the strains and stresses of workaday life and enjoy a really relaxing holiday. Apparently such cares are, however, nothing new, because as long ago as 1891 a guide-book described the area as:

> a delightfully quiet and health giving retreat for those desirous of escaping for a season from the din and bustle of city-life. The air is clean and bracing, the beaches well adapted and the water supply is excellent. There are many beautiful walks and drives in the neighbourhood and golfing links are close at hand. These advantages, coupled with the fact that the place is equally easy of access by rail, road or sea would seem to bespeak for it even greater popularity than it presently enjoys.

Surprisingly, none of the embryo resorts around the shores of the East Neuk developed in the way suggested by this 19th-century

Elie is one of the Firth of Forth's most popular ports for pleasure boating.
Kingdom of Fife Tourist Board.

writer with spas such as those found at the Yorkshire resorts or the piers of the Lancashire Coast, so happily today they are still the scene of bucket and spade and paddling holidays rather than places of 'hi-de-hi' style, ready-made entertainment.

First of these holiday hideaways is Earlsferry, so-named because it was from here that Macduff, Earl or Thane of Fife, of Shakespeare's *Macbeth* fame, sailed to and fro across the Firth to North Berwick. At one time regarded as a little resort on its own, it is today more or less one with its equally charming neighbour Elie. Sometimes the latter place-name used to be spelt Ely or even Ellie, but no matter which, it is derived from 'a liche' meaning out of the sea or out of the water, which is a fine description of it. Indeed it is built so close to the Firth that the walls of many of its houses are bathed by its waters, even although Chapel Ness to the west and Elie Ness to the east do protect it from the worst of the winter west and south-westerly gales. It was on just such a wild day in 1586 that James Melville, the brother of the more famous Andrew, arrived and later wrote about 'landing frae a boat at the Alie, efter a maist weiriesome and sear day'.

Only three years later, a charter confirmed the right of 'the inhabitants and visitors to play the gauf', a claim re-affirmed in 1832 after a long and expensive legal case. Ever since, Ely and Earlsferry have been synonymous with the game and the 1891 guide-book gives an interesting description of the course as it was a century ago.

> Elie and Earlsferry is a fourteen hole links course with magnificent turf and several very trying hazards. The course has in recent years been much improved, and the narrow neck where the outgoing and incoming lines of play coincided has been got rid of. It is known to fame as the training place of the famous Simpson family, Jack, Bob and Archie, as well as of Douglas Roland, the mightiest driver of the time. The fourteen hole course starts from the Elie Club House and the eleven hole round from the Forresters. On the way to the first hole from Forresters, dangers arise from two bunkers, a disused well and a cart track. At the fifth, the Sea Hole, there is a nasty ridge of rocks. At the sixth, known as The Bent, two cart tracks, a long stretch of reeds or rushes from which it takes its name and a bunker, bar the way. Next at the seventh, known both as Kincraig Braes and The End, a very disagreeable half hid bunker extends across the course and on the way to the ninth, The Quarries, two deep hollows with rocky sides, have to be crossed. The record score is fifty six, but seventy is good! There is a ladies' course in the Elie Recreation Park.

While golf will always be the real reason for holidaying in Earlsferry and Elie, there is also plenty of antiquity in the area to keep history buffs exploring happily. The parish church, for instance, dates from the end of the 17th century, but stands on the site of a much earlier place of worship and there are several curious memorial stones built into its walls. The steeple dates from 1726 and there were many renovations in 1831. The most eminent of its ministers was the Revd Robert Trail. He was born in 1603, the year of the Union of the Crowns, and after studying at St Andrews University went to France to complete his education. He returned to Scotland in 1630 and became the chaplain to the famous Marquis of Argyll. He became minister at Elie in 1639 and played a very active role in church life. He remained the town's parish minister for ten years, but in 1649 accepted a call from Greyfriars in Edinburgh. In the bitter conflict which later divided the church in Scotland, Trail took the side of the Covenanters. For his active support of their cause he was summoned before the Scottish Parliament and in 1663 was ordered to be banished from

Summer sailing is a happy holiday pursuit at Elie. Kingdom of Fife Tourist Board.

the country. He sought sanctuary in the Netherlands, where he died in exile.

Two hundred years later controversy again split the church in Scotland over the question of congregations' rights to choose their own ministers and, after the Disruption of 1843, half of Elie's worshippers quit the parish church to form the new Free Kirk under the leadership of their chosen preacher, the Revd Walter Wood. His long ministry in the town was marked in 1887, the year of Queen Victoria's golden jubilee, by the opening of the Free Church.

Quite what the Revd Mr Wood might have thought of all the Sunday activities at Elie's old harbour makes the mind boggle, but it is certainly at weekends that the little port's modern watersports centre is at its busiest, from the beginning of May right through until the end of September. Expert tuition is available for those who want to try dinghy sailing, canoeing, water skiing and windsurfing. The brilliantly coloured sails of the windsurfers make the harbour scene particularly bright and summery. For other visitors, who simply want some fun and relaxation, Elie Watersports also offer inflatable rides and even a Mediterranean-style pedalo.

All of this active participation is quite a contrast to the days when up until the outbreak of the First World War, paddle steamers used to berth alongside Apple Rock pier so that their passengers could enjoy a sedate walk ashore along the causeway for a brief visit to Elie. The causeway was built during the 1850s by William Baird to link what had until that time been a little tidal islet, known as the Elie of Ardross, to the mainland. This made it easier to transport ashore the cargoes stored in the thick stone-walled, four-storey high granary building, which still dominates the harbour scene and acts as a reminder that Elie once had a commercial trade rather than just catering for water sports enthusiasts as it does now.

That holiday-makers are able to enjoy all the leisure opportunities available at Elie harbour is thanks to the generosity of the Nairn family who formerly owned it and gave it to Elie Town Council in 1955. Faced with Lord Wheatley's ill-conceived plans for the reform of local government and the abolition of caring local town councils in favour of large impersonal regional administrations on the grounds that they would save money, Elie's Provost and Magistrates in 1974 very wisely transferred control of the harbour to a locally controlled trust. In 1993, it assumed the added responsibility of controlling the outer harbour, when the area between the headlands at Chapel Ness and Elie Ness was also given into its care by its former owner, the Baron of Elie and St Monans, Baron Vipiana.

Returning across the causeway with its views of Elie's fine sandy beaches, on the shore side the historic Ship Inn makes an ideal spot to stop for a drink, or better still a full meal, as its food has been honoured by a prestigious Egon Ronay Award and definitely lives up to it.

In Elie there are two beaches which are seaside award winners with water of top guideline standard. They are separated by the harbour causeway. The main one stretches to almost a mile of golden sand, ideal for young families, but after the children are beyond the bucket and spade stage, the smaller one on the opposite side offers more scope for exploring. Called Ruby Bay, it has lots of rock pools where happy hours can be spent crabbing. Shells often found on Forth beaches include whelks, limpets, barnacles, cowries, tower shells, pelican's foot, mussels and cockles.

Leaving behind the beaches and busy little harbour, from Elie a

Boats on the slipway is something no longer seen in St Monans since the closure of Millers, Scotland's oldest shipbuilding yard, in 1993. Kingdom of Fife Tourist Board.

path leads along the cliff-top to two ruined castles. One was Ardross, which was the stronghold of the Dishington family who had royal connections with King Robert I. The second was Newark Castle, which was once in the possession of the famous 17th-century Scottish Royalist, General David Leslie, the victor of the Battle of Philiphaugh. Almost 300 years after, at the beginning of the 20th century, distinguished Scottish architect Sir Robert Lorimer surveyed the ruins with a view to restoring them as a suitably impressive home with appropriately magnificent seascapes for shipping magnate Sir William Burrell of subsequent Glasgow art gallery fame, but the project never got under way, Burrell residing instead at Hutton Castle, near Berwick-on-Tweed.

The cliff-top trail then continues round to the north-east to St Monans, which truly lives up to its Latin motto 'mare vivimus', meaning 'we live by the sea'. Its name is sometimes also spelt St Monance, it is said because the English railway engineers, who put it on the map, did not know any better, but today the original version is back in fashion and rightly reminds visitors of the wee town's ecclesiastic origins. Tradition claims that during the 6th century, a holy man called Moinenn travelled all the way from his birth-place in Pannonia in Hungary to convert the heathen Irish to Christianity. He became Bishop of Clonfert in County Galway and after his death was beatified. It is believed that when the Vikings invaded Ireland, Celtic missionary priests rescued his bones and brought them with them when they came to Scotland. Their travels eventually brought them to Fife, where, struck by its peacefulness, they dedicated a small church to him at this spot on the shore, which then bore the name Inverory or Abercrombie. Paying a pilgrimage to St Monan's tomb gained the reputation of healing pain and suffering and this was put to the test by no less a person than His Majesty David II. In 1346 the Scottish king fought at the Battle of Nevill's Cross, where he was hit by two arrows, one of which stuck in his flesh. The wound began to fester and in agony David came to pray at the tomb of St Monan. Despite its terrible barbs, the monks managed to remove the arrow and the grateful king gave royal instructions that from then on the tomb be protected by the building of a much statelier church. Construction of the new church began in 1362 under the supervision of Sir William Dishington of Ardross Castle and by 1370, St Monans had its impressive parish kirk, which is still its pride and joy to this day.

The church, however, has had a long and chequered history. Originally a place of worship for the Dominican Friars, it was attacked and partially destroyed by English invaders, who sailed up the Forth in 1544 during the Rough Wooing following the Scottish refusal to promise that the infant Mary Queen of Scots would one day marry their Prince Edward. After the Reformation in 1560 the damage was repaired and it became a Protestant place of worship and a century later in 1646, the official parish kirk of St Monans. During the 18th century, only part of it was used for services and other areas fell into disrepair but it was eventually restored by celebrated architect William Burn who is also mentioned earlier for his work in Leith. He supervised work on it for two years between 1826 and 1828. The church as it is today is the result of a further very fine renovation in 1955 by architect Ian Lindsay.

The church at St Monans is very much a sailor's place of worship, set as it is facing the open water of the Firth with nothing between it and the waves, but the rock-strewn foreshore. Outside, the salt-laden sea air has over the years taken its toll of the stonework, but inside the light lime walls and ceiling look virgin white illuminated by the light of the Firth streaming in through the clear glass windows, which seem more appropriate than any patterned stained glass could possibly be. The church is, however, not without its splashes of colour, for above each arch are picked out the brightly decorated coats of arms of various famous Scottish families including the local Leslies and Dishingtons. Round the walls are 12 consecration crosses marking where the holy water was sprinkled when the church was first dedicated and representing the 12 stations of the cross, where Jesus stopped on his final journey to Calvary.

Of particular interest is the fine model of a full-rigged ship which sails high above the sailors' aisle. Hanging model ships in an honoured place in church is a custom maintained in countries on both sides of the North Sea, with noteworthy examples in the ornately decorated Cathedral in Aalborg, the starkly contrasting, modern, golden, brick-built Grundvelt's Kirk in Copenhagen and, nearer home, in the neighbouring Old Parish Kirk and Carriden Kirk, both overlooking the Forth in Bo'ness and just down river in the little church built in Blackness, as a place for the crews of the Royal Naval ships to come ashore and worship.

While its church is still a showpiece, the surrounding town has fared less well and sadly St Monans is now very much the Cinderella of the East Neuk. The little town's decline is the result of the closure of its once-famous shipbuilding yard, which was the oldest in the whole of the British Isles, dating back all the way to the year after the defeat of the Jacobites at the Battle of Culloden. It was then, in 1747, that the Miller family began building boats in St Monans and they continued to do so proudly for no fewer than eight generations. James N. Miller and Sons Ltd specialised in building all kinds of small craft, from fishing boats to both sailing and motor yachts, with occasional additional orders for pilot boats and Admiralty launches for the Royal Navy. The local workforce, drawn mainly from St Monans itself and neighbouring Elie, Pittenweem and Anstruther, were all skilled craftsmen. They all knew their trades, from carpenters and cabinet makers to painters and plumbers and built each boat using traditional methods and tools handed down from father to son. Materials, too, were traditional, from oak and larch for the fishing boats to more expensive teak for the decks and rich mahogany for the finishing touches to the yachts. It was said you could always tell a Miller boat without even looking at its maker's plate. The attention to detail was enough to speak for itself. Miller's experience of building fishing boats capable of withstanding the rigours of the North Sea added to the safety of the St Monans yard's yachts, many of which won prizes in ocean races.

The launch of a Miller vessel was always an exciting event in St Monans, with the town's Virgin Square crowded with both local folk and visitors to see the latest addition to the yard's list being trundled from the building sheds behind Shore Street and down the slipway into the harbour. For the launch of bigger vessels constructed in the main shed immediately to the east of the harbour, a section of railway sleepers on the pier could be lifted out to provide direct access to the water. As well as boat building, Miller's also had a flourishing engineering business, manufacturing capstans and winches for export to ports in many parts of the world, but the end came for this once prosperous family firm when it was taken over in the 1980s, first by MacTay from the Wirral in Cheshire and then by Mowlem, before being traded back to MacTay once more.

St Monans' centuries-long history of shipbuilding finally came to an end in 1993 with the closure of the yard. Some of the men used their redundancy money to open their own business and keep the Miller name alive in a small way along the coast at the docks at Methil, but for St Monans the glory days of launching sturdy fishing boats and sleek yawls and ketches such as the *Cayenne*, the *Ceol Mara 11* and the *Old Fox* were finally over.

Former owner of the yard and Provost of the town, Mr W.P. Miller, would be birling in his grave if he could see the devastating effect the closure of his family firm has had on St Monans. The smaller boat-building sheds are soon to be demolished to make room for seven new houses, which will help a wee bit in the town's revival, but the derelict, giant, grey shed on the quayside, welcome when it provided jobs, is now just a massive blot on the Firth seascape.

'The world's biggest doocot', is how Harbour Master, 64-year-old Robert McMurray describes it, as he watches the pigeons fly in and out. Mr McMurray is about to retire, but he has a dream, which if turned into reality would ensure a happy ending for St Monans' Cinderella story. For Mr McMurray, who is himself a boat owner, wants to turn the east end of the harbour into a marina, not just for local sailing enthusiasts like himself, but to welcome yachtsmen from the Scandinavian countries and other parts of Europe, who will come to the Forth in increased numbers, after the re-opening of the Forth and Clyde Canal, as part of Scotland's Millennium plans, opens up western waters to them:

> At present they have to sail right up the Forth, below the bridges to Port Edgar, before they can make landfall, but I'm sure they would be very pleased to tie up here for a run ashore after their North Sea passage, if we had a well equipped marina to welcome them. And it need not cost a fortune to construct, simply a sill across the harbour mouth to retain two metres of water and at low tide a floating pontoon for them to moor alongside. The marina would create activity in the harbour and this would in turn bring back holiday visitors. At present motorists drive down the hill to the harbour, find there is nowhere for them to park and depart without bringing any trade to the town's shops and businesses. This too can all be changed at little expense by demolishing the shipbuilding shed and using the space for a harbourside carpark with wonderful views right out across the Forth. During the winter months the carpark would not lie empty as it could also be used to provide hard standing for the dinghies and yachts, while owners who prefer covered storage for their vessels could be easily catered for by retaining one of the shipbuilding sheds on the other side of Virgin Square.

For Harbour Master McMurray's ideas to become reality requires Fife Council, in faraway inland Glenrothes, to realise the potential which St Monans offers. To change pantomimes from *Cinderella* to *Sleeping Beauty*, the Council needs to wake up and change from being the Wicked Witch, as it is regarded at present by many older residents in St Monans for simply seeing the old fishing port as a convenient hide-away to dump its problem tenants as it has been doing allegedly in council-owned flats and become the Good

Fairy, who can grant the local inhabitants' wish to breathe new life into their community.

In the meantime, St Monans continues to decline, with its harbourside cafe, its only bank and several of its shops all shut. Only the town's post office is truly busy, doling out weekly government benefits to St Monans' unemployed. Despite its down-at-heel appearance, compared with other East Neuk towns such as Elie and Anstruther, St Monans clearly has many buildings which deserve preservation and restoration, as the National Trust for Scotland has already done for some under its Little Houses scheme.

One of the most interesting of these is Harbour Master McMurray's shoreside home, which, along with its adjoining neighbour, was originally the town's Anti-Burgher Chapel. The date stones on the two houses show the property was originally built at the start of the 1700s and they were used as a place of worship for about 50 years. The Anti-Burghers were one of many small religious groups who have always flourished in Scottish coastal towns and like most of them showed little Christian love for their neighbours. During their frequent and lengthy services the Anti-Burghers even went so far as to post one of their younger members upstairs at the round window in the gable wall to keep lookout and give warning if any of their rival sects appeared on the scene and if they did were ready to sally forth with sticks and clubs to ward them off. As often still happens with small religious groups in the East Coast ports, some of whom will not speak to their neighbours or eat at each other's tables, after about half a century the Anti-Burghers of St Monans quarrelled in turn amongst themselves and broke up into smaller splinter groups of worshippers, each certain that their way and only their way was the rightful path to heaven. Their church with its sea views was then divided into homes. Today it is divided into two houses, each with interesting features such as the well in the garden of one and the typically Fife fore-stairs jutting out in front of the other, but at one time all of the rooms on all four floors, including the attic, were occupied by different fishermen's families, mostly with many children, making it a veritable rabbit warren of a building.

Those were the days, of course, when the fishing flourished in St Monans, but today the only trade is carried on by two small prawn catchers, as the port's last fishing boat was sold in 1997.

Set high to catch the wind, the St Monans' Windmill provided power to pump the river water into the town's salt pans, whose product boosted the district's economy in former years. Kingdom of Fife Tourist Board.

Fishermen and seals have always been traditional enemies, but today another bit of life is added to the St Monans' harbour scene by regular visits from the Seal Survey Unit's zodiac inflatable. Originally based at Cambridge University, the members of the seal research team are now based at St Andrews. For convenience, they keep their vessel in one of the buildings at the little industrial estate up on the hill behind the town and use the slipway at the harbour for their voyages along the shores of the Firth and out to the Isle of May, where there is a large colony of seals.

A traditional Forth industry of which St Monans has a reminder is the salt trade, because on the bend of coast which curves round

Pittenweem harbour's fishing boats are still as tight packed as herring in a barrel. The vessel in the foreground is registered in Kirkcaldy. Kingdom of Fife Tourist Board.

towards Pittenweem stands the reconstruction of a stone-built windmill. The connection between a windmill and salt production may not at first be apparent, but all becomes as clear as the salt crystals themselves when it is explained by the very well-illustrated information boards that the reason it was originally constructed here overlooking the shore was to provide the power needed to pump the water from the Firth into the large shallow iron pans where it was slowly evaporated into salt. Production of salt by evaporation from sea water does still continue in some parts of the world, such as Lanzarote in the Canary Islands where the sun does the job, without the need for costly coal, whose increase in price partially helped put the Scottish salt industry out of business. The windmill, with its conical pointed, black witch's hat slate roof, is now a distinctive landmark on the Fife shore. It is just a pity that its red sails no longer turn.

While salt making is now a thing of the past, for those on holiday who think there is nothing more interesting than watching others hard at work, the harbour at neighbouring Pittenweem is definitely the answer. For of all the little harbours along this stretch of coast, it is Pittenweem which truly retains a workaday feel to it as the home of much of what remains of the Fife fishing fleet. Not that Pittenweem is not also a pretty place to visit. With its historic homes, many now in the protective care of the National Trust for Scotland under its Little Houses Scheme, it definitely is, as proved when it caught the eye of film-maker Alan Rickman, who featured its red pantiled roofs and harled, colourwashed walls as a background for his screen production of *The Winter Guest*, starring mother-and-daughter team, Phyllda Law and Emma Thompson, but it is the fact that the harbour here is still in active daily use that gives it a special attraction.

With its modern fishmarket right on the West Quay, the early morning is the best time to visit the crowded harbour, as the day's catch is swiftly and efficiently auctioned. Catch the fishing prices at five to one on BBC Radio Scotland or read them at leisure in the columns of the Aberdeen *Press and Journal*, the only morning newspaper in the world with its own dedicated fishing correspondent, and it all seems a very calm and orderly affair as you learn that boxes of haddock sold for so much and boxes of lemon sole for a wee bit more, but down here in the dawn light it is fast and furious as the fish are auctioned and as soon as sold, seem to melt away as fast as the ice, which keeps them fresh.

Out in the harbour itself there is also lots of action as the brightly-painted fishing boats seem to copy the fairground dodgems as they jostle for position in its narrow crowded waters. Each has its registration code letters on the bow, usually 'KY' for Kirkcaldy or 'LH' for Leith, but look out for the occasional visitors whose home ports are further north, such as Buckie and Peterhead. East coast registration marks which you may see include A, AH, BF, BK, BCK, BU, FR, INS, ME, PD and WK. See if you can successfully link the letters with ports they represent. The numbers after the letters indicate individual boats.

Back to Pittenweem, however. Its name means the 'Place of the Cave', and the long narrow cave can still be visited in Cove Wynd. The cave is traditionally linked to the 7th-century Saint Fillan and is still looked after by the local Scottish Episcopalian Church. On the subject of churches, steep Cove Wynd climbs up to the remains of the 14th-century Augustinian Priory, to which the brothers of the order came from the earlier one out on the Isle of May. After the Reformation the remains of the ancient Priory were not treated very reverently by the local inhabitants, who not only appear to have used various parts of them as stables and even stores for their herring barrels, but do not seem to have been averse to acquiring some of their stones to incorporate into the walls of their own homes. The Priory buildings and their surrounding grounds originally occupied between two and three acres of the hillside overlooking the Firth. The main entrance seems to have been from the east facing the Great House. The Prior of Pittenweem is first mentioned as long ago as 1220 in a charter of that year and one of the last was John Rowle, who was a Lord of Session during the reign of Mary Queen of Scots and who accompanied the Regent Moray to visit her at the French royal court in 1550.

Following the Reformation and after Mary abdicated in favour of her young son, who became James VI, William Stewart, the Captain of the King's bodyguard, obtained a charter giving him the rights to the Priory of Pittenweem. Later in 1606 the Captain's son, Frederick Stewart, persuaded King Jamie to turn his lands at Pittenweem into a temporal lordship and to grant him the title of Baron Pittenweem. He transferred the superiority to the Earls of Kellie and the title died out.

By then Pittenweem was as staunchly Protestant as any other place in Scotland and worship had moved to the parish church near the remains of the Priory at the east end of the main street. It appears, however, to have actually originated as part of the Priory and to have been converted from its earlier use as a grain store for the monks. On its west side the church tower, with its ballustrated top, its short spire and its two bells dated 1663 and 1742, seems also to have had an earlier use as its base appears to have been Pittenweem's Tolbooth, which contained the local courtroom and the town jail. It was there, despite Pittenweem's long ecclesiastic history, that local sentiment gave way to superstition and women suspected of the abominable crime of witchcraft were imprisoned. The last of them was Janet Corphat.

On a more respectable note, Pittenweem's market cross, with the town's coat of arms and the date 'July 4 day, 1711' stands at the foot of the tower.

These accoutrements of burgh status are a reminder that Pittenweem does indeed have a long history of local government. It was granted the status of a Burgh of Barony way back during the reign of King James III at the end of the 15th century and his grandson, James V, issued a fresh charter to this effect in 1526. In the year of his death, 1542, the same Stuart monarch created Pittenweem a Royal Burgh and this was again ratified by his great grandson, Charles I, on the occasion of his own and only royal progress through Scotland in 1633. During the troubles of the 1640s many of the Pittenweem men fought and died at the Battle of Kilsyth, the port being so badly hit by their loss that many of its fishing boats were left without crews and rotted away in the harbour. The local economy was in such a bad state by the time of the execution of King Charles I in 1649 that Pittenweem and East Anstruther further along the coast, jointly petitioned Parliament for help. Even after Oliver Cromwell, as Lord High Protector, was officially ruler of the country, Royalist sentiment remained sufficiently faithful to the Stuart cause to guarantee King Charles II a truly regal welcome to the town on 15 February 1651, when the young monarch rode through it on his way to spend the night at Anstruther House. A contemporary account states:

> The Provost and bailies convoyed the King from the West Port to Robert Smith's yett, where a table was laid with refreshments including some great buns and other breads of the best order, baked with sugar, also eight to ten gallons of good strong ale and many wines.

When His Majesty left, 'Andrew Tod on ther kirk steeple had signalled to the battery of 36 cannon, so that they could all be shot at once.'

In 1736, Pittenweem gained a certain notoriety as the place which sparked off the famous Porteous Riots. This came about because of a running dispute between one of the town's seafarers and alleged smuggler, Andrew Wilson, and the local gauger, as the custom's collector was known. According to Wilson, the said official had repeatedly confiscated his goods and reduced him to a state of bankruptcy. Together with another local man called Robertson, he therefore lay in wait for the Customs collector and together they robbed him of all of the week's customs and excise dues for the port of Pittenweem, 'to reimburse himself for his losses', as Wilson put it at his subsequent trial in Edinburgh. Despite such an eloquent plea he was found guilty and publicly executed in the Grassmarket at the foot of the Castle Rock. While the Pittenweem sailor failed to save his life, his case against the unpopular Fife tax collector had won over the sympathy of the Edinburgh crowd, who staged a riot in the crowded streets of the

Pittenweem's fishermen mend their nets with the old port's historic harbourside homes in the background. Kingdom of Fife Tourist Board.

capital's Old Town. As sticks were flourished and stones hurled, the Town Guard was called out and their Captain, John Porteous, ordered them to load their muskets and fire into the crowd, resulting in the deaths and injury of 30 people. Captain Porteous was in turn arrested and sentenced to death and on 8 September the crowd again congregated in the narrow Grassmarket to see him publicly hanged. As the time for the execution came and went, the Edinburgh mob again turned nasty as rumours spread that because of his position in the city, Porteous had succeeded in cheating the hangman. By the time the Magistrates announced that Porteous had indeed petitioned Queen Caroline, who was at the time acting as Regent for King George II, but had only been granted a six-week stay of execution, the crowd were in too angry a mood to listen and, robbed of the pleasure of seeing Porteous officially put to death, decided to do the job themselves. Swiftly, they rushed up the hill to the Tolbooth in the High Street, next to the High Kirk of St Giles, burnt down the doors, dragged the hapless Porteous from the condemned cell and hanged him from a dyer's pole.

On a more peaceful note, Pittenweem's other claims to historic fame include that it was the birth-place in 1721 of the Revd John Douglas, who became Bishop of Salisbury and, of nautical note, in Victorian times it was the birth-place of the Henderson brothers, whose Anchor Line steamships challenged the Cunarders as they raced across the North Atlantic.

Similar rivalry at that time used to divide Pittenweem from its near neighbour Anstruther and there is still a bit of it between the two ports, but nowadays house building has almost linked the two places. In the past, however, there were even fierce divisions within Anstruther itself, the Dreel Burn dividing the Parish and Royal Burgh of Anstruther Wester from Anstruther Easter and the latter in turn being split off from what looks to the stranger just like its eastern extremity, Cellardyke, which formed a separate burgh with its immediate inland neighbour, Kilrenny. To add to the confusion, Cellardyke was sometimes known as Nether Kilrenny, that is Lower Kilrenny as in The Netherlands, meaning the Low Countries of Europe. In the end, local government re-organisation in 1929 at last brought them all together under the banner of the longest town-name in Scotland as The United Burghs of Kilrenny, Anstruther Easter and Anstruther Wester. After all of that mouthful it is interesting to discover that folks these parts still abbreviate Anstruther to Ainster.

Furthering local rivalry, for hundreds of years Anstruther and Cellardyke each had its own fishing fleet. In the middle of Queen Victoria's reign, however, the Anstruther fleet having grown too large for its little harbour, the government was persuaded in 1866 to provide funds for the much larger Union Harbour. Construction of it proved a very arduous task, as frequent storms interrupted work and swept away what had already been achieved, but in the end, in 1877, it was completed at a cost of £80,000, a large sum in those days. As it was constructed to the east of the old one in Shore Street, Easter Anstruther, its better facilities and sheltered waters protected by a western breakwater and an eastern pier 1,200 yards long proved sufficiently attractive to lure the Cellardyke fishermen to berth their boats there as well.

Anstruther harbour used to be crowded with fishing boats, but most have moved to Pittenweem, leaving plenty of space for pleasure craft. Kingdom of Fife Tourist Board.

Although it covers an area of all of 13½ acres, making it the largest fishing port in Fife, and was designed to cater for around 500 fishing boats, the new Union Harbour must often have been crowded, because the report of the Fishery Board for Scotland for 1883 states that the number of fishing craft of all classes belonging to the Anstruther District was 830. Even taking into account that Anstruther District officially took in all ports from Buckhaven to the south side of the River Tay, it gives some impression of how busy the new harbour must at times have been. It was designed to cope with vessels of from 200 to 500 tons and to allow them safe entrance for three hours on either side of each day's two high tides. The 1883 Fishery Board Report records that fishing vessels were divided into three categories by tonnage and that the aggregate tonnage of the first class largest vessels in the Anstruther District was 9,646 tons out of a total of 10,663. The value of the boats was estimated at £66,960, their nets at £95,584 and their lines at £14,132, making a total investment in the fishing industry of £176,676.

Anstruther District was one of 26 areas into which the Scottish fishing industry was divided and it was the most prosperous with an eighth of the fishing fleet having it as their port of registration.

These 830 boats employed 3,491 fishermen and boys, of whom 2,050 had their homes in the district. The fishing also provided almost as many jobs in ancillary industries, with a further 2,362 men and women earning their living as fish curers and coopers making the barrels in which to stuff the herring which they salted so that they could be exported across the North Sea to the Scandinavian countries and other parts of Europe, especially Holland.

During this century, Anstruther's fishing fleet has mainly relocated to the harbour at Pittenweem, but the port is still the site of Scotland's Fisheries Museum, housed in an attractive huddle of 16th- to 19th-century buildings at Harbourhead, directly overlooking the port where all of the action used to take place. The white-harled, red-pantiled, three-storey corner block, which is known as St Ayles Land, has a long history of links with the fishing. Its last private owners, the Cunningham family, operated a prosperous ships' chandler's supply business and leased other parts of the premises round the three sides of its courtyard for fishermen's stores and net lofts, while the courtyard itself was used for hanging up and drying the nets. The old wooden structures on which the nets were strung were known as gallows, and some of the original ones still survive.

It was local interest in preserving the history and telling the story of the fishing industry which led to the museum being founded in 1969. Since then it has expanded to cover every aspect of the Scottish fishing industry, ranging from industrial salmon fishing to whale hunting in the Arctic and later in the Antarctic, as well as all of the shore-based jobs which were needed to support them. All of this is presented in a lively, attractive manner with the opportunity to stand in the wheelhouse of a modern fishing boat and imagine you are the skipper, as you listen to the ship-to-shore radio and other full-scale displays, ranging from the inside of a typical fisher-home to a fishmonger's shop.

The museum also has wonderfully comprehensive collections of oil and water-colour paintings and black and white photographs illustrating every aspect of life in the fishing industry, both at sea and ashore, as well as a well-stocked library, the latter open to interested visitors by prior appointment. In the whaling section, look for the log books of the Scottish whalers and search the margins for the black flukes drawn to indicate a successful catch.

Although most of its fishing fleet has gone, Anstruther is still home to the Scottish Fisheries Museum. Kingdom of Fife Tourist Board.

The museum also has its own collection of actual vessels on display in a neighbouring former shipbuilding yard and afloat in the harbour. Among the 15 boats is a Fifie, one of the typical wooden-hulled fishing boats, which were a familiar sight in East Coast ports throughout the first half of the 20th century. She is the *Reaper*, whose keel was laid in 1901 and was first registered in 1902 as FR 958. She later transferred to Lerwick, where she was reregistered as LK 707. In 1975, she was purchased by the Fisheries Museum, and after over 20 years of work, has now been fully restored and registered again as FR 958 and is now able to go to sea again to sail to special events in neighbouring ports. With her smart black and white painted hull and her two red sails she attracts a great deal of attention wherever she berths.

Adding further interest to Anstruther's Union Harbour is the fact that it also boasts Scotland's only lightship museum in the distinctive shape of the North Carr. She is open for casual visits, but much more interesting is to take a conducted tour, which not only takes you through the crew's quarters including the mess room and galley and officers' cabins, but below decks to the engine room and even the chain store.

Despite the North Carr and the other 200 lights ranging from lighthouses to illuminated buoys, which the Commissioners for Northern Lights carefully tend around the coasts of Scotland and the Isle of Man, tragedies do sadly still happen at sea and the Scottish Fisheries Museum is particularly proud to have been chosen to be the home of the Memorial to Scottish Fishermen Lost At Sea.

The fact that even more lives have not been lost at sea is the result of the sterling service of the volunteers of The Royal National Lifeboat Institution, which was founded by Sir William Hillary in 1824. Anstruther men have been manning their local lifeboat since Victorian times and their present craft is an impressively powerful Mersey class vessel capable of going right out into the North Sea, as she is often called upon to do, and in marked contrast to Fife's other lifeboat, an Atlantic 75, which is based at Kinghorn to cater more for inshore emergencies. Both crews are always pleased to welcome visitors and to tell them more about the lifeboat service of which they are so justifiably proud.

Anstruther has always bred fine sailors such as Fisher Willie, the nickname for Laird William of Anstruther who in the Middle Ages ran his own private navy. With the men from his Fife estate as crew he put to sea 'wearing a shirt of mail beneath a woollen doublet, while enormous boots encased his nether man', and thus clad engaged the enemy English, the rival craft often getting so close that hand-to-hand sword fights took place. Later in the 19th century, Anstruther was the birth-place of Rear-Admiral William Black and a wall memorial was erected to him in the church at the east end of the town. Mention of the church, is a reminder that Anstruther's most famous son was not a seaman, but that distinguished theologian, Dr Thomas Chalmers, who at the General Assembly of the Church of Scotland in 1843 led the famous Disruption, by leading around half of the other ministers and elders out of St Andrew's Church in Edinburgh's George Street to demand congregations' rights to choose their own preacher, rather than having one foisted onto them by the local laird and thus founded the Free Church of Scotland. Dr Chalmers' brave act is still recalled by his statue in George Street at its junction with Castle Street. There he stands proudly, still defiantly reading his open Bible and with his back appropriately to the Church of Scotland's still very establishment-looking headquarters at its famous 121 George Street address!

Motor launches from Anstruther ply regularly to and from the Isle of May during the summer months. Kingdom of Fife Tourist Board.

The Anstruther kirk is also the burial place of Professor William Tennant, still remembered in these parts not for his distinguished academic career, but as author of the rollicking poem, *Anster Fair*, which describes all that took place at that annual event held in a field to the north of the town beside the road which leads out to St Andrews and vividly describes all the local characters who gathered to do business there. Professor Tennant tells of his heroine, Maggie Lauder, living in 'The East Green's best house'. The Green has long gone, and with it the building of which he wrote, but the place-name remains and a house on the street leading along from Anstruther to Cellardyke is still pointed out as the famous Maggie's home.

Cellardyke is a popular wee holiday place, and deservedly so, with views out across the Firth to the Isle of May, which visitors can explore thanks to daily sailings from Anstruther Harbour. Nearer at hand, Cellardyke's grassy cliffs have for generations offered exciting adventure for the younger generation, but they are now also well catered for by the enterprising East Neuk Outdoor Activity Centre, whose enthusiastic young instructors tempt participants to try everything from climbing and abseiling to, naturally, water-based activities such as canoeing and sea kayaking. For those who want to explore further afield, the centre

179

offers both coastal walks and, for the more ambitious, cycle expeditions. All age groups and the physically challenged are catered for and unaccompanied children are welcome. Activities take place everyday from April to September, more or less regardless of what the spring and summer weather offers, but for those who prefer to retreat indoors on less fine days, the East Neuk's only secondary school, Waid Academy, is converted during the summer holidays into Waid Recreation Centre, offering good facilities for swimming, badminton, table tennis and carpet bowls.

While Anstruther and Cellardyke offer much for holiday visitors throughout the whole season, try especially to visit the latter when it is colourfully flag-bedecked for the summer Saturday, when caravan dwellers and local residents get together to enjoy celebrating the Crowning of the Sea Queen.

CHAPTER 8

FROM SETON SANDS
TO TREASURE ISLAND

S eton Sands — the name has a certain ring to it and it might well have become as famous as Filey, Skegness or any of the other English holiday camp-sites, because it was here on the shores of the Firth of Forth that the whole idea was born, long before Billy Butlin thought of it. The site overlooking the two-mile stretch of sandy beach at Seton began simply as a popular site for Boys' Brigade camps under canvas in the years immediately after the First World War, but soon the lads' parents also heard about the delights this seaside holiday had to offer and decided to come too. Like the boys, some of them brought tents and pitched them on the site with its lovely views out over the Firth, but others found accommodation in the old former War Department ambulances and other vehicles, which Farmer Bruce, the owner of Seton Mains Farm, good naturedly allowed onto what had previously been an unused scrubby piece of his land.

Then, in 1922, he began getting letters in the post asking for places to stay and so he began renting out some former railway carriages, which he had acquired and had hauled onto the foreshore site. Thus was founded Seton Sands Holiday Camp and soon it was attracting thousands of visitors. Those from Edinburgh came mainly for weekends, but as more Scots began to get one week's paid holiday each year, many Glasgow families, instead of going 'doon the Watter fur the Fair', daringly began to venture further afield for their yearly break and came all the way to East Lothian. Some of the excellent fish and chip shops which are still to be enjoyed at Port Seton Harbour opened to feed the hungry holiday hordes and the local council realised the potential for expanding the local economy.

Seton Sands' big break came in 1933 with the opening of its huge open-air swimming pool, which became one of Scotland's most popular holiday attractions. Trams from Edinburgh brought thousands of people out all the way from the city, not only to swim, but also to spectate and enjoy the water carnivals which became a feature of the Seton Sands summer season. While most visitors came by tram or by train to the little railway station which the place had in those pre-war days, some of the richer ones arrived by air. For when the tide was out, the long stretch of beach was for a time used as the landing strip for an air taxi and charter service operated by the famous Scottish Motor Traction Company (SMT). When the little planes were not hired, they were used by the enterprising company to offer visitors short sight-seeing pleasure flights round the bay and out over the Forth.

From the mid- to late-1930s, holiday homes of every description, from humble huts to much more ambitious chalets, filled the site. Even after the Second World War, Seton Sands continued to grow until its peak season in 1948, when there were 700 homes, plus another 200 tents crowded onto the site beside the Forth. For the little Forth resort the height of its season was crammed into a period of six hectic weeks and that year, from the Edinburgh Fair during the first two weeks of July, through the Glasgow Fair Fortnight and on into the first two weeks of August, there were never fewer than 3,000 people in residence.

Perhaps surprisingly, 50 years later, despite the coming of jet package holidays to the Spanish Costas and other places which can promise more guaranteed sunshine than the Costa Forth, Seton Sands still attracts a loyal following, thanks to a large extent to the far-sighted management policy of the Bourne Leisure Group, which now owns what is termed Seton Sands Holiday Village as one of 19 holiday centres, which it operates around the coast of the United Kingdom. For Bourne Leisure has not only totally upgraded its holiday homes at Seton Sands to an extent which would make them unrecognisable to the converted railway carriage dwellers of the 1920s and 30s, but has found the secret of appealing to modern holiday families by providing welcoming indoor attractions for all age groups. A private, tropically-heated, indoor, lagoon pool, complete with separate splash area for children has replaced the old public outdoor baths and instead of jammy pieces as a chittering bite, there's now the well-prepared food and drink of the Aqua Bar and Restaurant, whose windows provide a grandstand view of all the action in the water. If the children ever tire of swimming, there is the Bradley Bear Club waiting to entertain them, while their older brothers and sisters have the Teen Challenge Club and the adults the evening discos, dancing and cabaret entertainment offered by Sundowners, one of the largest and best-equipped entertainment venues on the East Coast. All of this is quite a difference from the homespun camp-fire sing-songs of past decades, but interestingly one of the most popular places to end the day at Seton Sands Holiday Village is the Inn on the Bay, with its views out over the Firth as the sun sets, which are still as entrancingly beautiful as they ever were.

Walking on along the coast, after the crowded concentration of Seton Sands, the scenery becomes much more rural. As the coast swings round into Gosford Bay, the view is pleasantly open, taking in the typical grassy links where the golfers of Longniddry enjoy their sport. Gosford Bay stretches for about two miles, its landward side guarded all the way by the Earl's Dyke, the impressive early Victorian stone wall, which marks the boundary of the Earl of Wemyss' huge estate with its great domed Adam mansion. On the other side of the coast road is a car park, which makes a pleasant spot to sit and look out over the river, or better still to get out and walk along the sandy links. At the east end of Gosford Bay the road cuts across the headland and takes only about a mile to Aberlady, but it takes double that distance to walk round the coast of Craigielaw. On the west side it is eaten into by little Shell Bay. The two nearby villas are Greencraig and Harlaw, the former taking its name from the wee island in the middle of Shell Bay. Both are part of Gosford Estate. Moving on east, the path passes Kilspindie Golf Course and then, as it turns into Aberlady Bay, follows the estuary of the little Peffer Burn, where it flows into the Forth at Craigielaw Point. This, confusingly, is the first of two streams both called the Peffer, which are tributaries on the south shore of the Forth. Both have their source close to each other near the East Lothian village of Athelstaneford of Scottish Saltire flag fame, but run in opposite directions, the second Peffer meeting the Forth near Whitberry Point to the north of Belhaven near Dunbar, of which more later.

It is out here in this lonely spot that the Victorian Earl of Wemyss built a rifle range to encourage his estate workers to enlist in the Army Volunteers, which he was largely responsible for creating in 1859. Highlight of this patriotic force's existence was the Great Review, to which thousands of the members of this 19th-century Dad's Army came to be reviewed at Holyrood House by Queen Victoria's consort, Prince Albert. Tragically, he died soon afterwards and it is in the uniform of a Field Marshall, which he wore on that occasion, that he is immortalised in the shape of the equine statue, which was dedicated by his devastated widow as Scotland's national memorial to him in the centre of Edinburgh's Charlotte Square. So great was the crowd, which once again included many of the Earl's men from Gosford, that it was reported that not a single blade of grass could be seen and there was total silence as the Queen addressed the people.

Craigielaw Point is an equally quiet spot, the calm only broken by the occasional cries of the birds for whom Aberlady Bay has since 1952 been protected as a nature reserve. Consisting of around 1,500 acres of sandy shore, dunes, mudflats, salt sea marsh and grass-covered links with a small stretch of trees, it is home to a wide range of wild duck and wading birds. The nature reserve takes in both sides of the bay and although these lands still belong to Gosford and Luftness Estates, public access is allowed and is in fact made easier by the wooden walkways which have been erected.

Most of the territory covered by the nature reserve is tidal, but the whole area seems so flat and shallow that it is hard to realise that Aberlady used to be the port for Haddington, just as further up the Forth, Blackness served inland Linlithgow and Torryburn served inland Dunfermline. Like these other out-ports, as they were known, Aberlady is an interesting reminder of how important water-borne transport was in past centuries and around the village there are still reminders of the days when boats docked here, from Ship House, with its sailing vessel carved above the door to the big, thick, stone-walled warehouse, which has recently been converted into attractive modern flats, but which was originally the granary, where cargoes of barley were stored by the local merchants, while they awaited the arrival of the sailing ships to export them. As a port with exports of grain and imports ranging from lime and fertilisers for the farmers' fields to fine wines for their cellars, Aberlady, of course, required the presence of the gaugers, the excisemen and their customs house, now known as Kilspindie House, still stands out near the golf clubhouse. Despite the presence of the customs officers, however, Aberlady in the past was famed for its smugglers, who operating in secret at dead of night from their premises in the Wynd, carefully avoided the payment of duty on goods as varied as salt to brandy.

The merchants' granary and warehouse in Aberlady has been beautifully restored and converted into attractive apartment homes. Anyone who believes all stones are the same colour should examine the rich hues of those which make up the thick walls of The Maltings below its traditional red pantiled roof.

Aberlady, with all its tales of smugglers, seems a very suitable home for that veteran teller of Scottish stories, Nigel Tranter. As one of the country's most prolific and successful authors, Mr Tranter has the unusual habit of writing his books on the hoof as it were, carefully recording ideas in his notebook as he walks the shores of the bay. There are certainly plots aplenty for his wonderfully detailed historic novels, right on his doorstep. It is from a spot on the shore of the Forth near Aberlady that King Loth, from whom Lothian takes its name, is reputed by tradition to have set his daughter, Thenew, adrift in a small open boat, after it became known at the royal court high on Traprain Law to the south of Haddington that she was about to bear an illegitimate child. Loth's daughter survived the ordeal and the boat was swept up river by a gale and eventually washed ashore at Culross, where she was rescued and given shelter by St Serf. Soon afterwards she

The painted sailing ship above the door of this cottage, which overlooks the main road through Aberlady, is a reminder that the village was once the port for Haddington. Nowadays Aberlady Bay has silted up and is visited not by ships, but by thousands of seabirds and waders, who benefit from it being protected as a nature reserve. The reserve is open every day to the public and well constructed wooden bridges and paths make it easy to explore.

gave birth to a baby boy. She christened him Kentigern, but when he grew up and travelled west to the village on the shores of the River Clyde which later grew to become Glasgow, he became much better known as Mungo and of course became the city's patron saint. Interestingly, his mother Princess Thenew has also left her mark on Scotland's largest city, because the title of Glasgow's largest indoor shopping mall, St Enoch's Centre, is derived from her name.

Another story, which has all the appeal of one of Nigel Tranter's historic novels, is that of Luffness Castle, situated just to the east of his home in Aberlady. The estate of Luffness is much older than that of Gosford and as a stronghold it once rated as one of the Keys of the Kingdom. The original castle was so powerful that in 1545 its cannon succeeded in preventing the landing of the invading English troops, who were aiming to march inland to relieve their fellow soldiers under siege at Haddington during the 'Rough Wooing' of the infant Mary Queen of Scots. King Henry VIII never forgot the role which Luffness had played in thwarting his army and two years later, after the decisive English victory at the Battle of Pinkie near Musselburgh, he had his revenge, when as part of the peace process, he insisted on its demolition. Henry had however reckoned without the sturdiness of the massive walls of Luffness, the base of which defied destruction and which a few years afterwards provided the foundation for the present late 16th-century fortified mansion. It looms over the main road which leads on into Gullane, which lies about half a mile to the south of the coastline of the bay.

Gullane is the most up-market of the seaside resorts on the Lothian shore of the Forth and, as befits its reputation, offers several first-class hotels. In alphabetical order, Bissets and the Golf Inn are both in the main street and both family-run, the latter in premises which have catered for travellers since coaching days. Greywalls, the Mallard and the Queens all overlook Gullane's famous golf courses and all have their devotees. Architecturally, Greywalls' Edwardian country house setting is of particular interest.

Gullane is considered so very posh that there are as many stories about the correct pronunciation of its name as there are about Edinburgh Morningside accents. Use 'Gulyn' if you want to be accepted. It is little wonder that Gullane has become such a popular residential and retirement village because it is a delightful little place lying sheltered in the lee of Gala Law. Today Gala Law is a great grassy mound, but originally it was a huge wind-blown sand dune. In the past, the dunes were one huge warren of burrows, to such an extent that the thousands of rabbits which inhabited them, were caught commercially and many of them were sent south to markets in England.

In the 17th century, the sands threatened to overwhelm Gullane and after a series of storms buried the 500-year-old St Andrew's Church and its graveyard, its congregation abandoned it and moved to worship in neighbouring Dirleton, from which the parish from then on took its name. Today, the problem of the wind-blown sand has been tamed and the sand confined to the bunkers on Gullane's four golf courses.

Most famous is Muirfield, over which The Open has been regularly played, most recently in 1992. Originally known as Hundred Acre Howe, Muirfield was laid out between 1890 and 1891 by the Honourable Company of Edinburgh Golfers, who had decided that Musselburgh Links had become just too crowded. Now tempted by the new railway stations on the line from Edinburgh to North Berwick, at Drem and Longniddry from which horse-drawn omnibuses were available, they were tempted to move further out to Muirfield, which, unlike the public common at Musselburgh, was a private estate. Having leased the land, the Honourable Company employed the renowned Tom Morris to design the course. To begin with it had only 16 holes, the idea that all golf courses require 18 being one which did not become firmly established until into the 20th century. An early description of Muirfield Green, as it was called during its first few years, states:

> It is naturally well adapted for the purpose, with tough, firm turf and has been skilfully laid out by old Tom Morris, who has taken full advantage of the bunkers and ditches, which are plentifully scattered about. The course, which is about two miles and seven furlongs round, will in course of time be a really good one. The most difficult holes at this new course include the bunkers at the 3rd and 5th, the length of the 6th, the bunker and trap at the 7th, the ditch and bad country at the 8th, the narrow line of play at the 10th and again at the 12th, where it is necessary to play your shot between bunkers and the water.

Mention of 'the water', which is now up to top guideline standard, leads us back again to the coast of the Firth. Gullane has one of the finest seaside award-winning beaches on the Forth. It is known locally as the Bents, from the old Scottish word for the coarse grass which binds together its dunes, and the sea buckthorn which also grows there is home to many songbirds. Out towards Gullane Point there is a little bay, where ironstone, hewn from the headland, used to be loaded directly into the holds of the Cadell family's barges to be shipped up river to the Carron Iron Works near Falkirk, in which they had a major investment. The fact that the ironstone could be taken aboard out at Gullane Point and discharged at the company's own wharf at the other end on the River Carron, without the need for any form of land transportation, greatly helped to keep down the price of this vital raw material. The spot where the ironstone barges were beached

Gullane and golf seem almost synonymous. Here some enthusiasts record their scores during an autumn round.

for loading on the shelving shore at Gullane Point was called Jovey's Neuk, after old Jehovah Gray, who was employed by the Cadells as their caretaker. He lived on the site in a stone cottage overlooking the Firth. Some stories say that he had a tame eagle as a pet, others that his companion in his lonely shoreside home was a parrot, which as a retired sailor he had brought back after his army years at sea, but all agree that he supplemented his pay from the Cadells by taking part in the smuggling trade.

Once round Gullane Point the appearance of the coast changes again, becoming more rocky, rising eventually to the cliffs known as the Hummell Rocks. Slightly inland rises Yellow Craig, which many local folk insist was the model for the famous Spy-glass Hill in Robert Louis Stevenson's popular *Treasure Island*. Certainly, the author knew this stretch of coast very well, thanks to his many childhood holidays in the area and it was here at Dirleton that he had his two heroes, David Balfour and Alan Breck reach the coast in *Catriona*, the less well-known sequel to his most famous adventure *Kidnapped*. Yellow Craig is now a nature reserve and there are often ranger-led walks out across the sand dunes, which introduce visitors to the birds and other wildlife of the area. The reserve also has a barbecue site just above the shore, which makes a delightful setting for an open-air party on a summer's night.

Just inland from Yellow Craig lies the village of Dirleton, another popular place with summer visitors. Many come simply to enjoy the hospitality of the Open Arms, overlooking the village green, but Dirleton's main claim to fame is as the site of the famous castle. 'Towers, and battlements it sees, bosom'd high in tufted trees', to borrow two of John Milton's most famous lines, is a graphic description of Dirleton, because even although its drawbridge is a modern re-construction, it has a truly medieval look and is very much the castle of children's picture books. It dates back all the way to the 12th century and parts of three of its towers date from this period, when it was the home of the Anglo-Norman family of de-Vaux, who were favourites of King William the Lion and King Alexander II. Despite a desperate resistance, in 1298 it eventually surrendered to the invading troops of King Edward I, under the command of Anthony Beck, the fighting Bishop of Durham. During the reign of Robert the Bruce it came into the possession of the Haliburtons, who made many alterations and additions. Later it changed hands again, becoming the stronghold of the Logans, who became Earls of Gowrie of Gowrie Conspiracy fame when they plotted the assassination of King James VI. This ill-conceived plot on the life of the monarch led to the name of Ruthven being proscribed by Act of the Scottish Parliament and to the confiscation of the castle, which was then bestowed on Sir Thomas Erskine, who became Lord Dirleton. During the civil war of the 1640s, Dirleton was held by a party of Moss Troopers, but in 1650 they surrendered to Oliver Cromwell's commander, General Monk, who bombarded the castle, turning it into the ruin which it is today.

Although Dirleton is a ruin, it is a fascinating one and one which is well worth exploring. Dirleton stands on a shelf of rock and it is interesting to study how advantage was taken of this defensive site, but its domestic arrangements and what life must have been like for the castle's inhabitants, from the lords and ladies of the ruling families to their horde of retainers and servant, are also interesting to consider. Look out for the stone-flagged kitchens and the deep, dark well and the ingenious way in which it was designed to supply water to different floors of the castle. Having climbed to the top of the castle, leave time to enjoy the grounds spread out below. After the restoration of the Stuarts in 1660, when Charles II came to the throne, Dirleton became the property of Sir

'Towers, and battlements it sees, bosom'd high in tufted trees.' These lines by John Milton seem an appropriate description for Dirleton Castle, whose impressive ruins and colourful immaculately tended gardens are open to visitors. Normal Historic Scotland hours and admission prices apply.

John Nisbet, the king's advocate and later it was bought by the Ogilvy family and ever since these times it has been famed for the beauty and colour of its gardens and lawns. As early as Victorian times a guide-book noted, 'The exquisite gardens and grounds are open to the public on Thursdays and this privilege is largely taken advantage of by driving parties from North Berwick.' Today, under the guardianship of Historic Scotland, the gardens are equally immaculate and their sheltered walled grounds are a very pleasant place to sit and enjoy the sunshine with which East Lothian, as one of the driest places in Scotland, is particularly blessed. The beehive-shaped, stone-walled doocot, which supplied eggs and fresh pigeon meat in winter for the lord of the castle's table, can also be seen, built neatly into the boundary wall of the castle. Three projecting ledges run round its circular sides. These were constructed to prevent rats and other vermin climbing up to enter and attack the pigeons. The birds flew out each day to scavenge for food and at harvest time ate lots of grain to the fury of the surrounding farmers who resented the laird's exclusive right to maintain a doocot, in their opinion at their expense.

Looking out from the heights of Dirleton Castle to the east,

Berwick Law dominates the scene and it is worth continuing this inland detour to climb to its grassy summit to take in the panoramic view of the Forth which it provides. A zigzag path snakes its way up the slope of this conical basalt plug, left exposed after the Ice Age swept away the surrounding sedimentary rocks. The top is 612 feet above sea level and from it the view stretches from the Lammermuirs in the south to Arthur's Seat, Edinburgh and the Pentland Hills to the west. Out across the water, the Firth is about 15 miles wide with the Lomond Hills clearly in view on the Fife shore to the north. Nearer at hand the Bass Rock, which is described in the next chapter, rises starkly from the Firth about four miles out to the north-east. More immediately, the peak of the Law is of interest as the site of the ruins of an early signal beacon and its famous arch, formed from the jawbones of a whale. Walking through them gives an impression of just how huge these magnificent monsters of the sea are and, while it is now politically correct to decry their slaughter, pause and remember just how brave the Scottish whalers, who from the middle of the 18th to the middle of the late 19th century sailed from the Forth on this dangerous quest.

While the climb from North Berwick to the top of the Law is well worthwhile for the view which it offers, if you want to examine and touch a whale's jawbones, without the exertion, there is also a similar whale archway at the southern entrance to Jawbone Walk in Edinburgh's Meadows. The city arch was erected originally as an attraction at the Great Edinburgh Exhibition, held on the Meadows site in 1886, where it provided an eye-catchingly different entrance to the Fair Isle and Zetland Knitwear Company's stall. Zetland comes from the Norse *Hjaltland*, meaning the High Land and although it is now almost always translated as Shetland, it did survive until 1975 and Lord Wheatley's reform of local government, in the title of Zetland County Council. Now it is only found in the title of the Marquis of Zetland, whose predecessor, Laurence Dundas, was responsible for the founding of Grangemouth and the siting of the eastern end of the Forth and Clyde Canal on the riverbank of his Stirlingshire Estate.

Zetland is the only entry under Z in Collins' *Encyclopedia of Scotland*, but by coincidence it is the letter Z, not at the beginning but at the end of a word, which provides the link with our next port of call, North Berwick.

The path to the tip of the rocky promontory at North Berwick harbour provides visitors with a bracing stroll and an excellent vantage point to admire the surrounding seascape and Craigleith Island.

For 'Scotland's Biarritz', was the proud title given to North Berwick by a 19th-century Victorian holiday guide-book. Aimed at the English upper-class visitor, for whom Scotland was in those days every bit as exotic a destination as the resorts of the Italian and French Rivieras, it enthused that:

> North Berwick's charming situation, noble views and healthy climate; its sea bathing, boating and golfing facilities and the numerous pleasant excursions, which can be made from it both by land and sea, have already made the town a favourite summer resort and it is yearly growing in popularity. North Berwick contains numerous handsome villa-residences and boarding establishments and several large first class hotels, the finest being The Marine, a noble edifice, erected at a cost of £20,000 in the Scottish baronial style and containing upwards of one hundred apartments. The marine is truly first class and conveniently situated only half a mile from the railway station at the West Links, where excellent golf may be enjoyed

The Marine is indeed still 'truly first class' under the banner of Trust House Forte's top of the range Heritage Hotels and its patrons can still indulge in rounds of golf on the town's three golf courses

Lobster creels piled up on the outer quay of North Berwick harbour are a reminder that a limited amount of fishing still takes place from it, but it is now mainly home to a flotilla of small dinghies and yachts. The East Lothian Yacht Club's headquarters is conveniently situated in the old three-storey warehouse building overlooking the harbour. Access to the clubhouse is by the typically East Lothian forestairs to the left of the building. Now there are promises from East Lothian Council that as some compensation for the closure of the town's once highly popular open air pool in the left background of the picture, boating facilities may be further improved by turning the site into a marina. The building with the large windows used to be a pleasant sun lounge in the days when North Berwick's popularity was at its height, but it too has been neglected by the local authority and like the swimming pool has now been closed. The site of the beach pavilion is designated to become the Scottish Seabird Centre, with video links to the gannet colony on the Bass.

and on the eight others in the near vicinity, but like most other Scottish seaside resorts, North Berwick has sadly suffered a general decline since the introduction of jet aircraft in the 1960s made possible the annual package holiday exodus to the sun of the Spanish Costas. While North Berwick has to a large extent lost the families who used to come to stay for their annual summer holiday week, or even, if they were very lucky, a whole fortnight, it does, however, still succeed in attracting many day and short-break visitors, who still enjoy a breath of sea air, the fun of playing on its well-maintained putting greens, its dramatic views out across the Forth and the never-ending fascination of its crowded dinghy-packed harbour. On a sunny, summer regatta Saturday afternoon, there can be few pleasanter places to be on the Scottish coast than North Berwick and the good news is that its facilities for small boats may soon be improved even further with the construction of a new marina adjacent to the old harbour.

The promise of the new marina is one piece of good news to come out of East Lothian Council's sad, unimaginative decision to close North Berwick's famous open-air swimming pool. The heated salt water pool in its rocky setting next to the harbour was a huge attraction during the 1920s and 1930s, with aquatic shows and galas in addition to its crowded public swimming sessions. Even during the 1950s it continued to attract reasonable attendances, but the coming of indoor pools in the 1960s and 70s, combined with the general fall in the number of holiday-makers visiting North Berwick, reduced its popularity. In the 1980s, the opening of North Berwick's own indoor pool took away still more swimming enthusiasts and, instead of seeing the health conscious 1990s as an opportunity to revive the open-air pool as an East Coast aquatic centre, the local authority took the decision to close it. The nearby shoreside pavilion site is to become the Scottish Seabird Centre, brainchild of local design consultant, Bill Gardner.

Despite the derelict condition of the open-air pool as it hopefully awaits redevelopment for use as a yacht and dinghy centre, there is still much to do and see around the harbour area, with its lobster creels piled high on the quayside. Steep, stone fore-steps lead up to the premises of the local yacht club, while the other red sandstone, former warehouse, buildings overlooking the harbour have been converted into spacious homes. Nose behind them and you find the headquarters of the local branch of the Royal National Life Boat Institution. The RNLI's North Berwick vessel is of special interest to young visitors. Christened *Blue Peter 3*, it was originally one of four inflatable in-shore lifeboats paid for from the efforts of the nation's children through one of the popular, well-known, television programme's famous Christmas appeals. While inflatable lifeboats of this kind have to be replaced every ten years and the original *Blue Peter* gift is now on show as an exhibit at the former Royal Naval Dockyard at Chatham in Kent, the programme still keeps its young viewers in touch with its successor at North

The North Berwick lifeboat being towed from the sea by the powerful 'all-terrain vehicle' familiarly known as 'the Honda'. This vessel, Blue Peter 3, *is the only* Blue Peter *lifeboat in Scotland.* Courtesy of RNLI, North Berwick.

Berwick and when last shown on the small screen in June 1997, the East Lothian-based lifeboat had notched up a total of 202 launches and saved 92 lives. Like her predecessor, the current *Blue Peter 3* is a 16-foot inflatable with a single outboard engine capable of 20 knots. She is manned by a crew of either two or three, drawn from the local lifeboat crew, who are all volunteers, and has proved an ideal vessel for the North Berwick lifeboat station, as she is ideal for rescues close to shore, where larger craft cannot operate. Her crew are justly proud of their record under-two-minute launch.

Despite its difficult entrance, North Berwick harbour has a long history and at one time, as well as fishing and pleasure craft, had a commercial trade exporting agricultural products and importing coal and what was discreetly referred to in the records as 'tons of guano', in other words the droppings of seabirds, which were highly prized as dung to fertilise their fields by the East Lothians farmers!

It was to the harbour at Hallowe'en 1589 that, under the cover of darkness, a fleet of small boats sailed down the coast of the

Firth from Cockenzie. It was under the command of the mysterious, black-cloaked figure of Dr Sin, but who the 94 local women crowding the boats knew by day was none other than their bairns' dominie at Cockenzie school, one John Cunningham by name. By night he, Jekyll-and-Hyde-like, swapped identities and became the menacing warlock under whose spell the mothers had fallen. That pitch black October night he was angrier than he ever was when he strapped their children by day, because they had taken longer to sail to North Berwick than he had expected and now they were late for a very important appointment. Furiously, he screamed at them to disembark and hasten along the high stone quay wall to the nearby parish kirk, where no less a figure than that of the De'il himself was waiting to receive them.

Despite his exhortations to hurry, his women followers shouted, danced and capered their way noisily along the quay, but on entering North Berwick Kirk, their shrieks and screams were suddenly silenced, for there, looming high in the pulpit, was the terrifying apparition of Satan, 'with goat-like beard and flowing tail', as a contemporary account describes. Today, it is believed that the Devil was in fact no less a person than the Earl of Bothwell, Francis Stewart in disguise, because the aim of the work of that dark night was to murder King James VI and his newly-wed bride, Princess Anne of Denmark, and if it succeeded, he stood to gain the throne of Scotland.

First it is alleged that the figure in the pulpit in the auld kirk ranted at the assembled throng for their late arrival and then addressed Warlock Sin and each of his woman witches by name, they all in turn replying, 'Here maister!' The contemporary account then describes how the Satanic figure then delved under his cloak and, in what appeared to be a horribly shrunken, shrivelled human hand, grasped a waxen doll, which was to represent King James in the black magic rites which followed. Swiftly, he wrapped the image in a piece of linen, which he boasted to the crowd had been obtained for him by one of the young serving-wenches at the royal palace at Holyrood and which he assured them had only recently been worn next to his skin by the king. Then, as they watched, he began piercing the figure with long, sharp needles and demanded that Dr Sin and each of the women come forward in turn to swear their desire for the death of the king. The account continues, 'Then on his command they openit up the graves, two within and one without the kirk and took off the joints of the corpses' fingers, taes and knees and partit them amangst them!'

Although Dr Sin and his coven of witches left the kirk at North Berwick and sailed back to Prestonpans before dawn broke, with so many people involved, it was not long before rumours began to circulate about their dreadful night's work and when they reached Edinburgh, King James ordered an immediate investigation. James Stewart, Earl of Bothwell fled into hiding on the continent, but Agnes Sampson, the servant at Holyrood, was questioned and confessed to supplying the piece of linen. Soon all 94 of the women from Prestonpans were arrested, but the king ordered that the trial concentrate on breaking the warlock, Dr Sin, alias the schoolmaster John Cunningham. Cunningham was conveyed to Edinburgh's jail, the grim, thick stone-walled Tolbooth in the shadow of the High Kirk of St Giles in Parliament Square. There the king had a torture chamber set up awaiting his arrival and came personally from Holyrood to supervise the proceedings.

It is claimed that it was at Cunningham's trial that the terrible thumbscrews were used for the first time in Scotland and that it was as a result of the intense pain which they inflicted that Cunningham amazed the court by confessing not only to having led the Satanic rituals at North Berwick, but also to being the instigator of another earlier attempt upon the lives of the king and his beautiful young Queen. According to the pain-racked Cunningham, this had taken place on the night when the king first brought his bride home to Scotland from the Danish court in Copenhagen. As the royal couple voyaged across the North Sea, Cunningham claimed that he had ridden from Prestonpans to the little East Lothian mining town of Tranent, where he had succeeded in catching a black cat, which he threw into a large sack which he had brought for the purpose. As the terrified beast struggled to be free, he tossed the sack over the back of his horse and spurred it back to Prestonpans, to which he lit his way by spiriting up four candles on the horse's lugs and another candle on the cane which the man who was with him had in his hand and together they gave him, 'sic a licht as if it had been daylicht.' Immediately they reached the shore at Prestonpans, Cunningham claimed he had thrown the cat into the waters of the river. As the poor animal drowned, he admitted that he had called upon Auld Nick, the De'il himself, to whip up such a storm that the royal vessel would be wrecked as she entered the Firth of Forth, so that both King James and Queen Anne would be drowned below the waves.

As the stunned Lords who acted as commissioners at the witch trial listened, a triumphant King James confirmed that he remembered only too well the gale and how he and the skipper of the royal ship had been surprised that, just as they should have reached the safe shelter of the Forth after completing their passage across the North Sea, they were hit by such an unholy blast. Now he declared that he knew the truth and was satisfied that Cunningham should pay the supreme penalty by being burnt at the stake at Castlehill the following day. Happy at the result of his day in court, James returned to Holyrood. As soon as the thumbscrews were released, however, Cunningham retracted his confession. When informed of this, a furious James immediately rode back to the Tolbooth and remained present while the Edinburgh executioner inflicted the severest forms of torture which he could devise. Each of Cunningham's nails were ripped off with iron pincers, then long needles were inserted one by one into each of his fingers and thrust in, right up to their hilts. When this failed to make the Prestonpans dominie repeat his earlier confession, his legs were forced by the executioner into the dreaded metal boots, which slowly and excruciatingly crushed his flesh and bones. Still Cunningham refused to confess, but King James declared that this merely proved without doubt that the Devil had taken possession of the schoolmaster's heart. Inevitably, Cunningham was declared guilty of the crime of witchcraft and was condemned to be publicly put to death by being burnt at the stake. In January, 1591, he was dragged up to Castlehill. There, at the foot of what is now the Castle Esplanade, watched by one of the largest crowds ever to witness an execution in the Scottish capital, he was securely bound to a tall wooden stake around which a large bonfire was already lit and smouldering. Then, as the flames slowly spread up and licked the body of the poor misguided Prestonpans dominie, the executioner stepped forward, and, placing a short cord round the teacher's neck, in traditional Scottish fashion, 'wirried', that is, strangled the life out of him, before the blaze reduced his remains to ashes.

As well as the ruins of the Auld Parish Kirk, with its graveyard where Cunningham and his coven of witches are alleged to have opened the graves, North Berwick also has several other sites of interest well worth visiting. These include the beautifully kept grounds of the 18th-century Lodge and the Glen, with its choice of walks from Dunbar Road down through the trees to the East Bay, or from its entrance, the Ladies' Walk along the high ground from where there are breathtaking views out over the Firth and right across it to the far shore and the low Lomond Hills of Fife.

Mention of the Ladies' Walk is yet another reminder of just what a popular watering spot North Berwick was in Victorian days, when one family which frequently holidayed in this East Lothian resort, was that of Robert Louis Stevenson. Young Louis was accompanied not only by his mama and papa and his two cousins, Charles and David, but always by his devoted nurse, Alison Cunningham, his beloved 'Cummie'. After days of packing and the filling of great wickerwork hampers with all the piles of carefully folded linen necessary for their summer stay on the coast, the Stevensons travelled from 17 Heriot Row, in Edinburgh's fashionable Georgian New Town, to Waverley Station to catch the train to North Berwick. These must have been among the young R.L.S.'s earliest train journeys and it is intriguing to wonder if they inspired one of his most famous poems, *From A Railway Carriage*, in which with his lines:

> Faster than fairies, faster than witches,
> bridges and houses, hedges and ditches;
> And charging along like troops in a battle,
> All through the meadows the horses and cattle:
> All of the sights of the hill and the plain
> Fly as thick as driving rain:
> And ever again, in the wink of an eye,
> Painted stations whistle by.

he so vividly portrays the rhythm of the huffing and puffing steam engine, whose arrival did so much to promote North Berwick as a seaside holiday resort.

Upon arrival in North Berwick, several carriages were required to convey the Stevenson entourage to the house in the Quadrant where they stayed through the months of August and September. These long summer weeks allowed R.L.S. and his cousins ample active days for bathing, exploring and fishing and what he later described as 'crusoeing', which appears to have been his delightful description for building camp-fires and cooking out and picnicking at the Leithies or Seacliffe or The Broad Sands or some of the other coves and crannies which made North Berwick such a boyhood summer wonderland. Again, Stevenson captured these special moments well in many of the poems in *A Child's Garden of Verses*, which, when it was first published in 1890, he dedicated to Cummie. In one of the poems entitled *Summer Sun*, he wrote:

> Great is the sun, and wide he goes
> Through empty heaven without repose.

North Berwick to this day is still big sky country with its sweeping seascapes and although the town has an excellent library and good local museum in Old School Road, which frequently put on special displays to honour Stevenson, it is really more by simply walking the streets, the sea front and the shore as he loved to do, that one can bring his spirit to life.

Of all the summer treats which North Berwick had to offer, young Louis' favourite was to set sail and visit the islands out in the Forth. This is an adventure which it is still possible to enjoy today.

On some summer days the motor launch *Sula*, on her voyages from North Berwick harbour to the Bass also makes calls at the islands of Fidra and Craigleith, where unlike the Bass it is possible for passengers to scramble ashore and enjoy exploring. Craigleith is just under one mile from North Berwick harbour and is over half a mile in circumference. Its black rocky surface reaches a height of 80 feet above sea level. Nearby is the little island affectionately nicknamed The Lamb, because of its shape in the water.

Exploring Fidra has the added attraction that it has a lighthouse, designed by the Stevenson family's firm, and also the ruins of a little chapel. Amongst those who did land on Fidra was Robert Louis Stevenson, who went out to the island to see progress on the building of the lighthouse. Ever since, there have been suggestions that rather than being inspired to write his *Adventures of A Sea Cook* or *Treasure Island* by the wee island in the middle of the pond in the gardens opposite his Heriot Row home, it was possibly sailing out to the real, horseshoe-shaped island of Fidra on that childhood summer holiday visit to North Berwick which gave him his model for the island to which the *Hispaniola* carried Jim Hawkins and Long John Silver in his most famous children's story. A glance at the map of Treasure Island in the first edition of the book does indeed show similarities to the outline of Fidra.

Certainly, as the sun dips in the west up river behind Fidra, it is not at all difficult to imagine that the island's highest point just has to be the prototype for Stevenson's Spy-glass Hill and that his famous lines, 'Here lies the hunter home from the hills and the sailor home from sea', while written far, far away on the Pacific Island of Samoa, also have a special significance for this part of the Firth of Forth, where R.L.S. spent some of his happiest summer days.

CHAPTER 9
THE BASS AND THE MAY

'Ane wounderful crag risand within the sea' is how Hector Boece, the 15th-century writer poetically described the Bass Rock in his *History and Chronicles of Scotland*.

Approaching the Bass is every bit as dramatic an experience nowadays for the thousands of holiday-makers who, each summer, voyage out the three and a half miles from the harbour at North Berwick aboard the MV *Sula*. The sturdy, little, traditional, wooden-hulled *Sula* takes her name from the Latin name for the gannets, who are the rock's most famous inhabitants.

The Bass lies about a mile and a quarter off the East Lothian shore of the Firth and as the *Sula* sails closer, its massive black bulk looms precipitously above her, rising to a towering height of 350 feet sheer out of the water. Its plateau-like top slopes southward rather like the roof of a house, or perhaps more appropriately, a high-rise apartment block whose narrow cliff ledges provide crowded homes for the gannets and other seabirds who have decided it is the ultimate desirable residence for themselves.

The gannet colony has been established on the Bass for hundreds of years, the earliest written mention of it occurring as long ago as the 12th century in no less than a Papal Bull issued in Rome and carefully preserved in Edinburgh's Register House. It refers to a dispute about the birds between the owner of the Bass and the Cistercian Nuns, who occupied the convent in North Berwick. Sadly, the holy sisters' interest in the gannets originated not from a St Francis-inspired love of ornithology, but from their much more monetary concern to safeguard the tithes which they jealously claimed from the sale of barrels of fat obtained from the birds, when they were slaughtered in autumn culls.

Even the gannets which survived the autumn cull were not safe because in the Middle Ages and until the 18th century, as well as providing a supply of oil, the young seabirds were looked upon as a welcome source of fresh food during the winter months and were served as a table delicacy in a similar fashion to the pigeons which occupied the doocots on the mainland, such as the one which the National Trust for Scotland has so beautifully restored at Phantassie near Preston Mill at East Linton. In Fleshers' Close, where the butchers plied their trade in Edinburgh's crowded High Street in the 17th century, fresh young gannets from the Bass were offered for sale at 20 pence each and it was recommended that they 'be rostit a little before the dinner'. When brought to table just as deer became venison, pig changed to pork and sheep to mutton, so the gannets were presented as solan geese. As such they were even featured on the menu at royal feasts at the banquets served at Holyrood Palace. Their fishy, oily-tasting flesh, however, was apparently not always to the royal taste, as King Charles II joked that there were two things he hated in Scotland: 'The Solemn League and Covenant and the Solan Goose.'

The introduction of root vegetables such as turnips for use as winter fodder following the Agrarian Revolution in the middle of the 18th century resulted in fresh beef, mutton and pork becoming available all year round, with a consequent decline in the demand for roast gannet, but their eggs continued to be sold for food until the end of Queen Victoria's reign and were considered as much of a delicacy as those of the quail are today.

In modern times, the estimated 18,000 gannets on the Bass are left in peace, if such be an appropriate way to describe their ear-piercing, operatic chorus of shrieks, screams and yells, with which they fill the air around the Bass during their spring and early summer breeding season, as they appear to quarrel endlessly amongst themselves and the other sea fowl who share their crowded, cliffside nesting places. There are many curious facts about the gannets. They select a mate for life when they are only about five or six months old, but appear to believe in a long courtship, as they often do not breed for another four or five years. Even then, the female lays only a single egg and within eight weeks of hatching, the fledgling is heavier than its parents, because of the high fat content in its body. When it leaves the nest and slithers and flops down into the water, it cannot fly and has to live off this fatty layer for several weeks until it eventually loses enough to be able at last to take to the skies and hunt for the fish which are to be its diet for the rest of its life at sea.

Other seabirds which compete with the gannets for space on the narrow shelves of the cliffs of the Bass include the miniature penguin-like guillemots with their white breasts and long black-feathered bodies, the much more colourful puffins with their red, yellow and blue faces, the glossy green cormorants, fulmars, razorbills, and herring and lesser blackbacked gulls.

Down through the centuries the Bass also had several different groups of human inhabitants, including priests, prisoners, soldiers and lighthouse keepers. One of the first to arrive was St Baldred. A dedicated follower of St Mungo, the patron saint of Glasgow, Baldred was given charge of several churches in East Lothian, including Tyinghame, Auldhame and Preston, which is now known as Prestonkirk. According to tradition, he rowed out all alone to the Bass to enjoy a place of solitude and periods of retreat from his busy church life on the mainland opposite. While on the Bass, he built for himself a simple, little, stone-built cell, shaped like a beehive. It is believed that his cell probably occupied the same site as the ruined medieval Roman Catholic chapel, which still stands on the middle terrace of the Bass, about half-way up the steeply stepped route which leads from the rock's only safe landing place on the south-east side, all the way up to the highest and largest of the three terraces on the sloping plateau summit. Intriguingly, the remains of the ancient chapel are situated immediately over a cave.

It is in fact possible at certain states of the tide to sail right through the heart of the Bass, as gale-driven waves sweeping up river from the east have, over countless centuries, slowly worn a cavernous channel. It stretches for about 170 yards in length right through the rock. Its roof is about 30 feet high, after dropping from an impressive 100 feet at its entrance.

From the ruins of the little church, which was built of stones both from the Bass itself and from others ferried across from quarries near Dirleton a little up river on the East Lothian coast, the pathway climbs ever steeper to the top terrace. All of a mile and a quarter in circumference, the top of the Bass has in the past been used both for grazing a small flock of sheep and for cultivating cabbages and other vegetables, but today much of its surface is covered with nettles, while its edges are being ever more encroached for extra nesting places by the rock's ever-expanding population of birds, whose droppings also seem to be having a deteriorating effect on the vegetation. In the past, the vegetables were grown to add some variety to the diet of the soldiers whose lonely duty it was to garrison the island and the remains of whose small fortress still defy the elements.

According to local tradition, the Bass was granted to the Lauder family by King Malcolm III in the 11th century, but the first written mention of their ownership is of part of the rock being granted to Robert Lauder by the Bishop of St Andrews in 1316. In return, the Lauders promised to supply a pure white wax candle for the altar of Tynghame Church every year in May on Whit Sunday. This charter, however, appears to have been a re-affirmation of the Lauder family's claim to the Bass, because it is known that before this time Robert Lauder, who staunchly supported Sir William Wallace and his fight for Scottish independence, defended it against the ships of the English King Edward I, the hated Hammer of the Scots.

Although it never became their permanent home, the Bass was for long the Lauder family's favourite stronghold, and, again in 1338 it wove its thread into the ever-changing pattern of Scottish history. In January of that year Dunbar Castle, which was the home of the Countess of March and Dunbar, who was better known as Black Agnes, was being besieged by the troops of the English Earls of Arundel and Salisbury's invading army. As the long siege continued, the position of the castle was becoming impossible to sustain as it was running out of supplies of both food and water. Then, on a dark winter's night, a daring expedition of soldiers from the garrison on the Bass set sail and slipped straight past the English naval vessels, which were supposed to be guarding the narrow entrance to the old harbour at Dunbar. Under cover of darkness, they quickly and quietly unloaded their cargo of food and their barrels of water, which were smuggled into the harbourside castle, before the men from the Bass sailed undetected back across the Forth to their island stronghold. Next morning, with great delight, Countess Agnes boldly sent a message to the English forces bidding them all to come to breakfast in her banqueting chamber at the castle. Thinking that their siege had therefore clearly failed and that Black Agnes must indeed be still very well supplied, Arundel and Salisbury ordered their soldiers to raise the siege and retreat, and the threat to Dunbar and the Scottish cause was removed, thanks to the courage of the men of the Bass.

Early in the 15th century in 1405, Prince James, the young son of King Robert III, lived for a time in secret on the Bass, until he could be sent to the safety of France, with whom Scotland had its famous Auld Alliance. The Earl of Orkney sailed to the Bass and embarked the boy aboard his ship, but the little crown prince never reached the French royal court, because on the voyage across the North Sea the rescue vessel was spotted and intercepted by an English naval ship and he was held in captivity for almost 20 years. When the exiled prince eventually returned home to Scotland and in turn became King James I he apparently never forgot his early childhood period of residence on the grim Bass, because it was to it that, in an attempt to keep his rebellious nobles under control, that he in turn exiled the powerful eldest son of the Duke of Albany, Walter Stewart.

During the troubled reign of Mary Queen of Scots, a century later, the Bass became an important fortification with a garrison of over 100 soldiers, some of them from her ally, France. Realising full well its strategic importance at the entrance to the Firth of Forth, the English navy of Queen Elizabeth attempted to capture the Bass in 1548 but failed and a further attack in 1549 was also repulsed. The Regents, Moray and Morton, both tried to purchase the Bass and it is suggested that they may have wanted it for use as an island prison for the disgraced Queen Mary, instead of the much easier reached castle on the island in the middle of Loch Leven, from which she managed to escape. Lauder, the owner of the Bass, who was a loyal supporter of Mary, steadfastly refused to consider their offers, and so we shall never know how Scottish history might have been changed had the ill-fated queen been imprisoned there, instead of ultimately in Fotheringay where she posed such a threat to Queen Elizabeth that she was ultimately sentenced to be executed by beheading in 1587.

Later, Mary Queen of Scots' only son and successor to both the Scottish and English thrones also tried to buy the Bass, but once again the Lauders refused to sell their sea stronghold. By the middle of the 17th century, however, the Lauders were experiencing financial difficulties and reluctantly parted with the Bass. In 1649, the same year that King Charles I, who had once tried to buy the Bass from them, was executed, they finally sold it to Hepburn, the Laird of Waughton.

Like most Scots, Waughton was horrified at the beheading of the king and used his new possession to support the Stewart heir to the throne, who was crowned Charles II at a coronation ceremony at Scone Palace. This he did by firing on every ship belonging to Oliver Cromwell which he spotted entering or leaving the Firth. Although the self-styled Lord High Protector was furious at this harrying of the ships of his fleet as they sailed between London and Edinburgh, Waughton resolutely refused to surrender and continued his campaign in the Forth for almost three years until 1652.

The next owner of the Bass was Sir Andrew Ramsey, Lord Provost of Edinburgh. He paid £400 for it and in 1671 made a very handsome profit when he was persuaded to sell it to the Scottish government for ten times that amount. The government was prepared to pay such a high price because it desperately wanted a really secure prison in which to keep captive the Covenanters. The only sin which these truly religious Presbyterians had committed was to refuse to worship and say their prayers in the fashion which the by then restored King Charles II and the government desired, but they were proving an irritating thorn in the Scottish establishment's flesh and so their leaders were rounded up and isolated on the Bass. They included one of the most dedicated of the Covenanters, John Blackadder, after whom one of the chambers in the ruined fort on the Bass is still named. It is a fitting tribute to Blackadder, for he steadfastly refused to recant his beliefs and in the end died there in 1686. His body was rowed ashore for burial in the parish church yard at North Berwick, where his grave is still a place of occasional pilgrimage.

Soon afterwards, the Bloodless Revolution of 1689 swept Charles II's son and heir, the Stewart King James VII of Scotland and James II of England from the throne, as there was a threat that his baby would one day make the British royal family once again Roman Catholic. This time, the Bass swiftly came under the control of the government forces loyal to the new Protestant King, William of Orange, or King Billy as he is still known to this day. Yet again, the lonely Bass was used as a prison, this time for those who became Jacobites and remained loyal to the Stewart side.

In 1691, of the young Jacobite prisoners managed to seize the Bass by a most audacious act. They waited until a ship bringing a cargo of coal as fuel for the island put in at the landing stage far below the fort. Normally when a supply ship arrived, half of the guards went down to unload it while the rest remained on duty, but coal was such a heavy commodity that, on this occasion, all of the 50-strong garrison went down to help. The Jacobites seized the opportunity and escaped from their cells. When the guards, dirty and sweating, climbed back up the steep path carting the wickerwork panniers of coal, they discovered to their horror, that the gate of the little castle was firmly barred against them and that the Jacobites were firmly in charge. As the Jacobites aimed a volley of shots at their former jailers, the soldiers scrambled back down the path to the landing place and as night fell and they lacked any other form of shelter on the Bass, begged to be taken off and ferried ashore in the grim covered hold of the little sailing vessel.

The Jacobites lost no time in turning their new possession to good use and, with fellow supporters to bring up their strength to 16, began a campaign of terror against all ships which came within range of their guns. As each vessel was spotted from the summit of the Bass, a boarding party was sent out with the threat that if the captain did not pay a toll to pass in safety, his ship would be shot at. During this time, the only vessels which were allowed to dock at the landing stage on the Bass were the French naval frigates, sympathetic to the Jacobite cause, which put in to keep them supplied with food and drink. Their defiance greatly annoyed the Scottish government in Edinburgh, which arranged to stage the execution of a captured Jacobite on the shore at Castleton within clear sight of the Bass, as a dire warning of the fate which awaited the prisoners and their supporters out on the rock, when they were eventually captured. Again, the government had acted without anticipating the daring of the Jacobites on the Bass, who turned their guns on the shore and succeeded in scattering those who had come to watch the hanging. In the end the Bass rebels were forced to give in, but they escaped a similar fate and indeed managed to arrange very favourable terms for their surrender.

The government did, however, exact its toll on the Bass itself, by determining that it should never again be used as a fortress and its fortifications were demolished in 1701. Before their destruction, the artist and writer Slezer visited the Bass and described the fortifications as consisting of a square tower with a curtain wall similar to the larger ones at Tantallon Castle over on the mainland coast of the Firth. On the Bass the curtain wall was constructed to defend the landing stage below. The top of the wall was crenellated with battlements so as to give suitable protection for the firing of the stronghold's guns and there was a half-moon battery similar to the famous larger one which overlooks the Esplanade at Edinburgh Castle. The steps and path up the rock were defended by three stout gates and the fort thus cut off the remainder of the rock from the landing stage.

In the tense run-up to the eventual Union of the Parliaments in 1707, the Scottish government was obviously worried lest the Bass should again possibly fall into Jacobite rebel hands and so, anxious to find a loyal owner, bestowed ownership of the rock on Sir James Dalrymple, Lord President of the Court of Session and first owner of the Barony of North Berwick. The Bass has remained in the hands of the Dalrymple family ever since and members of the public are not allowed to land without permission, which is usually only granted to properly organised expeditions with a specific purpose for visiting it.

The Bass is, for instance, a particularly interesting place for geologists to study. Like the neighbouring islands and Berwick Law on the mainland opposite overlooking North Berwick, it consists of igneous fire-work formed over 300 million years ago during the early Carboniferous Era. The Bass occupies the site of one of the many extinct volcanoes which once used to erupt in this part of what is now Scotland. Its mouth became choked with its own molten lava, which when it became extinct formed a plug. When the Ice Age covered Scotland in its freezing glacial blanket it rubbed and wore away the volcanic ash and the softer sedimentary rocks. As the glacier retreated, it left behind the stark black, bare-butted remains of the Bass as it is so starkly revealed today. The igneous rock of which it consists used to be described as Clinkstane, because of the distinctive noise which it used to make when struck by a geologist's hammer, but it is now, somewhat less imaginatively, known as Phonolite.

In Victorian times the rock of the Bass became a distinct hazard to the ever-increasing number of merchant and naval vessels sailing in and out of the Firth of Forth. It was therefore decided that it was necessary to construct a lighthouse on it and the contract for its design went to the famous family of lighthouse engineers, the Stevensons of Robert Louis Stevenson fame. The tall new lighthouse on the Bass was completed in 1902, the year after Queen Victoria's death. It cost £8,087, ten shillings and a very exact four pence to erect and its light first beamed out on 1

November of that year. The lighthouse, which like all others around the whole coast of Scotland and the shores of the Isle of Man, is maintained by the Commissioners of Northern Lights, and is now automated. But for over eighty years lighthouse keepers did monthly spells of duty, before enjoying a two-week spell of shore leave with their families. Each day, throughout their month of duty, the chief keeper and his assistants had to climb the spiral turnpike stair to the top of the lighthouse's 67-foot high whitewashed circular tower to clean the lamp which was originally powered by paraffin produced by James Young's Scottish mineral oil industry. The intensity of the light was described as 156 candelas and with its elevation 150 feet above sea level, its six white flashes every half minute could be seen for a distance of 21 miles.

When the Bass was a manned lighthouse station it was serviced once each fortnight by the lighthouse tender *Pharos*, sailing out of Granton. On each visit it landed fuel for the light, food and water and all other necessary supplies from paint to cleaning materials and the relief keepers, before ferrying ashore the men who had completed their four-week term of duty. During the alternate week when buff-coloured funnelled *Pharos* did not call, the keepers were supplied with perishable provisions such as milk, butter and fruit together with letters from their wives and families and any other post for them by a once-a-week call by motor launch from North Berwick, a duty which the *Sula* latterly performed, adding to the interest and excitement of the passengers on some of her summer cruises.

The Commissioners for Northern Lights also established a powerful fog-horn on the east side of the Bass and it is linked to the lighthouse by a handrail to help the keepers reach it if necessary even on stormy windswept days. Its signal is three blasts at four-second intervals.

There were, however, also many fine sunny days on the Bass and during them, to pass the time after completing their duties, the lighthouse keepers kept two small gardens, one in the sheltering ruins of the old prison and the other high on the top terrace. Near the latter is a small well, about three feet wide and seven feet deep, which is filled by rainwater. As it is, however, very polluted by bird droppings, it is hard to imagine that it could ever have been used for drinking water and was therefore presumably only used to provide water for the garden plants.

Most notable of the plants on the Bass is, however, not a cultivated one but the wild tree mallow, which grows to a height of six to eight feet and whose red flowers make a brilliant splash of colour. Another notable feature of the summit is a cairn of stones which marks its highest point above the waters of the Forth, far below.

What the name Bass means is a puzzle. Perhaps it is derived from the Gaelic *Bathais*, meaning a foreland. This suggestion is strengthened by the fact that in the pronunciation of *Bathais*, the 'th' is silent. Another suggestion is that it is named after a person, a man named Bass, who is mentioned in the *Chronicles of the Picts and Scots*. Most likely, however, is that it is derived from a Celtic word meaning a conical-shaped rock.

No matter which, the Bass is certainly a fascinatingly mysterious rock to sail around and it makes one of Scotland's most impressive inshore voyages. Another can be made to the mouth of the river, sailing out to the Isle of May.

The Isle of May

The Isle of May is the guardian of the entrance to the Firth of Forth. After a rough crossing of the North Sea, or the German Ocean as this shallow, stormy stretch of water was formerly known until the outbreak of hostilities at the start of the Fist World War made it simply too politically incorrect to do so, there can be few more welcoming sights.

The May's exposed position right in the mouth of the Firth means that it is not always possible to land safely on it, but the best chance of doing so is to sail out from Anstruther Harbour. The *May Princess* takes about an hour for the voyage and her skipper knows exactly how to inch her into one or other of the two recognised landing places. Both bear names connected with the island's religious past and whether he chooses to come alongside at Kirkhaven or Altar Rocks depends on weather, wind and tidal conditions. It is a voyage well worth making.

The island is situated approximately six miles out from Anstruther and about 11 miles north-east by north of North Berwick on the southern shore of the estuary. It is about a mile long by quarter of a mile in breadth and covers an area of slightly over 140 acres, of which 14 are accounted for by the foreshore. Its shores are rocky and, indeed, in places precipitously cliffy, the

50,000 puffins breed on the Isle of May between April and July every summer. Courtesy Colin Aston and the *Maid of the Forth*.

highest point at the western end of the island being 150 feet above sea level. In general, however, the surface of the island is flat, a reminder that the name May is derived from the Celtic word for a plain, as in County Mayo in Ireland and in the name of the Castle of Mey, Queen Elizabeth, the Queen Mother's holiday hide-away home in Caithness.

For such a windswept, salty sea-blown place, the Isle of May is a surprisingly green and fertile place and in the past was often used for grazing sheep, as shepherds believed that a spell on the island greatly improved the quality of their beasts' fleeces.

Nowadays, the main reason most people sail out to the May is to view the 150,000 seabirds which nest there, including the colourful puffins who make it their home from April to the end of July each year, but the May also has a long history. It starts as early as the 8th century when the Fife missionary, St Adrian, or St Hadrian as he is sometimes known, was killed there by marauding Danish Viking warriors around the year 875. The heathen Danes also killed all of his followers, who had followed him all the way from Hungary. Their martrydom is described by Wyntoun in his *Original Chronicles of Scotland*.

The island continued its religious connections when in the 12th century King David I founded a priory on it and the crumbling remains of some of its stone walls can still be seen. The king dedicated it to all of the Christian Saints, but probably chose the site because he recognised it as an especially holy place as a result of the massacre of St Adrian. He granted the priory to the Benedictine Abbey in Reading, in Berkshire, on condition that this English religious establishment maintained nine monks on the Scottish outpost to say mass daily for him and his predecessors and successors on the Scottish throne. The priests journeyed north and eventually sailed out to the May, where to their credit they kept up this remote religious establishment for over a century. Before he died, King David also gave them the Manor of Pittenweem and they also founded a Benedictine Priory there. During this period, the May became a place of pilgrimage for women who could not bear children, with the promise that a visit to this far-flung priory would cure their infertility.

In 1269, the Priory of May was purchased from the Benedictine Order by Bishop Wishart of St Andrews and in 1318 all the rights to the island church were transferred to the Canons of St Andrews. Around this date, daily worship in the little priory on the Isle of May appears to have ceased, monks from the religious houses in St Andrews only sailing out to it for special services during the summer months. Even these acts of worship came to an end with the Reformation in 1560 and from then on the May belonged to several different families.

The history of the Isle of May is also the history of its lighthouses. The first, which was one of the earliest around the shores of Scotland, was erected in 1635 by the then owner of the island, Alexander Cunninghame of Barnes. He had shortly before obtained a royal charter to the island from King Charles I during his one and only visit to Scotland in 1633. In partnership with James Maxwell of Innerwick, over on the mainland to the south of Dunbar, he constructed a three-storey tower with a brazier at the top. Each evening at dusk a fire was built and kept fed with coal to produce a light throughout the whole night. To keep it burning every night throughout the whole year 380 tons of the stuff had to be ferried out to it annually and to pay for this a duty was imposed on all ships sailing through the waters between St Abb's Head to the south and Dunottar to the north. The light was not very effective, however, as in poor weather conditions, when it was most needed, it was scarcely visible and when gales blew up the Firth, the fire was often extinguished by the howling wind.

There was particular discontent about the warning light on the May after the Union of the Parliaments in 1707, because despite the fact that Great Britain was now officially one country, the island's owners still insisted on charging English- and Irish-owned vessels double dues, just as they did all other foreign vessels. The tax, however, on all shipping continued to be imposed until after the end of the Napoleonic War in 1815 and 15 years earlier in 1800 was let for as high a sum as £1,500. Despite the fact that the light was improved during this period by the simple method of burning more coal, it was not sufficient to save two of the Royal Navy's frigates, HMS *Nymphon* and HMS *Pallas*, which in 1810 ran aground on the south shore of the Firth near Dunbar. At the court of inquiry into their loss it was stated that the wrecks occurred because both captains were misled by the glow of the fire of a limekiln at Skateraw near Torness, on the East Lothian shore, which was glowing much more brightly and effectively than the official light out on the May.

The May lighthouse was afflicted by ill luck on several other occasions. Its first lighthouse keeper was drowned off the island in rough seas. His death was said to have been caused by witchcraft and over on the mainland in Anstruther a local woman called Effie Lang was arrested and ultimately charged with the crime. She was accused of using her black magic powers to raise the viciously violent storm, which resulted in the keeper's drowning. Although she had never in her life set foot on the Isle of May, she was in the end found guilty of the 'horrid and abominable crime of witchcraft', and ordered to pay the penalty for her dreadful deed. She was therefore duly executed by being put to death by being strangled, after which her body was burned at the stake.

Later, towards the end of the 18th century, tragedy struck again. Passing ships reported that the light on the May was out and when this was investigated it was discovered that the keeper, his wife and their five young children all lay dead in their beds. They had died from carbon monoxide poisoning, having breathed in the fumes from the fire fuelling the light, too many coal cinders having been allowed to build up, thus cutting off the ventilation.

When the Barnes' family estate including the May was sold, the island was purchased by Scott of Scotstarvet in Fife. It was later inherited by General Scott, whose daughter, the Duchess of Portland, in 1814 sold it to the Commissioners of Northern Lighthouses for the amount of £60,000. Partly because of the wreck of the *Nymphon* and the *Pallas*, which it was reckoned had cost the government £100,000, an Act of Parliament was quickly passed authorising the Treasury to loan the Commissioners £30,000 to finance the building of a new light.

The Commissioners immediately contracted Robert Stevenson, founder of the famous Stevenson family of lighthouse engineers, to build a new light. To house it he built the baronial style tower, which still dominates the island scene to this day. The lantern room, which crowns the structure, is 240 feet above sea level and originally its light was oil-fired, with fuel refined specially by the Scottish shale oil industry. The stones required for this impressive new lighthouse were prepared for assembly by masons working in the Bell Rock construction yard on the shore at Arbroath and then shipped out to the island. The work of building the new lighthouse took less than two years and on 1 September 1816, the old coal-fired beacon was finally extinguished and the new light switched on for the first time. Situated on the north-east side of the island, its light was described as, 'A group flashing white, showing four flashes in quick succession every half minute.'

Even before it was eventually electrified in the mid 1880s, its original paraffin burning light could be seen from all points of the compass for 21 miles around. The light is situated at a height of 240 feet above sea level at latitude 56.12 degrees and longitude 2.36 degrees west and from it the compass bearing for Fife Ness is 'North by east, half east at a distance of five miles' and for the Staple Rocks off Dunbar is 'West by half west, distant ten miles.' The light now flashes white for 20 seconds every minute. The May also has a powerful fog-horn to give audible warning to approaching vessels.

Later, a second light, known as the Low Light, was built on the island and came into use in 1843. Using the signals from both lights enables ships more easily to obtain a fix on the island and thus more accurately calculate their positions.

As well as all the data on its technical side, the May lighthouse in the days before automation, had its domestic side, Stevenson including in his plans two houses. The larger of the two accommodated the principal keeper and his family, while his assistant and his family had the smaller one. There were also guest apartments so that members of the Commissioners or the staff of Northern Lights could stay on the island. This sometimes happened because weather conditions changed and they could not be safely taken off, but on some occasions during summers in Victorian days some also chose to stay on the May for short holidays. The island has its own underground supply of fresh water from five wells, including one dedicated to St Adrian, but all other supplies had to be ferried out from Granton. For the keepers and their families, spells of duty lasted for four weeks, before they were relieved. They were then ferried back to Granton where they enjoyed a month ashore at the lighthouse keepers' cottages.

The Northern Lighthouse Board's tender, *Pharos* still calls at the island, but not so regularly since the May, like all the other 240 navigational lights around the coast of Scotland, has been automated. The present *Pharos*, which was launched by Fergusons of Port Glasgow on 11 December 1992, is the latest in a long and proud line of no fewer than ten lighthouse tenders to bear this very appropriate name. Her immediate predecessor, also called the *Pharos*, which was built in 1955, is still in service, but sailing thousands of miles away in very different waters. Renamed *Amazing Grace*, which seems an appropriate name for a Scottish-built ship, she is now operated by Windjammer Barefoot Cruises. Based in Nasau in the Bahamas, Windjammer use her to supply their fleet of six tall ships operating throughout the Caribbean and this takes her island hopping on a regular four-week-long route from Antigua to sun-kissed Virgin Gorda. In addition to all the food and other cargo needed to keep Windjammer's fleet of sailing ships at sea, the former *Pharos*, now with her hull painted an unfamiliar white, also carries 94 passengers in the cabins, formerly occupied by the lighthouse keepers on the way to and from their off-shore postings. Her new owners describe her as 'the workhorse vessel of the fleet', but go on to tempt American passengers by noting that:

> her fine appointments were still elegant enough to play hostess to the British Royal family and on her wanderings through the islands to Trinidad in the south and back to Grand Bahamas in the north, she still carries on the tradition of old world charm and elegant service.

Interestingly, considering the important role which *Amazing Grace* now plays in servicing sailing ships in the West Indies, her successor, the present Leith-based *Pharos*, has also had the honour of carrying HRH Princess Anne, the Princess Royal, when she sailed out into the Forth in July 1995 to inspect the hundred vessels of the Tall Ships fleet off Inchcolm before they sailed out past the Isle of May to sail across the North Sea to Bergen in Norway.

When the new baronial style lighthouse was completed in May 1816 its designer, Stevenson, was persuaded by Sir Walter Scott, not to demolish the original beacon tower, 'but to ruin it a la picturesque', which is what was done, so that it too can still be seen as an object of interest to this day and as the oldest light of its kind in Great Britain.

Earlier, prior to 1790, 15 fishermen and their families lived on the island and during this period it was the custom of the other fishermen of Fife to gather on the island each summer for an annual celebration. Unfortunately, the merrymaking one year ended in the capsizing of one of the visiting fishing boats, with the loss of all on board including many of the fishermen's wives and girl friends. As a result of this tragedy, the yearly summer party on the May was subsequently discontinued.

One early visitor to the May was Ferguson, the Scottish poet. He travelled out to the island from Dunbar on a sailing ship called *The Blessed Endeavour* and was inspired by his short stay to write the following lines about it:

> And now we hail the May, whose midnight light,
> Like vestal virgin's offerings undecay'd,
> To mariners bewildered acts the part,
> Of social friendship, guiding those that err,
> With kindly radiance to their destined port.
> Here the verdant shores
> Team with new freshness, and regale our sight
> Sequester'd for the haunt of druid lone,
> There to remain in solitary cell.

Today most visitors to the Isle of May come to see its vast flocks of seabirds and, as they disembark, each boatload is met by one of the wardens of Scottish Natural Heritage, who briefs them on what to see and where it is safe and unsafe to venture. The wardens are also available to answer questions and there are also orientation boards at both landing places.

The best time to visit the May is from April to July, when the sea cliffs are crowded with the nests of breeding guillemots, kittiwakes, razor bills, shags and terns, but the most popular show-stealing stars are undoubtedly the 'clowns of the sea', the island's 50,000 puffins. It is easy to see how the little puffins with their white breasts and faces tipped with red, yellow and blue huge beaks and bright orange feet got their nickname and also their other one of the 'Sea Parrots', for they do have a decidedly comical appearance as they bob in and out of the burrows which they dig for themselves. Way back in history the Norsemen called puffins Lundi and it was from this that their breeding ground off the west coast of England, the Island of Lundy got its name. Then, in Scotland, in earlier centuries they were called, Coulternebs, meaning coloured noses and to this day in some parts of Scotland they are referred to affectionately as Tammie Norries.

Watching the puffins flying back to their burrows on fish-bearing missions, it seems amazing that they are always able to immediately identify their own hole in the green turf, but who is to know if they ever actually make a mistake and quickly pop back out again? At the end of the breeding season the puffins fly off, some being known to go as far as the North Atlantic and are rarely seen near land throughout the whole winter. Then, come the early spring they return to the May to start the whole cycle again. Some of the puffins have now happily moved up the Firth to nest on Inchcolm and a few have also been seen as far up river as Inchgarvie, below the Forth Bridge. Considering how rare they are in North America, with a few breeding pairs attracting thousands of keen ornithologists to Camden in Maine, it is wonderful how established the puffins are on the Forth. Perhaps this is an aspect of Scottish birdlife which could be advertised more to attract tourists who are interested in bird watching, rather than them heading for the Farn Islands off the coast of Northumberland as they tend to do at present.

The island also has a large flock of eider duck, who are famed for the softness of their down and feathers. The Forth colonies of eider are growing and are considered of importance on a European scale. Another particular success on the May are the shags or green cormorants. Although recorded as nesting on the island as far back as 1828, this smaller version of the better-known cormorant appeared to die out, until one nesting pair returned in the 1950s. Since then the colony has expanded steadily each year, until there are now around 1,000 breeding pairs. The shag is difficult to tell apart from the better-known cormorant, but it is smaller, has no white on its face and has a short crest of feathers.

Another attraction for nature lovers visiting the May is the island's increasingly large herd of grey seals, who are best seen at low tide, when they love to bask and sunbathe on the rocks. The increase in the number of seals is not so popular with the fishermen, who insist they devour a disproportionate amount of fish stocks.

There are no trees on the windswept May, but there are lots of wild flowers, ferns and grasses for botany enthusiasts to study. The flower which is most associated with the island is the sea-pink, vivid clumps of which grow profusely amongst the short grass along the cliff tops. Adding to the colour are pink campion, red campion and sea campion, purple thistles, flowering clover, golden buttercups, bright yellow dandelions and white flowering nettles and, to soothe any fiery nettle stings, the antidote, curly green dock leaves are also present.

As the point which marks the entrance to the Firth, the Isle of May makes a good place to consider some of the statistics about the Forth. From a width of only a mile at Queensferry, the estuary has increased to a width of 19 miles, measured from Fife Ness across to Dunbar. Ten miles further inland, off Elie, there is only a distance of eight miles between the Fife and Lothian shores, then further up river it widens to a maximum 16 miles between Leven and Prestonpans. The depth of water in the Firth also varies greatly. Along the Fife shore, the bed of the estuary slopes down swiftly to a depth of an average of ten fathoms, 60 feet within one and half miles of land. The same steep slope is found on the Lothian shore, from the island of Fidra out to the sea. Further up river from Fidra, on the south shore, the drop is much more gentle and off Musselburgh, ten fathoms is only reached nine miles out. The channel, more than ten fathoms deep, extends almost from shore to shore at the mouth of the Firth but going up river does not widen after Elie has been passed. Depths of 30 fathoms are only found at one or two points in the Firth and the North Sea only reaches a depth of 50 fathoms 60 miles out from Fife Ness. Surprisingly, the deepest part of the whole Firth is in the narrows between Queensferry and North Queensferry, where there is a trough more than 20 fathoms deep for almost two miles and at one point it plummets to a maximum of 42 fathoms, over 250 feet.

Tides on the Forth run very fast, reaching a speed of two and a half knots, that is almost three miles an hour. These strong currents are caused by the rise and fall of the tide, the difference at some times of the year between high and low water being all of 20 feet. The Forth is tidal as far inland as Stirling and the water in it remains salt almost as far as the little village of Cambus near Tullibody, three miles upstream from Alloa.

Until the end of Victorian times, small ships regularly sailed as far up river as Stirling, and Alloa retained its commercial shipping until the 1970s and its neighbour South Alloa on the opposite shore still had small tankers discharging at it until into the 1980s. Nowadays, however, Grangemouth is as far as ships go and it is to or from its large port that the majority of ships passing the May are heading. The May makes an ideal lookout point from which to spot the ships which sail these waters. The pattern of shipping has changed over the years, with fewer naval vessels since the closure of Rosyth as Scotland's only Royal Naval Dockyard. You are also less likely to see poet John Masefield's 'Dirty British coaster with her salt caked smoke stack', as the cargoes these little vessels used to carry have now been containerised. The sight of container ships with their 'boxes' stacked almost as high as the wheelhouse on their bridges is now a frequent one and there is nothing dirty or salt-caked about these modern vessels. They sail on a regular timetable between Grangemouth and major continental ports such as Antwerp, where they connect with much larger container vessels sailing across the Atlantic to the USA and Canada and to other worldwide destinations.

The oil tankers sailing up and down the Forth have also changed, from the small vessels up to 30,000 tons which used to import crude oil from the Persian Gulf and other foreign sources for processing at British Petroleum's Grangemouth Oil Refinery, to the 100,000-ton plus giant vessels which now export North Sea fuel from the company's Hound Point Terminal. Seen from the shores of the May as they sail up river to collect their cargoes, these vessels seem to soar mountainously above the waves, but sailing back out into the North Sea with their tanks brim full, most of their massive size is hidden below the surface.

The level to which ships can be loaded is indicated by the white Plimsoll line, which used to be painted right round their hulls, but which is now only indicated amidships. It is named after the Victorian Member of Parliament, Samuel Plimsoll, who led a campaign to improve safety for sailors, at a time when unscrupulous owners often overloaded their ships because if they sank they were covered by insurance. Plimsoll helped not only in this way, but also by inventing flexible-soled canvas shoes to make it safer for sailors climbing the rigging and to this day, such footwear still bears his name.

Safety, and again in particular safe footwear, is a priority when planning a visit to the Isle of May. To get the most out of a visit to the island, sensible walking shoes or, even better, stout boots with ankle support and soles with a good grip are essential. Even on summer days, wear warm clothing and carry a waterproof, as the crossing, which takes from 45 minutes to an hour each way, can be both cold and wet and the wind off the North Sea often means that it is cooler on the island than back on the mainland. Pack a picnic with more sandwiches than you usually prepare and several bars of chocolate or other sweet treats, because sea air is guaranteed to give you an appetite and climbing the island's rough paths uses up a lot of energy. The whole expedition out to the May usually lasts around five hours and there is no place to buy either food or drink on the island. Bring a flask of hot tea or coffee, plus a container of at least a litre of drinking water. Plain water is much more refreshing and better for avoiding dehydration, than either fruit juice or carbonated drinks and, yes, there are lavatories on the island. In the interests of the many nesting birds, dogs are not allowed on the island. On the other hand, children are welcome to visit the May, provided they are accompanied by a responsible adult, who should ensure that youngsters appreciate the danger of natural hazards and that they must keep to marked paths and well away from cliff edges. Bearing these provisos in mind, a day on the Isle of May can prove a very memorable outing for families with older children interested in birdwatching and other aspects of river life.

CHAPTER 10

AND SO TO CRAIL!

And so to Crail, the final town on the Fife shore of the Firth. Crail, however, is not so much a simple full stop but more a definite exclamation mark! For Crail is emphatically a place of infinite fascination, well worth venturing all this way out to the most easterly tip of Fife to find and explore.

Crail occupies two sides of a gulley and tumbles so precipitously down to its snug harbour that cars are no longer allowed to make the steep descent to its old stone quays. Parts of the South Pier date back to the 16th century and approaching on foot from the east on a snell winter's day, it looks as if the white-capped waves crashing in from the North Sea seem determined to demolish it, but within the harbour wall is a sheltered haven. Merchants are recorded as plying their trade from Crail harbour as early as the first half of the 9th century, with fishing and fish curing already established businesses. Most of Crail's trade was with the Low Countries of Europe and it is even claimed that the good folk of Holland came here to learn the best way to salt the herring which are still considered the great appetiser on Dutch menus. In their turn, it was Dutch engineers who designed the harbour and local tradition insists that they included several women amongst their number.

While women engineers were striking this early blow for female liberation, in an equally interesting role reversal, it was definitely the local fishermen who perfected the little Fife port's culinary delicacy, the famous Crail Capon. The Crail Capon consisted of the best of the catch of North Sea haddock, carefully gutted but not split, then hung up to dry on tall wooden frames along the harbourside until slowly cured by the sun and the salt sea air. Tastes change and today there are no Crail Capons on offer on the quayside, but signs offer visitors plump, fresh lobsters and crabs, cooked while they wait. A guide-book published in 1890 notes that Crail was 'providing lobsters, crabs and whelks for the London market', but nowadays most of those not consumed locally are exported to France, where there is a ready demand for them.

Largest of the buildings on the quayside, the Customs House, is a reminder that Crail has long had its international trade, but although it was used for a time during the 17th century for collecting the dues and excise money and thus justifies its name, this impressively restored building was for most of its long life a wealthy merchant's home. Look high on the west gable wall and you can still see where the goods, which its owners imported, were winched up for safe storage on the fourth floor. Even higher is the little attic window and it is a pity that when the National Trust For Scotland did the building up in the 1950s they did not make a wee stair up to it, instead of being content with access through a tight little trapdoor hatch, because it is from way up there that the best views are to be had and it is surely from there that the merchants must have keeked out to spy their ships coming safely home to harbour. 'Keek' is, of course, derived from the Dutch tongue, a reminder of which is the fact that the Rockefeller family's mansion near Rip Van Winkle's Sleepy Hollow in Upper New York State is called Kykuit, because it does just that, across the spectacular cliff-lined valley of the Hudson River. Crail's Customs House has another Dutch feature in the unusual lintel above its door, with the painted carving of a small sailing sloop in the middle. There is a possibility that it may not always have been an external feature but may have been borrowed at some time in the past from an interior hearth fireside mantelpiece. Mentioning fires, the Customs House's tall chimneys are also of interest, reached as they are by steep corbiestep gables at the foot of which the initialled corbie stanes are a reminder of the house's original owners.

Tucked in the sheltered lee of the Customs House is little Lobster Cottage, whose red-pantiled roof recalls the fact that these colourful features of so many homes along both shores of the Forth also came originally from the Netherlands and helped provide a more comfortable voyage home for the crews of the sailing ships. This came about because of the nature of their trade. Sailing out across the choppy North Sea, their holds were well-filled with heavy cargoes of Scottish coal and salt. These were sold at a good profit in Holland and the proceeds used to buy the fine silks and spices brought home from afar by the ships of the Dutch East India Company. This was very much a case of 'guid gear gaes in sma' bulk' as these expensive luxury items fitted easily into the wooden

Tiny Crail harbour is a first port of call for many European yachtsmen who sail across the North Sea to visit the Forth. Kingdom of Fife Tourist Board.

kist in the captain's cabin, leaving the ship's holds empty. Rather than sail home light with the ship riding high out of the water, thus adding to the risk of a stomach-churning sea-sick-making crossing of the North Sea on the way home or simply filling the holds with uneconomic ballast to keep their ship steady in rough seas, the wily Scottish skippers (which is yet another term derived from the Dutch) learned that there was a good market at home for both red pantiles for roofing and equally attractive white and blue Delft pottery tiles for round fireplaces and for other interior decoration, thus adding to the colour and interest of Scottish homes.

Lobster Cottage is itself a colourful place because its walls are lined with the works of its artist-owner, Roger Banks. These, however, are not seascapes, but precisely detailed paintings of flowers, because Roger is famed as a botanic artist, who specialises in portraying the rare plants of the foothills of the Himalayas. In between expeditions to his beloved mountains, however, Roger did until recently find time to be Crail's harbour master. In between acting as a 'marine traffic warden', as he describes himself, for the many pleasure craft from dinghies to 40-foot yachts which seek a berth in the crowded harbour during the summer season, Roger found plenty of time during the quieter months to turn his harbour master's office in the old two-storey building opposite Lobster Cottage into additional studio space in which to work on his paintings, as the Forth's fine light filled the room. Like Skagen on the tip of Denmark's North Jutland, where the North Sea meets the Baltic, Crail has always attracted artists. Sir Muirhead Bone, that fine craftsman of the Glasgow school, made a particularly fine etching of the old town. Crail was also the home of that artist in words, Scottish author Oswald Wynd. One of his stirring plots tells of the work of the deep sea salvage tugs, a reminder that one of the most famous of the real-life ones, the *Turmoil*, was Forth-built by Henry Robb of Leith. *Turmoil* rescued Captain Kit Carlsen in his crippled heavily listing cargo vessel, *Flying Enterprise*, in 1952, and two years later succeeded in bring the surviving stern half of an oil tanker safely into the Firth of Clyde.

Back in Crail, the harbour master's office adjoins another interesting harbourside house, Peppers Cottage. While this title might at first glance be thought to complement the salt which used to be exported from Crail harbour, it actually takes its name from a former elderly resident whose somewhat fiery temper earned for him, and later his home, this unusual nickname.

The two-storey, white-harled homes of other former fishermen, which have become mainly holiday hideaways, climb up the wynd from the harbour to the Nethergate. Here on the high ground above the shore it becomes apparent just how rich a little place Crail once was, with attractive, well-built stone properties on either side and even more imposing ones to be found in neighbouring Marketgate. 'Gate' in both of these place-names is derived not from the French port as in so many Scottish towns, but from the old word *gait* meaning 'stride' as is also found in Bergen, Stavanger and other Scandinavian towns. Here it does indeed take quite a number of paces to cross either Nethergate, meaning Lower Street or even broader Marketgate, which, as the name suggests was where Crail's traders and farmers from the surrounding Fife countryside set up their stalls each week. Crail had the right to hold such markets from the earliest times, because it was one of Scotland's first Royal Burghs and the ancient Market Cross still stands as silent witness to all the deals which were done,

Lobsters and crabs are still landed regularly at Crail's historic harbour.
Kingdom of Fife Tourist Board.

announcements which were made and wrongdoers who were
publicly punished at this spot.

Crail's royal connections date right back to the time of King
David I, who liked to stay at its castle, only a few scant ruins of
which remain. While the stonework of the castle has crumbled,
Crail's regal links are well documented in the town's papers,
including a charter granted by Malcolm IV, who reigned from 1153
to 1165. His successor, William the Lion, also came to stay at Crail
Castle and three of his surviving charters are signed as having been
written in the town. One hundred years later, in 1310, King Robert
the Bruce signed the all-important charter for Crail itself, making
it a Royal Burgh. Crail's affairs as a Royal Burgh were conducted

by the Provost and his Bailies from the Town House, which dates from the 16th century and still flanks Marketgate. On the far side are the foresteps which lead up to the first floor. Today, weeds sprout from the sides of their paved steps, but in the past they would never have got the chance to grow as this was the busiest place in the town. Everything from council meetings and criminal trials were held here, beneath the town clock in the distinctly Dutch-shaped belfry, whose bell was ferried across from the Netherlands and hung up aloft in 1520. The final touch to the Town House is its unusual but very appropriate, fish-shaped, weather vane.

Crail has an equally ancient church history. Its parish kirk dates from the reign of King David II. A carved stone, built into the inside of the west wall for preservation, after being trodden upon for over half a century as a paving slab, is thought to be the Old Cross of Crail to which early pilgrims came in the belief that touching it would cure their ill health. Sir David Lyndsay of *The Satire of the Three Estates* fame wrote, 'And sum in hope to get thare hail, Rynnis to the auld rude of Kerrail'. Until 1517 the church owed allegiance to the Cistercian Nunnery in Haddington across the Firth in East Lothian, but upon the petition of Sir William Myreton and his gift of a handsome endowment, the prioress agreed to it being erected into a collegiate church dedicated to St Mary, with 'a provost, sacristan, ten prebendaries and a choirester'. It had nine altars and ornaments, vestments and silverware in abundance, which are all carefully listed in the church records printed in 1877 and held in the Advocates Library in Parliament Square in Edinburgh.

All of the Crail kirk's treasures, however, appear to have disappeared at the time of the Reformation, when its leader John Knox chose it as the place from which to campaign. Following its success, Crail's first Protestant minister was the Revd John Melville, brother of the more famous Andrew. To begin with, however, his ministry did not apparently go altogether smoothly, because in 1561 he complained that certain persons threatened to 'take hym owt of the pulpit by the luggis and chase hym owt of the town'. Most famous of Crail's ministers was the Revd James Sharp, who in the 1650s went on to become Archbishop of St Andrews. Outside in the kirk's graveyard are many carved and sculpted tombstones, which give details of many of Crail's former inhabitants. Of particular interest is its Mort House, built in 1826 to try to thwart the efforts of the Resurrectionists, the infamous body-snatchers, who could earn good money by supplying corpses to the Professor of Surgery at St Andrews University's School of Medicine for his students to undertake their anatomy experiments. The fresher the body, the higher the price which the Resurrectionists could demand and so, as Crail churchyard was only nine miles away, it was clearly worth targeting. The Mort House was therefore erected to provide shelter for the relatives of the deceased, who were expected to sit up each night and maintain guard for three weeks after the burial, until the corpse was of no further interest to the body-snatchers. Often, rather than undertake the wearisome task themselves, the relatives employed a couple of the old men of the parish to keep watch. They paid them with nightly bottles of whisky, which no doubt kept up their spirits!

The Mort House was the resting place in February 1830 of one of the town's most curious residents, Helen Ross, who was nicknamed the Rich Beggar of Crail. Helen Ross was born in Crail in 1755. At the age of 22 and still unmarried, she bore an illegitimate son to Peter Hunter, a married farm labourer at Denbrae near St Andrews. For this misdeed, she was hauled before the Kirk Session of Crail and publicly rebuked. Despite this, she was befriended by the church minister, the Revd Andrew Bell and, when she took to a life on the road to escape the criticism and wagging tongues of Crail, it was to him that she periodically returned to bank the money which she appeared to have had the happy knack of gathering on her travels.

On one occasion she arrived at the manse in Crail and asked him to look after what she described as her 'twa-three bawbies', before handing over a bag full of gold and silver coins, which, when counted by the minister's daughters, Amelia and Margaret, amounted to over £200, a large sum in those days.

Helen's wanderings took her to Dundee and then all the way north to Caithness, before roaming south to Portsmouth and back through Cheshire to Ayrshire, Lanarkshire and finally Linlithgow. Her support over all these years from the Crail minister proved invaluable, because when the magistrates in several places on her travels became suspicious of how a beggarwoman could have gathered such a fortune, he and his lawyer son, John, always wrote defending her honesty. In 1799, for instance, they forced the authorities in Ross-shire to return to Helen the sum of £60, which they had confiscated from her. John Bell wrote, 'Helen Ross's habits and life have been very singular. She has been a wanderer from her childhood and during that time she has amassed a considerable sum of money, which, so far as I know, has all been honestly come by.'

One of the last mentions of Helen's stravaigings occurs in the records of Linlithgow in December 1829, when, because of her ill health, she was ordered to return to her birth-place, Crail, so that as a beggar her death should not become a cost to West Lothian's Royal and Ancient Burgh. Little did its magistrates ken that the wee beggar wifie from Fife was a comparatively wealthy woman, as the will which she shortly afterwards drew up in Crail revealed. This was a second will, drawn up apparently because of her anger with her second illegitimate son, Alexander, who had a short time before brought dishonour upon her family by being found guilty at Dundee Police Court on a charge of theft. She therefore left the whole of her estate of £262 18s 7d to his young half-brother Peter, who lived and worked in Crail as a sailor and fisherman and who had his home with his wife's in-laws, the Flemington family at 33 Shoregate, overlooking the harbour. No. 33 is the property which is now home to that previously mentioned colourful character, artist and former harbour master, Roger Banks, and his equally locally well-known and liked, delightful, little, pug dog, Clytie.

Helen Ross died a month later, on 26 February, and a furious Alexander disputed his mother's will, claiming half of her small fortune. He took his case all the way to the Court of Session, but in the end on 24 June 1830 had to be content with a settlement with his brother which gave him £50. Meanwhile, their mother's body lay in the Mort House for just over two months until it was finally buried in a lair in her father's grave in the churchyard on 27 April 1830. Such a long delay was apparently not unusual, as Erskine Beveridge, writing in his *Church Memorials of Crail*, which was published in 1893, states that to prevent desecration of the dead by the dreaded body-snatchers, coffins were kept in the deadhouse for up to six weeks in summer and three months in winter before being buried. He adds that the church officer, the Beadle, always secured new graves with an iron mortsafe and that the churchyard was guarded at night by men with loaded firearms.

Two years later, in 1832, Peter used the money which he obtained from his mother's will to better himself by buying the Largo Inn, to which he moved with his wife, Margaret, and the surviving five of his eight children. His sixth child, Thomas, married a Largo lass, Christina Morrison, and after living in Dundee and Elie they finally moved to Earlsferry, where he established a successful business as a carpenter. Their son, Thomas, became one of the many Scots to emigrate to the Scotland of the South Seas, New Zealand, where he became the successful owner of a chain of general stores in the area around Christchurch. He made one return visit to Scotland and during it had erected a tombstone in Newburn Cemetery, four miles inland from Elie. The inscription on it reads simply 'Sacred to the memory of Christina Morrison, wife of Thomas Hunter, who died in 1847. Erected by their son, Thomas, New Zealand.'

The other side of the Rich Beggar of Crail, Helen Ross's family, also ended up down under in the New World, but for much less honourable reasons. For, despite gaining the £50 from his mother's hard-earned estate, her son, Alexander Ross, continued with his life of crime for which she had tried to disown him. On his fourth court appearance in Dundee on yet another charge of theft, he was declared of 'habit and repute a thief' and was sentenced to seven years transportation. On 16 July 1837, at the age of 48, he was one of 270 male prisoners who set sail on the convict ship *James Pattison*. By day, Alexander and his fellow prisoners were allowed up on deck, but as soon as dusk descended they were ordered below decks and the guards battened down the hatches until the following morning. Below in the holds, Alexander and his companions were each allowed a space 18 inches wide in which to bunk down to sleep. The *James Pattison* docked safely in Sydney three and a half months later on 25 October and Alexander served the whole of his sentence in New South Wales. He received a Certificate of Freedom on 22 November 1843, but whether he settled in Australia or returned to Scotland is not known.

Back in Crail, Helen Ross's life-time supporter, the Revd Andrew Bell, wrote the entry for the town, which was published in the First Statistical Account of Scotland in 1793. In it he wrote:

Of the character of his people, a minister ought to speak with caution. In no material feature do the people here differ from their neighbours.

The credulity of former times with respect to witches is almost extinguished. The practice of inoculation for smallpox has been much retarded, partly by religious scruples and partly by the expense of medical aid. When dressed they are decently neat rather than fine. If they are not remarkable for their sobriety and industry, neither do they deserve to be stigmatised as dissipated and idle. Their ideas and sentiments are gradually acquiring a greater degree of liberality. As subjects they are peaceable and loyal and by no means fond of 'meddling with those who are given to change'.

Across the road from the kirkyard, in Marketgate, the town well, gifted to his birth-place by wealthy Glasgow merchant and Justice of the Peace, Andrew Mitchell, was originally erected to mark Queen Victoria's jubilee. For those who fancy something a little stronger to drink, Crail is well supplied with hostelries including the historic East Neuk and Golf Hotels and the Marine with its fine sea views. Crail has been popular as a holiday resort since Victorian times and the number of visitors was greatly increased after the coming to the town in 1883 of the East Fife line of the North British Railway. The fares for the 34-mile journey from Edinburgh's Waverley Station was first-class return ten shillings (50p), or six shillings and eight pence single, while third class cost only five shillings and eight pence return, or three shillings and four pence single.

During the 1880s, Crail's population was around 1,500, but during the summer months this almost doubled with visitors. One of its main attractions was the excellent golf which it offered, its Golf Society, founded in 1786, being the seventh oldest in Scotland. Another favourite pastime for these Victorian visitors was walking and one of the most popular expeditions was the two and a half mile walk to the north-east to Balcomie Castle and Fife Ness. The 16th-century castle tower was incorporated into Balcomie Farm House and retained as a useful landmark for ships navigating the Firth. Beyond Balcomie and half way between it and the Ness, the walkers always stopped to admire Dane's Dyke. Stretching across the neck of the promontory, it took its name from having been erected to protect the camp which the Danish warriors once built at the Ness, but it is now recognised that the barrier is mainly a natural phenomenon to which the Vikings probably added by gathering boulders from the nearby shore. Even earlier than the Vikings, recent archaeological excavations at Crail Golf Course have shown that the area was inhabited from as early 8,000 BC, probably by nomadic hunters.

Another attraction which the Victorian holiday-makers also liked visiting, was the cave, where tradition maintained that King Constantine was slain by the Vikings. Today, Fife Ness still attracts visitors mainly interested in its plentiful population of seabirds, but it is mainly famed as the windswept site of one of Scotland's best-known Coast Guard Stations, whose name features on the Shipping Forecast broadcast three times every day on BBC Radio Four.

As one of the weather reporting centres which are situated right round the coast of the British Isles, details of wind speed and direction, visibility and barometric pressure and changes, are collated at Fife Ness and sent by computer to Eskdalemuir, where all of the Scottish information is gathered before being passed on to the Meteorological Headquarters in Bracknell, where each of the five-minute long Shipping Forecasts is put together. The data from Fife Ness is incorporated in the forecast for inshore waters broadcast in the latter part of the bulletin, which, apart from being essential listening for all mariners, also has such a cult following that a photographic exhibition illustrating the 32 sea areas which it covers, toured the country in 1998 and *Sailing By*, the tranquil piece of music used to introduce the midnight 45 transmission, has become a best-selling CD. It is difficult to explain why The Shipping Forecast has such devoted listeners: perhaps it is the tones of Charlotte Green and the other announcers who read it so precisely that it can be relied upon to end to the second and never overrun; perhaps it is the poetic nature of the names of the shipping areas, from Trafalgar, Biscay through Forth, Tyne, Dogger all the way round the coast of Britain to Dover, Sole and Lundy; perhaps it is simply the feel-good factor of lying safely tucked up and berthed in bed and knowing that there is no need to face the hazards of the high seas; or perhaps it is just reassuring to know that as long as The Shipping Forecast goes out on time, then all must definitely be well with the world.

In the big, light and airy control room at HM Coastguard Fife Ness, there is little time for such romantic thoughts. It has a much busier, practical and workmanlike atmosphere as the uniformed officers go quietly and efficiently about their duties. In the background is the constant chatter of the VHF ship-to-shore radio.

Twenty-four hours a day the emergency channel is closely monitored. In 1997, the coastguards at Fife Ness logged a total of 309 incidents, ranging from one involving a naval vessel to two dealing with children who had got into trouble while playing in the Firth on inflatable toys. The largest category of emergencies coped with involved powered pleasure craft, of which 49 got into difficulty, followed by 41 incidents involving sailing yachts and dinghies. Adding to the variety, Fife Ness had to organise help for four rowing boats and one lone canoeist. Sixteen vessels were stranded, six capsized, 56 suffered engine failure, seven fouled their propellers, 18 were caught by adverse weather conditions, one went on fire and one sank. Thirteen people got cut off by the tide, six people got stuck on cliffs, six swimmers had to be rescued and three divers got into difficulties. In all, 322 people received assistance and 126 were rescued thanks to the alertness of the Fife Ness Coastguards and the close and efficient liaison which they maintain with the other emergency services, the locally based RNLI lifeboats and the rescue helicopters at RAF Lossiemouth and RAF Bulmer in the North of England.

The 'ness' in Fife Ness is derived from the French *le nez* meaning 'the nose' and this most easterly point on the shoreline of the Firth of Forth pokes its nose out to such an extent that from the glass-surrounded operations room at the Coastguard Station it is possible to see round an arc of 280 degrees. This wide sweep takes in from Scurdy Ness lighthouse near Montrose in the north, through the mouth of the River Tay, past the Isle of May and right on down to the south, past North Berwick and Dunbar to St Abb's Head. Fife Ness is the co-ordinating centre for the lifeboats at Broughty Ferry, Anstruther, Dunbar and Eyemouth and inshore lifeboats at Broughty Ferry, Kinghorn, Queensferry, North Berwick, Dunbar and St Abb's.

As an executive agency of the Department of Transport, Coastguard District Controller, Hugh Shaw, has Three Sector Managers at St Andrews, Granton and Eyemouth. Under their direction there are Coast Rescue Companies made up of well-trained local people at Carnoustie, St Andrews and Leven in St Andrews Sector; Kinghorn, South Queensferry, Granton and Fisherrow in Granton Sector; and Gullane, North Berwick, Dunbar, Cockburnspath, St Abb's, and Eyemouth in Eyemouth Sector. To make certain they are always prepared, each Coast rescue team takes part in four emergency training drills every year. Each Coast Rescue team is equipped with powerful rocket maroons capable of carrying a line to any vessel in distress. Once the line is attached, a hawser is secured between the ship and the shore and this is used to set up the breeches buoy so that, if necessary, the crew and any other people on board can be brought to safety ashore.

From the shore at Crail on a clear day, when Fife Ness is reporting good visibility, the south shore of the Firth can just be seen and it is to there that the following chapter moves on.

CHAPTER 11
FROM TANTALLON TO TORNESS

'**Y**e might as well try tae ding doun the walls o' Tantallon as build a brig tae the Bass', is how the folks of East Lothian used to sum up what they considered an impossible task.

Even today, in its ruined state, Tantallon on its cliff-top peninsula site looks impressive and when it was at the height of its power with its massive stone curtain walls intact it must indeed have been a formidable fortress. As an old poem put it:

> Tantallon vast, broad, massive high and stretching far,
> And held impregnable in war.

Tantallon's origins are unknown, but with the crashing waves of the Firth forming a natural moat on three sides, it must have seemed a natural place for a castle. One story is that it was originally fortified by the Thanes of Fife so that they could command both sides of the Forth. It first comes into prominence, however, as a stronghold belonging to the mighty, powerful Douglas family, who were second in Scotland only to the Royal House of Stewart. Tantallon came into the possession of the House of Douglas in 1371, when they acquired the Barony of North Berwick. For a time, indeed, North Berwick was known as Castleton.

From the fact that it was the Good Sir James Douglas to whom King Robert the Bruce entrusted the mission of carrying his heart on a Crusade to the Holy Land, the family's emblem became, appropriately, a vivid scarlet red heart and it was carved above the entrance to Tantallon as Sir Walter Scott described in his famous epic poem *Marmion*, when he wrote,

> Above the rest a turret square
> Did o'er the Gothic entrance bear
> Of sculpture rude a stony shield,
> The Bloody Heart was on the field,
> And in the chief three mallets stood,
> the cognisance of Douglas blood.

After King James II murdered William, Earl of Douglas in 1452, his successor, the ninth Earl, rose in rebellion against the monarch,

Tantallon Castle with its impressive defensive curtain walls looks seaward towards that other guardian of the entrance to the Forth, the Bass Rock, whose white-painted lighthouse can be seen on the cliffside below its sloping plateau. Cruises round the Bass are operated from North Berwick Harbour by the MV Sula.

but was defeated. All of the Douglas family's possessions, including Tantallon, were declared forfeit but later, in 1493, Tantallon was reconfirmed to the Douglas family, when Archibald Douglas received a royal grant of it from King James III

Archibald's successor married the widowed Queen Margaret, mother of the young King James IV. Having tried but failed to influence the youthful monarch, Douglas retreated to Tantallon. There he was surrounded by the royal forces, James himself directing the siege, but Tantallon held out until after Douglas successfully departed and sought safe refuge in England. Even then Tantallon stood fast, only surrendering when the governor Douglas had, left in charge, accepted a bribe from the king.

King James then set about strengthening Tantallon still further with a new gate tower and parapets along the battlements. After he was defeated at the Battle of Pinkie near Musselburgh in 1542 and died soon afterwards at Falkland Palace across the Firth in Fife, however, Tantallon again came into the possession of the Douglas family. In the following year, upon his return from exile, it was restored to the Earl. Douglas then proceeded to fortify it still further raising its towers to their impressive height, which so struck Scott as he again describes in *Marmion*. He writes:

> Broad, massive, high and stretching far,
> And held impregnable in war,
> On a projecting rock they rose,
> And round three sides the ocean flows.
> The fourth did battled walls enclose
> And double mound and fosse.

Less romantically than Sir Walter put it, it is correct to say that Tantallon is an enclosure castle with curtain walls, vast in comparison to an earlier Norman-style motte and bailey castle or a later, tightly-constructed Scottish Border peel tower. Tantallon was reduced to its present ruinous state by the bombardment of Oliver Cromwell's General Monk and his Roundhead Republican troops in the 1650s. Just as its impressive sweep of fortifications appealed to the romanticism of Scott, who was surely Scotland's first tourist board chief, Tantallon still draws many visitors. Most come on sunny, summer days to climb on its walls, laze on its lawns and perhaps throw a coin for luck into the depths of its well, but to truly capture the spirit of Tantallon, try exploring it on a wickedly cold winter day with the grey blanket of a North Sea haar enveloping its towers.

It would have been on such a winter day that the little building in the shelter of Tantallon's landward side came into its own. For this was the castle's doocot, the stone-built, glass-roofed pigeon loft, designed to provide the castle's residents with fresh meat, after the winter slaughter of the cattle and sheep and the salting away of their beef and mutton. Tantallon's lectern-style doocot is very different from the two mentioned earlier at Aberdour and Dirleton castles, for unlike them it is rectangular in shape and built of rougher stones. Doocots of this style were usually built facing south so that their birds could come out to sunbathe on the roof. The collapse of the roof at Tantallon allows the nesting boxes built in the interior compartments to be seen

No doubt the castle kitchen's doocot pie would be washed down with fresh ale and today some of the best beer in Scotland is brewed just down the coast from Tantallon at Belhaven Brewery. Before Belhaven is reached, however, there is much to explore along the coast at Auldharne and Scoughall, which is pronounced

Barns Ness Lighthouse looms over the white harled houses, where its keepers used to stay with their families before it, like the more than two hundred other lights around the coast of Scotland in the care of the Northern Commissioners of Lights, was automated. Its light which can be seen for 21 nautical miles is now programmed by computer from the Commission's headquarters in Edinburgh's George Street.

'Scole'. This is where the famous East Coast missionary St Baldred had his headquarters. In his day, Auldhame occupied such an important place in the life of the early church that it was recognised as a separate parish and, although it has long disappeared, Baldred had a little kirk here. He also, however, worshipped regularly in the churches in the two neighbouring parishes of Hamer and Tyninghame and when he died all three congregations wanted the honour of having his body lie in mourning and it is claimed that by a blessed miracle the saintly man did indeed manage to divide himself into three separate corpses.

While Auldhame Church no longer stands, the area still has plenty of place-names referring to its missionary priest, from St Baldred's Holy Well to St Baldred's Boat, a rock formation out in the bay, while the name of the little harbour called the Gegan is believed to be derived from the Churchman's Haven. Nearby above the beach is also the ruin of Auldhame Priory, but while this definitely sounds like another church connection, it was actually a fortified mansion built after the time of the Reformation, simply taking its name from St Baldred's earlier association with the district.

239

The neighbouring farm to Auldhame, Scougall, however, did begin life as a small chapel. As a farm, it grew to become one of the most prosperous on the East Coast and it was here that Robert Louis Stevenson spent several boyhood holidays as it belonged to his relatives, the Dale family. There is a tradition that it was in front of the fire in Scougall farmhouse that Stevenson first heard the story of how folks in these parts, on dark stormy nights, when winds used to whip the coast, lured sailing ships onto the rocks by displaying misleading lantern lights and that this gave him the idea for his story called *The Wreckers*. Thus, although he did not set his tale on the shores of the Forth it is probable that the rocky reef called the Great Car, with its warning beacon flashing in the dark below his holiday home at Scougall Farm, provided him with the inspiration to write it. No doubt this tale is one of many told round the camp-fire at the regular Scripture Union summer camps held at Scoughall in recent years and which have made this rugged spot on the East Lothian shore of the Firth as special a place for modern children as it was for R.L.S. as a boy in Victorian times.

Shortly afterwards, the shore turns sandy again with the Peffer Sands, where the second of East Lothian's two Peffer Burns flows into the Firth. After the mouth of the Peffer, the coast remains sandy with the Ravenshcugh Sands bordering the Tyninghame Estate. They end at Whitberry Point, amongst whose rocks is the formation known as St Baldred's Cradle. Round the tip lies one of the finest stretches of beach along the whole of the Firth, with two miles of fine firm sand running all the way from Tyne Mouth to Belhaven Bay. Through the middle flows the East Lothian River Tyne, from which the Duke of Haddington's Tyninghame property takes its name.

Beyond lie the two coastal villages of West Barns and Belhaven with the Beil Water separating the two and giving its name to the latter, which means the harbour on the Beil. Picturesque little Belhaven was indeed originally the safe harbour for Dunbar, although the sandy shallows off its mouth always made it a notoriously difficult little port to enter. Today, Belhaven is even more silted up but its fine stretch of sandy beach is much appreciated by both residents and visitors alike, who also enjoy its fine golf links and the excellent walks and nature expeditions made available by the John Muir Country Park, much of whose landscaped parklands have changed little since they were laid out in the 18th century.

After Belhaven, the coastline changes again from sandy beach, which is a seaside award winner with top guideline standard water, to rocky promontory and although it is less than a mile by the main road from the village to Dunbar, it is worth following the longer footpath round the shore to St Margaret's Head to admire the view of the waves crashing against the rocks of the Long Craigs. From out here it is also much more possible to appreciate Dunbar's position jutting out into the Firth, than it is simply driving directly into town. Alexander Carlyle gave a vivid portrait of it when he wrote:

> It stands high and windy, looking down over its herring boats, over its grim old castle, now much honey-combed, a grim niched barrier of whinstone sheltering it from the chafings and tumblings of the blue German Ocean. Seaward St Abb's head, of whinstone, bounds your horizon to the East; while West, close by, is the deep bay and fishy little village of Belhaven.

While, as mentioned, Dunbar did for centuries depend on its little neighbour for its port, attempts were made over the years to make Dunbar itself a safer haven. During the time of the republican Commonwealth in the 1650s, the Lord High Protector's government gave £300 to improve the harbour, which was from then on known as Cromwell's Harbour. It was, however, not until it was replaced in 1844 by the new Victoria Harbour, that Dunbar really became important as a port.

Compared to the old harbour to the east, the new one had a much safer entrance and was far more spacious, large enough indeed to accommodate over 300 fishing boats, when Dunbar was at its height as a herring port. It cost £16,000 to construct, of which half was paid by the burgh and half by the government's Fisheries Board. During the latter half of the 19th century, huge quantities of herring were landed at Dunbar. Many of them were transported fresh by rail for sale on the British market, but even more were gutted, salted and packed into barrels to be shipped from Dunbar across the North Sea to the Scandinavian countries where they were a popular delicacy at the famous cold table. Outwith the herring season, the Dunbar fishermen caught plentiful quantities of North Sea cod, which were sold both in Edinburgh and London.

Today Dunbar's Victoria Harbour seems far too large for the dinghies and other small pleasure craft which are its main users.

241

The crumbling ruin of Dunbar Castle overlooks Victoria Harbour. Of particular interest is the castle block house as Dunbar was one of the first to be fortified with canon and it is now the earliest example of its kind in Europe. The block house overlooking the Firth is now difficult to reach because of the collapse of the stone bridge, which formerly connected it with the main part of the castle and because of the ruinous state of the whole site it is not open to visitors.

Overlooking it are the few remains of the town's red sandstone castle and it is hard to imagine that its walls once provided hospitality for several royal visitors. The castle is mentioned in historic records as early as 858, when it is described as having been destroyed by King Kenneth II. Two centuries later, it was granted in 1072 by King Malcolm Canmore, the husband of Queen Margaret of Queensferry fame, to his kinsman, Patrick, Earl of Northumberland. Patrick had fled from the English royal court following the Norman Conquest in 1066 and became the progenitor of the family of Gospatricks, Earls of Dunbar and March. March is an interesting term. It means border, as in the famous Riding of the Marches ceremonies which are such a colourful feature of life in Kelso, Galashiels, Hawick, Selkirk, Linlithgow and other Scottish towns each summer. Its use in the title of the Earls of Dunbar is particularly important as it is a reminder that Dunbar was essentially a border town, guarding the

Dunbar's Victoria Harbour looks far too large for the dinghies and other pleasure craft moored in it, but once it was crowded with fishing boats as one of Scotland's busiest herring fishing ports. An interesting feature of the harbour was that it was at its entrance that tidal conditions for the whole of Scotland were measured. The tidal observatory set up here in 1913 was one of two covering the whole of the British Isles, the other being at Penzance. They were controlled by the Ordance Survey and the data which they collected was used to produce tide tables for ports right round the coasts of the United Kingdom. The observatory was closed in the early 1950s. At the harbour the Creel Restaurant offers excellent seafood dishes.

approach to Scotland from Newcastle and the north-east of England.

In the Middle Ages, Dunbar Castle was considered to occupy a most important strategic position, the key in fact to eastern approach from England into Scotland and so it often featured in the tides of war which swept to and fro across the Borders. In 1296 there was a major battle at Dunbar, which resulted in a victory for the English with King Edward I, who arrived the following day, taking possession of the castle. While The Hammer of the Scots came to Dunbar victorious, the reverse was true of his son and heir. For it was during his flight, after his defeat at the Battle of Bannockburn in 1314, that Edward II arrived at the castle pursued by the Scots under Sir James Douglas. It is said that the anxious Edward was received 'full gently' by the keeper of the castle, the ninth Earl, Patrick, as he waited until the tide was right for one of the local fishing boats to help his escape by carrying him south of the Border to land him safely at Bamburgh in Northumberland.

The most famous siege in the history of Dunbar, when 'Black Agnes' held out in defiance of the Earls of Arundel and Salisbury, has already been described in the chapter on the history of the Bass Rock, but there are still many dramatic events to describe in the history of the castle. George, the tenth Earl, who succeeded to the title in 1369, became one of the most powerful nobles in Scotland and a formidable rival to the House of Douglas. Intrigue and jealousy stirred up by the Douglases forced the Earl to flee to England, where he was supported by King Henry IV. A truce was agreed between the Earl and the Douglases and he returned home to Dunbar in 1408.

His son, George, succeeded him in 1420 and soon found that his wealth and power as keeper of Dunbar brought him into conflict with King James I. When Earl George and his son travelled south to England, the king grabbed the opportunity to seize the castle. When the Earl returned home he was arrested and at a Scottish Parliament held in Perth his estates were forfeited to the crown. Dunbar was then conferred by King James II on his second son, Alexander, third Earl of Albany.

Dunbar remained a royal fortress until the reign of Mary Queen of Scots and it was to it that Mary, early on the morning of Tuesday 12 March, 1566, rode after the brutal murder of her favourite and secretary, David Rizzio, a crime in which her second husband and cousin, Henry, Lord Darnley, was implicated. It is said that the Queen arrived so unexpectedly that the Governor of Dunbar was taken by surprise, but still managed to provide Mary with a hearty breakfast. Despite his hospitality, however, shortly afterwards the Queen ousted him and put Lord Bothwell in charge of the castle. Bothwell and Mary were soon to enjoy a close relationship, following Darnley's murder at Kirk o' Field, where Edinburgh University's Old Quadrangle now stands in Edinburgh, a deed in which they were both alleged to be involved. To add even further to the scandal, ten weeks after Darnley's violent death following the explosion at Kirk o' Field, under the pretence of abducting her, it was to Dunbar that Bothwell brought Mary. What a willing accomplice in the abduction had the Queen been was summed up as neatly by 16th century historian and tutor to her son James, George Buchanan, as by any sub-editor on the present day *Hello* magazine, when he wrote, 'They remained ten days in the castle at Dunbar, with no great distance between the Queen's bedchamber and that of my Lord Bothwell's.' In the end, however, Mary and Bothwell determined that it was time to return to Edinburgh where at that castle their forthcoming marriage was announced. The news soon spread through Edinburgh and beyond and the reaction was so hostile that the Queen and Bothwell had to flee.

At first they sought refuge at Borthwick Castle, but on the morning of the unlucky 13 of June 1567, they arrived back at Dunbar, with the Queen disguised in male attire as a page boy wearing doublet and hose and complete with thigh-length riding boots and spurs. This, Mary's third visit to Dunbar, was to prove her shortest and her last, because both she and Bothwell stayed only one night, before riding off to try to gather support. They failed to gain enough and the following day were defeated at Carberry Hill near Musselburgh. Before surrendering to the Confederate Lords, Mary bid a hasty farewell to Bothwell, who rode back alone to his castle at Dunbar. Soon afterwards, he put to sea to sail away, thwarted and defeated, to exile in Denmark. So ended the important role which Dunbar played in Scotland's most famous and most tragic royal romance. For the old castle overlooking the Forth it was a sad ending. As Mary fled across the Solway and sought refuge from her cousin Queen Elizabeth in England, it was taken over by the Regent, Morton, and, on the instructions of the Scottish Parliament, it was submitted to systematic destruction, after its cannon had been removed and transferred to the castle in Edinburgh.

Dunbar was, however, still to play one more significant part in Scottish history, when almost a century later Oliver Cromwell fought a major battle, two miles away from the castle on the high ground overlooking the town at Doune Hill. There, his Commonwealth troops faced the Scottish Covenanter Royalist supporters of King Charles II under General Leslie on 3 September 1650 and at Dunbar Drove or the Tuesday Chase, as it became known, won an overwhelming victory. Of the Scottish force of 20,000 men, 3,000 were slain and another 10,000 taken prisoner and the way was then wide open for Cromwell to advance and establish himself in Edinburgh Castle.

Dunbar's long High Street still has a distinctly historic feel to it. In the middle is the port's old, mid-17th-century Tolbooth. This two-storeyed, stone building with its dormer-windowed attic and

Dunbar's ancient Tolbooth with its slate clad wooden steeple brings a sense of history to the town's High Street. The flag flies at half mast in respect for the death of Diana, Princess of Wales in September 1997.

wooden spire served not just as town council meeting place, but also as both courtroom and jail for those who at their trials were found guilty. Much larger and grander at the end of the High Street stands Lauderdale House. It is actually the back which faces the street, but even it is finely decorated with, in the centre, below the roof, a large and finely carved Egyptian sphinx, which in heraldic terms is officially described as 'couchant with extended wings', meaning roughly that it is crouched as if ready to fly off into the East Lothian sky. This very impressive town house was originally built around 1740 by Captain James Fell, who was the local Member of Parliament. It was passed on to his son, but he was less successful in his career and sold it to the Duke of Lauderdale, hence the name. In 1780, he employed Scotland's most famous architect, Robert Adam, to improve and enlarge it and he created its present imposing appearance. Lauderdale house was purchased in 1859 by the government, who converted it into a headquarters and barracks for the 2nd Brigade, Royal Artillery and the parkland, which surrounded it, became the parade ground for the district's volunteer army reservists, who were raised and organised by the Earl of Wemyss from his family seat up the coast beyond Aberlady at Gosford and whose local connections were suitably commemorated by their title of the Haddingtonshire Militia.

Someone with a Dunbar connection who made a much more peaceful contribution to history was John Muir. Muir is actually much better known in the United States of America than in his native Scotland, but it was in Dunbar that he was born in 1838 and there are, at last, plans to turn his childhood home, which still stands in the High Street, into an appropriate memorial to this great man. For it was as a pioneer of nature conservation that Muir persuaded the American government to establish the first of the country's now world-famous National Parks in California's spectacularly beautiful Yosemite Valley. That was in 1890 and the idea proved so successful that as well as all the other National Parks in the USA there are now around 3,000 others worldwide, although Scotland did not acquire its first around Loch Lomond until 1997. To be fair, however, it must be noted that Dunbar has, for almost 30 years, had its own John Muir Country Park, complete with its staff of countryside rangers to protect the stretch of the shore of the Firth of Forth which first inspired the young naturalist during his childhood years and its facilities do much to interest visitors, especially families and school groups, to take an interest in the coast and its plentiful wildlife. As well as pupils from local schools, many of the children who enjoy lessons in this open-air classroom come from further afield and use the former primary school in the nearby village of Innerwick as a residential outdoor studies base.

Coming from inland towns, these youngsters' weekly programme often includes the excitement of a visit to Dunbar's lifeboat station. Dunbar has two lifeboats. At the local RNLI boathouse headquarters on the corner above the harbour is housed a D-class inflatable ready to be launched to cope with any inshore emergencies. The Dunbar lifeboat crew, however, also have to be prepared for rescue calls from out in the North Sea and so, in addition, they have been provided with one of the RNLI's latest deep-water boats with a speed of 25 knots and a range of 250 miles. This impressively powerful Trent class vessel is moored along the coast at Torness Harbour, where deep water means that her six-man volunteer crew can respond to any emergency call and have her out to sea within minutes. Almost 47-feet long, the Trent at Torness is one of 21 similar vessels based around the British coast, including a neighbouring one at Eyemouth.

One sailor who appreciated the power of both the Dunbar and Eyemouth Trents and the skill and courage of their crews is Douglas Stewart, Skipper of the 68-ton *Mayflower IV*, who was 100 miles out in the North Sea, when his vessel lost steering in stormy, severe gale force nine conditions. His 'Mayday' call was answered by both the Dunbar and Eyemouth lifeboats and, despite atrocious conditions, with waves 24 feet high often breaking right over the *Mayflower IV*, their combined efforts ensured that she reached harbour safely. Later, in a thank you letter praising both crews, Skipper Stewart wrote:

> Dunbar lifeboat made an outstanding job in rough seas. My crew and I feel the lifeboats have proved beyond a doubt their outstanding efficiency and the capability of the design of the Trent — Well done to both crews and boats.

While the sleek, streamlined, ultra-modern Trent is always on standby ready to help ensure safety at sea, only a few hundred yards away along the coast, looming over her mooring is historic Barns Ness Lighthouse, which has been helping to do likewise for over a century. Unlike lighthouses around the coasts of the United States, British ones do not have individual distinctive colour schemes, known as 'Day Marks', but nonetheless Barns Ness is a familiar landmark to all who travel either up or down the A1 or speed by on the electrified Edinburgh to London railway line. For many years, Barns Ness Lighthouse was the highest building for miles around, but now its pristine whiteness is overshadowed by the ugliness of the nearby cement works and the bulk of Torness Nuclear Power Station.

CHAPTER 12
FROM TORNESS TO THE SEA

Looming space-age-like above the lighthouse at Barns Ness is the silver silhouette of Torness Nuclear Power Station. Rising starkly, straight out of the golden harvest fields which border this stretch of the coast, there is something chillingly James Bondish about this intruder into the East Lothian countryside. Its owners, Scottish Nuclear Ltd, are however determined to portray a far more environmentally friendly image of their plant and so Torness goes out of its way to welcome visitors to its multimedia information centre with tours several times every day throughout the year, apart from the Christmas and New Year period. These tours allow visitors to explore the inside of the works. Viewing galleries look down right into the huge Reactor Hall. At its heart is the reactor core, with its vertical channels for the control rods and the vital fuel. The fuel consists of small pellets of uranium dioxide, a hard ceramic compound form of uranium. These uranium dioxide pellets are sealed into stainless steel tubes, one metre long. When all of this fuel is in place the control rods are slowly removed from the core. More and more neutrons thus become available to cause fusion, until eventually a self-sustaining chain reaction is started. From the viewing galleries it is also possible to see into the clinically clean, silent control room, where the plant's engineers maintain the reaction at precisely the required level by lowering and raising the control rods. The heat produced by the chain reaction is carried away by the carbon dioxide which is pumped through the core at great pressure. The carbon dioxide gas is then pumped throughout the boilers containing thousands of metres of steel tubes, through which pure water is pumped. The hot gas surrounds these tubes and the water inside boils to produce supercharged steam. This is then piped to the large blue and silver turbine which drives the two generators, which together produce an amazing quarter of the whole of Scotland's electricity requirements. Indeed, along with Scottish Nuclear's similar power station on the west coast at Hunterston on the shores of the Firth of Clyde, the firm now supplies half of the electricity used in the whole country.

The golden harvest field contrasts starkly with the silver space age silhouette of Torness Nuclear Power Station, which stands out against the stormy September sky out over the Firth.

All of the electricity produced at Torness and Hunterston goes directly into the national grid, approximately three-quarters of it to Scottish Power and the remaining quarter to Scottish Hydro Electric, which supplies the north of the country. In total, Scottish Nuclear employs around 1,600 staff, over a third of whom work at Torness.

Scottish Nuclear does not deny that all methods of generating electricity have some environmental impact. It claims, however, that a nuclear power station like Torness has the advantage that compared with its conventional fossil-fuelled equivalent, such as the traditional coal-fired Cockenzie, which has already been mentioned, or Longannet further up the Forth between Culross and Kincardine on the Fife shore, for the size of its output, it emits negligible quantities of carbon dioxide and far less of the polluting oxides of nitrogen and sulphur. Still, however, there remains the concern about the risk of radiation. To this, the reply at Torness is that nuclear energy is actually one of the smallest sources of radiation to which the population of this country is exposed. According to Scottish Nuclear it amounts to less than one thousandth of the total, of which the biggest percentage, totalling 86 per cent, comes from naturally occurring background radiation and most of the remainder being accounted for by the use of X-rays by hospitals and by dentists in their surgeries.

Torness is thus officially the friendly giant which dominates this stretch of the East Lothian coast. By coincidence, it is also where almost half a century ago almost 200 of nature's giants, the whales, inexplicably beached themselves on the sands at the foot of the cliffs at nearby Thorntonloch.

It was on the morning of Sunday 14 May 1950 that the wireless news carried a report that two local school boys had made the horrific discovery the previous evening and that the whales were all still alive. The radio broadcast created a huge amount of interest and by lunchtime all the roads in the area were jammed with traffic as around 40,000 people arrived to try to see the whales. MacMerry Aerodrome near Dalkeith even offered whale-spotting flights. On the ground, cars were parked all along the verges beside the A1 as their drivers and passengers walked across the fields and clambered down the cliffs to see the spectacle of the stranded whales.

Down on the sands the local police, supplemented by special constables, tried to keep the sightseers back from the whales, but were totally outnumbered and the great black beasts were soon surrounded by curious onlookers. Although many of the monsters, which were later identified as being pilots of up to 12 tons in weight, were stuck only a few yards from the water's edge, there was no organised attempt to save any of them. Some members of the crowd did try desperately to keep some of the whales alive by pouring water from children's pails over the brutes, but this was obviously futile and soon many were clearly dying.

In stark contrast to the tragic scene unfolding on the beach, an ice-cream van arrived and began selling cones and wafers to the sightseers. As dusk slowly descended on that warm May Sunday afternoon, the crowds began to go home. By then, over 100 of the whales had struggled to breathe their last and as darkness fell officers of the Scottish Society for the Prevention of Cruelty to Animals decided to shoot the remaining 78 animals to put them out of their misery.

Next day, East Lothian Public Health Committee convened to decide how to tackle the massive task of removing the carcasses of all the whales. In those days when rationing was still in force, five years after the end of the Second World War, nothing was wasted and firms despatched lorries from as far away as Tyneside to collect the whales for processing into animal food. There were even suggestions that the whale steaks should be sold for human consumption, as they had been a welcome addition to the Scottish diet during the immediate post-war years, but the authorities banned this. It took until the middle of the following week for the last of the carcasses to be removed. It was never discovered why such a large school of whales had run aground at Thorntonloch. Suggestions included the possibility of polluted water having confused the whales or that perhaps they had swum too far inshore while in pursuit of a shoal of fish. Another idea was that the pilots had been chased ashore by larger killer whales, but nothing was ever proved. To this day, occasional whales are still stranded in the Forth, but thankfully not on the tragic scale as the disaster at Thorntonloch. Most recent of the whales to die in the river was the much publicised Moby, who after over a week swimming up and down between the Forth Bridges and Bo'ness finally swam up river beneath Kincardine Bridge and became trapped on a mud bank off the village of Airth. Moby's huge skull has been preserved at Deep Sea World at North Queensferry and the entire skeleton of the whale can be seen at the Museum of Scotland in Chambers Street, Edinburgh.

Shortly beyond Thorntonloch, the large signs back on the main A1 road indicate the boundary of East Lothian and the start of the Berwickshire stretch of the coastline. Almost immediately at the large roundabout, the second exit road leads a short distance along the top of the cliff to a small car park. Here it is necessary to abandon the car if you want to discover the delights of picturesque Cove Harbour, because apart from a rough private track there is no vehicle access. A sign carved in the shape of an anchor at the point where the track descends steeply to the shore also reminds visitors that the little Cove is privately owned. Originally part of the Dunglass Estate, it was given to Berwickshire Council, whose successor Borders Council sold it to Ben Tindall who formed the Cove Harbour Preservation Trust. The sign, however, indicates that visitors are welcome so long as they keep their pets under control and make certain to take all of their litter home with them.

As mentioned above, Cove Harbour Trust is led by well-known, distinguished, Edinburgh-based architect Ben Tindall. As an associate of Prince Charles, Mr Tindall has been involved in His

Royal Highness's scheme to develop a modern environmentally friendly village on the Isle of Barra in the Hebrides. He has equally forward-looking ideas for the picturesque little secret harbour at Cove, or The Cove as the local people from the Cockburnspath district call it.

One of the first improvements which Borders Regional Council successfully completed was the provision of well constructed wooden steps to lead visitors safely down the steepest first stretch of cliff onto the track which twists its way down to the shore and it is worth the hike down to reach the water's edge. Before going down, however, make a point of finding the huge sandstone boulder tucked away in the north-east cliffside corner of the car park, because its siting here was a project which brought together lots of history enthusiasts and craftsmen from Cockburnspath and all along the coast to preserve one of its most unusual curiosities. For a niche carved into the big boulder now provides a safe haven for the historic barometer which the Laird of Dunglass Estate, Sir John Hall, gifted to the local fishermen, in the 19th century so that in these days, long before the broadcast of regular shipping forecasts, they could produce their own before deciding whether to set sail along this dangerous stretch of rocky, hazardous coastline.

The fishermen who berthed, anchored or beached their boats in the shelter of The Cove paid rent to Dunglass Estate in kind in the form of haddock or herring for the Laird's table. In the 17th century, shoals of herring swam into the Forth every August. This annual influx of the silver darlings provided a rich harvest for the fishermen from The Cove and other Forth fishing boats also put in at the little harbour to land their catches. As early as the early 1670s, the Laird of Dunglass tried to improve his harbour, in order to persuade more fishermen from further along the coast to move and centralise fishing at The Cove, but a great storm in January 1674 wrecked his efforts.

In the 1750s, the owner of Dunglass, Sir John Hall, tried again to make The Cove safer. Rather in the same way that applications are now made to the Lottery Commission, he obtained a grant of money from the fund established by the government from the sale of forfeited Jacobite estates, after their owners were defeated at Culloden in 1746. As a result, he was able to spend the then considerable sum of £450 on the construction of a breakwater to protect the entrance, but it was swept away by a north-easterly gale. This 18th-century period of improvement did however result in the construction of the tunnel to give access to the shore. An entry in the Summary of Accounts for the Dunglass Estate reads, 'By work at Cove shoar 21 August 1752 to 15 June 1753, hollow road and cellars, £68 18s 6d.' Originally the tunnel was wide enough to allow a horse and cart to pass through and reach the shore, but it has subsequently been narrowed, especially at the seaward end. The cellars running off it were originally dug in order to try to exploit a narrow seam of coal and use it to supply the Dunglass Estate. Later they came in very useful for the fishermen to store their lobster creels and other gear, but they have all now been blocked off for safety reasons.

One of the local men who worked for the Dunglass Estate during this period of construction at The Cove was Alexander Somerville. It was very unusual at this time for a labourer to be able to read and write, but the largely self-taught Somerville later wrote a book, which he entitled *The Autobiography of a Working Man*, in which he describes the work at the harbour. It might have been better if he had remained an estate worker, because when he went on to enlist as a soldier, he was court marshalled and sentenced to the dreadful punishment of a military flogging of 200 lashes on his bare back from the cat o' nine tails, although he may have been spared some of the final strokes.

Back in Scotland during this period following the Jacobite Rebellion, the government at Westminster continued with its programme of ideas to try to ensure that Scotland remained at peace by improving economic conditions by encouraging the provision of more jobs. In 1765, an Act of Parliament brought into being The Improvement of Fishing and Manufactures Scheme and again the Laird of Dunglass, Sir John Hall, showed his great astuteness as an estate owner by applying within months in 1766 for a grant. This he indicated he would use to allow him to bring a group of Banffshire fishermen south to base themselves at The Cove for a year to train more of the men on his estate to take up the white fishing. In his successful bid Sir John also promised that the fishermen from the North East would in turn benefit greatly by being taught the tricks of catching lobsters and crabs and other shellfish in the inshore waters along the Berwickshire Coast, which was an area of fishing in which The Cove men already excelled.

Writing in a letter to the Earl of Findlater, who was one of the administrators of the improvement scheme, Sir John added to his case for financial support by pointing out that 'more valuable than white fishing is the catching of lobsters for the London mercatt, which can never be overstocked'.

Almost a century later, the extension of the Edinburgh to Berwick railway, which had first been opened as far as the border in 1846, all the way south to London in 1850, with the opening of the Royal Tweed Bridge and the building of a station on this main line at Cockburnspath, gave both the lobster fishing at The Cove and the salmon net fishing along the coast a considerable boost as the steam trains meant that the daily catch could be on the tables of the smartest city restaurants within hours of being landed. Originally, the railway line at nearby Pease was the steepest gradient anywhere between Edinburgh and London. Later, when Penmanshiel Tunnel was constructed, it became the steepest section.

By the time of the coming of the steam trains, far fewer herring were being caught in the Firth and from the 'one hundred herring boats', reported in the First Statistical Account of Scotland, discharging their catches at The Cove at the height of the season in the late 18th century, the number dwindled greatly as Victorian times progressed.

On 14 October 1881, the fishing from The Cove and all the other fishing ports along the Berwickshire coast received a blow which was especially devastating because of its tragic suddenness, when it was hit by a horrendous hurricane. The morning of that fateful autumn day dawned fine and bright and despite the fact that the big barometer, upon the cliff near the Coastguard Cottages, was showing exceptionally low pressure, using their local knowledge of the weather, the fishermen decided to put to sea, with five boats setting sail from The Cove.

For several hours they fished successfully but by late morning the sky out over the North Sea looked menacing. It was darkening rapidly and by noon was described as 'inky black.' The Cove boats all began to make back to harbour but too late; there was not enough time. For within minutes they were battered by hurricane force winds. In a lifetime at sea The Cove crews had experienced nothing so severe.

As the hurricane whipped in towards the coast, the people of

Cockburnspath hurried to the cliff top and in horror watched through the wind-lashed spray, at the tragedy unfolding before their eyes.

The Cove herring fisher, *The Snowden*, which was working furthest out, capsized first with the loss of all six of her crew. The inshore lobster fishers, *Velox* and *Pearl*, ran for the shelter of Pease Bay, a little further down the coast. Despite the enormous breakers crashing into its beach, both reached the shore, but each lost one of her crew. The final two Cove boats, *Freedom* and *Renown*, which had been fishing inshore to the north were blown out of sight. The crowd on the cliff feared the worst. Both boats were, however, shortly afterwards swept ashore at Skateraw, near Torness, but with very mixed fortunes. All six of the crew of the *Freedom* survived, but the three men aboard the *Renown* were all drowned. In just over one hour, The Cove had lost 11 of its fishermen, the Fairbairn family suffering the most deaths. Further down the coast at Eyemouth, 129 lives were lost and the port's museum tells the story of what is still known as disaster day. There is also a monument in the park to the memory of the fishermen and boys who were drowned on that October day.

The Cove is truly a secret harbour. Invisible from the cliff-top above, it is entirely hidden from sight at the foot of the cliff. This surely is the kind of place that deserves to have been written about by John Buchan in one of his famous adventure novels. Even without Buchan's help, it does not take much imagination to people Cove's tiny harbour with sailors and fishermen of times gone by and with nearby Brandy Bay, surely some at least of them must have indulged in the smuggling trade. Nowadays, two inshore boats still fish out of The Cove. Operated by the Gray cousins, one of whose ancestors perished in the hurricane disaster, they are still as skilled as ever at knowing where to find the finest lobsters and the meatiest crabs and still land their daily catch at The Cove, as generations of their family have done before them.

Today, The Cove has more visitors than ever before because it is almost, but not quite, the end of a long adventure for many enthusiastic long-distance walkers who undertake the famous Southern Upland Way, which snakes its way right across the Borders of Scotland from Portpatrick on the west coast. As the walk is billed as running from coast to coast, when it reaches Cove it seems to come to its natural conclusion but the planners of the

212-mile route, which has been open to walkers since 1984, decided that it should end officially about a mile and a half inland at the village of Cockburnspath. This is perhaps a wise choice, for unlike the Cove with its old, early 19th-century buildings, the largest of which is the herring curing house built by Sir John Hall, Co'path as the locals know it, has, importantly, a welcoming inn in which to drink a celebratory dram or two to mark the feat, or should that really be feet of successfully walking right across the country.

Even for those who have not walked the entire length of the Southern Upland Way, Cockburnspath with its village store and traditional pub with its white-harled walls, is well worth making a detour to visit and it also provides access to the Berwickshire Coastal Route to continue south. The road is carried over the depths of the precipitous gully of Pease Dean by Pease Bridge, which when built in the 18th century was claimed to be a world record holder. For, at a height of 140 feet, it was considered one of the wonders of the age and was at the time the highest bridge in the world. The four-arched structure is 16 feet wide and 300 feet in length. It was certainly very well built by the local Dunglass Estate, for unlike many other bridges in the Borders, including those carrying the main railway line between Edinburgh and London which were swept away by the terrible torrential floods which devastated the district in August 1948, it survived intact and today huge 40-ton trucks trundle safely across it.

The bridge carries the Berwickshire coast road south to what should be the next point of interest on the shoreline, Pease Bay, but in comparison with lovely little Cove, it is in fact a great disappointment. For after taking the trouble to drive through the waters of the ford, which provides a hopefully exciting entrance at the foot of the cliffs to Pease Bay, it turns out to be a dreary caravan site, whose numerous static and touring vans mar the view of its beautiful beach, whose sands are presumably what their owners come to enjoy. Many local people still remember the bay before the coming of the caravans, when the only campers were the Scouts, Guides and members of the Boys' Brigade, whom the farmer allowed to pitch their tents in the sandy field overlooking the beach and the sea.

Someone who still has vivid memories of one of these never-to-be forgotten weeks under canvas at Pease Bay is that grand old man of Edinburgh Scouting, Leslie Pringle, who in his booklet, *From Dry Land to Wet Sea*, writes:

> Unlike the disastrous weekend of the previous year, the 28th Liberton Troop's summer camp at Pease Bay was a resounding success. It was an excellent site, hard by a mill stream and on good natural grass and not a motor car in sight. By this time I considered myself a pretty good cook. Not being so keen on going on Sunday church parade, I talked the skipper into letting me stay back and make the lunch. It was while I was stirring the lentil soup to make sure it did not stick to the dixie and burn, that a shadow fell on the fire and a deep voice said. 'That's grand soup you have there lad.' It was the local bobby and he gratefully accepted a bowlful.
>
> 'That's your good turn for the day,' he told me as he left, 'for I was famished.'
>
> It proved to be a useful encounter for a couple of months later while camping there with my brother and sister, I had driven the car up the hill to collect a container of water and was just filling it up when up hove the same policeman on his bicycle. He did not recognise me as the soup stirring Scout and said in stentorian tones, 'Aye, aye, and how old are you son?'
>
> Maximising my age as much as possible, I answered, 'fifteen and three quarters.'
>
> 'Do you know you have to be seventeen before you can drive a car?'
>
> 'Yes'.
>
> 'I'll have your name and address.'
>
> 'You liked my soup.'
>
> 'So it's you is it? I didn't recognise you in that old jersey. Aye, it was good soup. Lentil wasn't it? Aye, well, just you jump into that car with your water and I'll forget I ever saw you, aye and mind that double bend at the bottom of the road. It's a devil.'

Nowadays, Pease Bay is the point where the Southern Upland Way, running down from Abbey St Bathans, actually reaches the coast and it is worth backtracking up the path which it follows through Pease Dean to enjoy its rich variety of trees and the many species of birds which they attract. The trees and the wildlife for whom they are home are fortunately protected as the Dean is a nature reserve under the care of the Scottish Wildlife Trust. It is just a pity that Pease Bay did not enjoy similar protection. The oatmeal mill, powered by the burn which flows down to the sea through Pease Dean, has long disappeared, but the mill whose big wooden wheel used to be driven by the neighbouring Douglas Burn still stands. Although now converted into a private house, its lade survives to delight the local ducks.

From the shore of the caravan park at Pease Bay, the narrow, steep, single-track road climbs back up to the Berwickshire coastal route road. Almost at the top, just before rejoining it, a side road to the right leads along the side of the cliff to Old Cambus Quarry. Today the disused quarry provides this part of Berwickshire with another claim to fame as the site of the world's largest turnip, or to be more precise, swede-processing plant. Developed by enterprising local farmers R. and K. Drysdale, who both grow the swedes in the surrounding Berwickshire fields and also import them from as far away as the continent in order to ensure a year-round supply, the ultra-modern plant delivers the vegetables to supermarkets throughout Britain. Interestingly, swedes take their unusual name from the fact that they were first introduced into Scotland from Sweden as a result of a most unusual voyage from the Forth across the North Sea. It was made by the Deputy Governor of the Bank of Scotland, Miller, who was a man of many interests. As a director of the famous Carron Iron Works, situated further up the Forth on the banks of its tributary, the Carron, he was responsible for the development of the factory's most famous product, the Carronade, the small short-muzzled cannon, which did much to enable Britain to win the Napoleonic Wars. He was also the man who, in 1788, put up the money to allow William Symington to experiment with the world's first paddle steamer, which led on to the construction of the pioneering iron-hulled Grangemouth-built *Charlotte Dundas*, which is remembered on the town's coat of arms. What is less well-known is that Miller himself carried out experiments on the use of paddle power for sea transport, but instead of steam power was trying out mechanical propulsion and that, the previous year, he had successfully sailed a manually-powered paddle boat all the way from Scotland across the North Sea and through the Baltic to Sweden. The Swedish king was so impressed that he summoned the enterprising Miller to an audience at the royal court in Stockholm. At it he presented him with a golden casket. Strangely, inside was a packet of seed for a newly discovered root vegetable. Miller brought them back home to Scotland, where he planted them and successfully grew the first crop of what he called swedes.

In Sweden on the other hand, they are known as *rutabagas* and interestingly in Berwickshire the local name for swedes is 'baggies'.

Robin and Kim Drysdale's business is a year-round one, with particularly busy spells leading up to the 25th of January, when chappit neeps and tatties are the order of the day on every Burns' Supper menu, and as Hallowe'en looms at the end of October. To cater for the latter, the Drysdale brothers have even developed a machine to top and tail the swedes, scoop out the heart and carve out the eyes, nose and mouth required to turn them into classic tumshie lanterns to delight guising weans throughout the length and breadth of the haunted Hallowe'en kingdom. Only the candle has to be added by hand. Hopefully, their endeavours will help protect our traditional Scottish custom on the scariest night of the year, from the insidious invasion of the American pumpkin lantern with all its foreign 'trick or treat' connotations.

Having climbed back up the steep road from the Quarry to the Cockburnspath to Coldingham coast road, a most unusual public telephone kiosk catches the eye. It stands at the next farm road-end leading down to East and West Mains and Redheugh Farm and was the first in Britain to be provided with a solar panel to provide it with electrical power. Unfortunately, the Berwickshire weather could not guarantee enough year-round sunshine and so it is now even more unusual, because in addition to the solar panel above its roof, there has now been added a windmill. What Berwickshire lacks in sunshine, this exposed stretch of coast at the entrance to the Firth of Forth undoubtedly makes up for in winds and now the call-box functions happily throughout the year, thanks to its two environmentally-friendly sources of power.

On the cliff-top below the telephone box can be seen a row of houses. These are the former coastguard cottages at Redheugh, which were built in the 1820s as part of a drive by the government to stamp out smuggling, which had become very prevalent in these parts because of the lack of supervision along the coast during the long period of the Napoleonic Wars during the opening years of the 19th century. In the Berwickshire volume of the Second Statistical Account of Scotland., published in 1834, the parish minister at Cockburnspath wrote: 'Smuggling was said to be prevalent in the parish but has now died out, especially since the establishment of a Preventive Station at Redheugh.'

Although described as cottages, the coastguard houses are two-storeyed and there are more of them at Redheugh than at either St Abb's or The Cove, which suggests this lonely stretch of coastline was more attractive to the smugglers than chancing landing their contraband at any of even the smallest of ports. The six coastguard cottages overlooking Redheugh's tempting little cove and the stretch of coast to north and south were originally part of the Dunglass Estate, but in the 1950s the then Laird of Dunglass, Frank Usher senior, sold them to an Edinburgh surgeon. In his will he in turn left them to his family, one to his wife and one each to each of his five children, who still regularly stay in them as holiday homes.

The coastguard cottages are reached by a path through the fields of Redheugh Farm. Redheugh means the Red Cliff and its name is a reminder of its red soil, which stretches round the corner from East Lothian, where its distinctive shade is such a familiar feature of the landscape. The soil and geology of Redheugh is especially interesting, as it was here that James Hutton, the father of modern geology, identified his famous Unconformity, whose curious rock formations helped to confirm his evolutionary theories. Hutton, who was born in Duns in 1726, first spotted this interesting geological feature at Siccar Point, while sailing along the Berwickshire coast and to this day it still acts as a Mecca for geologists from all over the world.

Redheugh is farmed by Tom Dykes, whose uncle Tom farmed it before him. He takes a very enlightened attitude to public access, because while pointing out how unsuitable the high and dangerous cliffs of this stretch of the coast are for the development of a coastal path, he has persuaded the Cockburnspath Community Council to encourage local landowners to develop what he describes as 'vertical' rather than 'horizontal' access to the sea at appropriate places of interest.

Before the Second World War, Redheugh was home to a salmon fishery whose fishermen, although some of them were married men, during the season led a bachelor existence in a smoky little bothy by the shore. Redheugh was ideal for the salmon fishers as there was enough room on the shingle in the cove below the cliffs to pull their boat safely up on the shore above the high tidemark. Sea salmon fishing is a perquisite of the Crown and the rights to fish each stretch of the Scottish coast were auctioned every three years, with some of the fishermen, who lived each year from

February to September at Redheugh, coming from as far away as the north-east coast of Scotland. The fishing was done by fixed nets, which were anchored to the sea bed and kept afloat by cork floats. The law strictly banned salmon fishing on Sundays. This meant that on Saturday nights, the ends of the nets had to be lifted so that any salmon which swam into them on the Sabbath could escape and swim free. The salmon fishers did, however, usually launch their boat on Sunday afternoons to sail up the coast to The Cove in order to do their weekly shopping,

The outbreak of war in September 1939 brought salmon fishing at Redheugh to an end. The old bothy by the shore, with its poles outside on which the nets used to be hung to dry and for repair, was destroyed by the soldiers sent to man a searchlight battery at this isolated spot on the coast, who ripped out all its woodwork to burn to keep themselves warm on winter days, when an icy wind blew in from the North Sea. Throughout the hostilities, local residents were banned from the coast, which was fortified with concrete defences to prevent enemy forces, and especially tanks, coming ashore. In addition, the sands of Pease Bay were sown with landmines. It was at Pease Bay that a wartime shipwreck occurred, when the *Magicienne*, a Swedish three-masted wooden sailing schooner with an auxiliary engine, grounded on the sands in 1940, shortly after the Dunkirk evacuation. As a Swedish vessel, the *Magicienne* was officially a neutral vessel and had large crosses painted on the sides of her hull to denote this. Her hull was finally blown up by the army. Another wartime casualty at Brandy Bay was the Romanian steamer *Verobormilia*. Her hull was bought by the Dunglass Salvage Company of Dunbar. It was broken up on the spot and the metal taken out by sea aboard the company's little vessel, the *Jacob George*. For a time during the war years, the shore at Redheugh and Pease Bay was littered with wooden pit props, intended to keep up the roofs of the underground workings of Scottish coal pits, but which had been lost at sea, when the ship carrying them was destroyed by a German torpedo.

One of the most spectacular wrecks on this stretch of coast occurred in 1958, when on a very foggy Saturday evening, the modern Swiss-owned cargo ship *Nyon*, which was outward bound from the Forth, ran fast aground on the rocks at the Soutar or Standing Man on the shoreline of the neighbouring farm of Dowlaw. Later in the night, the swirling grey North Sea haar, which

The MV Nyon, *fast aground on the rocks off Dowlaw on the Berwickshire coast in November 1958, defied the efforts of two salvage tugs. After a month of fruitless efforts the Dutch salvage experts, sliced through the vessel, leaving her bows trapped on the rocks, but freeing the rest of her to be towed back to Rotterdam. There she was carefully reconstructed, only to sail out into the English Channel where she was involved in a collision and sank.* Picture by Tom Dykes Sn., courtesy of Margaret Dykes.

had blanketed the coast, cleared, and the Auxiliary Coastguards, who included several of the local farmers, discovered the *Nyon* with all her lights ablaze, clearly visible from the shore in perfectly calm water at the foot of the cliffs. By this time, the lifeboat was also alongside, but her German captain refused to abandon ship, as to do so would have been to have surrendered his vessel as a salvage claim. Surprisingly for such a new ship, the *Nyon* was later found not to have the radar equipment which could have saved her from running ashore.

Next morning her master shouted ashore an appeal for concrete, with which he hoped to plug the gaping hole in the *Nyon's* bows, where they had ploughed onto the rocks. Despite the fact that it was a Sunday morning in 1950s Britain, when nothing opened for business, supplies of concrete were eventually obtained from Berwick-upon-Tweed. In the days before the coastguard acquired any four-wheel-drive vehicles, the concrete was ferried down to the stricken vessel by farm tractor. By this time the local coastguard had managed to get a line aboard the *Nyon* and this was used to transfer the bags of cement out to her crew. In the end, they used several tons of cement to try to plug the hole in her bows where the rocks had ripped into her, but all to no avail. Her skipper still refused to be taken off, choosing to remain aboard until the *Nyon's* owners could arrange their own salvage effort with the help of Dutch experts. Their efforts were hampered by the fact that the *Nyon* was sailing light when she grounded and therefore there was no cargo in her holds which could be jettisoned to try to lighten her and float her clear. Helped, however, by calm seas the Dutch salvage engineers worked on for a whole month into December to try to free her from the rocks, but even with the combined efforts of two powerful tugs, she obstinately stuck fast. In the end, the Dutch experts decided on a bold plan. They cut through the forward section of the ship, leaving the bows trapped on the rocks, but enabling them to float off the remainder of the ship, which the tugs towed all the way to Rotterdam. There, the *Nyon's* bows were reconstructed. Once completed, she set sail again, under the same captain, but shortly afterwards was involved in a collision and sank in the English Channel, possibly the only ship which can be claimed to have been wrecked twice.

Shortly afterwards, a Scottish fishing trawler followed the fated *Nyon* onto similar rocks at Dowlaw, but she was more fortunate and was safely refloated. About ten years later, in 1969, a wee flavour of *Whisky Galore* came to this stretch of the Berwickshire coast, when the German ship *Carlo Porr*, in a severe gale, lost overboard a 4,000-gallon whisky container which she was carrying as deck cargo. The huge cask was washed ashore on the shingle near the Green Stone on the shores of Dowlaw, but if the good folks of Cockburnspath might have been planning to emulate the islanders of Little Todday in Sir Compton MacKenzie's famous story, their hopes were sorely dashed, when it was discovered that the *Carlo Porr* was inward bound at the time of the accident and that the whisky container was therefore empty. While this may have left a somewhat sour taste in the mouths of the Berwickshire folk, it is indeed an ill wind that blows nobody any good and the fact that the large container was made of stainless steel, made it valuable and well worth salvaging. This was eventually achieved by cutting it up on the shore at Dowlaw at the spot where it had grounded and removing the scrap metal by sea.

Dowlaw is pronounced 'Doolaw', but it has no connection with doos or pigeons, although they, along with crowds of crows and flocks of seagulls, raid its fields in the spring at seedtime. Dowlaw does, in fact, acquire its name from a corruption of the Gaelic *dhu*, meaning black and the word *law*, meaning a hill and is an apt description of the change in the colour and type of soil which this hilly farm possesses, in comparison with the red soil of its neighbour to the west, Redheugh.

Another feature of interest about the lands of Dowlaw are that they include the high cliff-top site of the few remains of Fast Castle, which was the basis for Wolf's Craig, the solitary and naked Border peel tower home of Edgar Ravenswood, one of the prominent characters in Sir Walter Scott's novel *The Bride of Lammermoor*. Fast Castle is indeed an appropriate setting for the action of *The Bride of Lammermoor*, because it is set precariously on a towering rocky crag, where Berwickshire's Lammermuir Hills end abruptly in a series of sea cliffs, over 500 feet in height.

A Victorian description of Fast Castle states:

Backed by lofty though receding hill slopes, the ruin presents one shattered side of a low square keep, with a still more dilapidated fragment overhanging the sea verge of its acclivitous site and is accessible only by a bridle path. Formerly it was even more isolated from the mainland as a chasm some twenty four feet in width could only be crossed by a narrow drawbridge. By whom this ancient fortalice was erected no satisfactory evidence exists to show, but history declares that in 1410 it was in the possession of one Thomas Holden and an English garrison. Holden was a sort of ancient brigand and rape and pillage occupied the time and talents of himself and his followers. In the year mentioned, however, he met with a severe and permanent check when Patrick, the second son of the Earl of Dunbar with one hundred supporters took the castle.

Fast Castle's most famous visitor was the little English Tudor Princess Margaret, who when aged only 14 was brought to Scotland to marry King James IV and spent one of the nights on her journey north, within its walls. The royal wedding was nicknamed the Marriage of the Thistle and the Rose and although it is of a later period, the market cross at Cockburnspath is carved on one side with a thistle and on the other side of the stone with a rose, as a reminder of the neighbourhood's link with this romantic incident in Scotland's history and that formed part of the Queen Margaret's dowry from her Scottish king.

Of the 16th-century history of Fast Castle, the Victorian guidebook says:

> For long one of the ancient fortresses of the Earls of Home, it passed from them by marriage about 1580. Thereafter it was tenanted by an individual, who according to Scott, was one of the darkest characters of that age, John Logan of Restalrig. He was implicated in the famous Gowrie Conspiracy of 1600 against King James VI, although his share in this plot was not discovered until nine years after his death, when the correspondence between him and the Earl of Gowrie was most unexpectedly discovered. Even after death the owner of Fast Castle was condemned for high treason, his bones being brought into court for this purpose.

Some accounts of the Gowrie Conspiracy maintain that had the traitors succeeded in capturing the king, they planned to hold him captive at the castle on the Berwickshire coast

Certainly at one time, Fast Castle appears to have ranked as a stronghold alongside Tantallon and Dirleton as one of the guardians of the entrance to the Firth of Forth, as it is mentioned on many early maps, but today there is very much less to see of it, probably because of its very exposed site and the viciously severe weather conditions, which its stone-built living quarters and outer protective curtain walls were subjected to over the years.

The site occupied by Fast Castle is truly a mysterious one, because for any castle to be viable, it required to have a well and an underground source of fresh water to supply not only the laird and his family and his retainers, but also their horses, which were vitally important for transportation in those days. Fast on its headland of solid rock at the end of its narrow peninsula appears at first sight to be entirely devoid of such a source. The way in which its early owners, the Homes and the Logans of Restalrig, overcame this deficit is most intriguing, because they discovered a freshwater spring below the low watermark way down at the foot of the cliff and used a small crane to winch up buckets full of water to the forecourt of the castle above. In addition to the spring of fresh water at sea level the rock, upon which Fast stands, is pierced by two large caves, both very difficult to access and adding still further to the feeling of intrigue about this remote site.

Yet another mystery is what provided for the financial upkeep of the castle. Tom Dykes, who as well as farming Redheugh also owns Dowlaw and the castle, which stands there, has an intriguing theory, which fits exactly with Fast's dominant position on the Berwickshire coast. For he is convinced that instead of depending on land rents, Fast earned its money from levying dues on all fish landed from these waters. From Fast Castle, any fishing boats working out in the North Sea could be easily spotted and no matter where their crews chose to put in to land their catches, a horseman from the castle could be on the scene before them to claim the estate's share of the fish.

Finally, Fast Castle's most well-known mystery is its famous missing horde of treasure. The persistent rumour that Fast's ruined site still conceals a very valuable horde dates back to a contract signed in 1594. The contract was between Fast's owner, Robert Logan of Restalrig, and John Napier of Merchiston, the world-famous inventor of logarithms. It states:

> as ther is dywarse reortis and appirancis that thair suld be within the said Robertes dwellinge place of fascastell asoum of monie and poise heid and hurdit up secritlie quhilk as yit is on fund be ony man. The sid Johne sail do his utter and exact diligens to serche and sik out and be al craft and ingyne that he dow to tempt trye and find out the sam and be the grace of god ather sail find the sam or mak it suir that na sik thing hes been thair.

Despite over 20 years of excavations by the Edinburgh Archaeological Field Society, no trace of the alleged treasure has ever been found, but more seriously, the work of the Society's enthusiastic members has revealed much of the detail of the castle's historic past and these are recorded in two books by Mary Kennaway and Keith L. Mitchell and these are recommended to readers who wish fuller information about this intriguing site. Fast Castle is the subject of a dramatic painting in the National Gallery of Scotland, Edinburgh, by the Revd John Thomson of Duddingston, who was a friend of Sir Walter Scott. He also painted several other prospects of the coast from here to St Abb's Head. The Edinburgh minister called his studio Edinburgh so that if any unwelcome caller threatened to interrupt his painting, his servant could truthfully say 'He's away to Edinburgh'!

Towering as it does above the entrance to the Firth, the crag on which Fast Castle is perched would undoubtedly make an ideal setting for television's old advertisement about the lady who loves Milk Tray, or possibly more appropriately for a new commercial featuring Drambuie on the rocks!

Beyond Fast Castle, the dramatic sea cliffs continue to dominate the scene through the lands of Lumsdaine. This is an inaccessible and dangerous area and so it is necessary to take the narrow twisting road which leads three miles to the next landmark, rugged St Abb's Head. This massive rocky outcrop is home to the largest cliff-nesting population of seabirds on the entire east coast. This, together with the fact that it is such an impressive guardian to the entrance to the Firth of Forth, makes it fitting that it is now safeguarded for the nation by being looked after under the auspices of the National Trust for Scotland, with a nature reserve run by the Wildlife Trust. The headland, which faces the North Sea, consists of three distinct summits, the highest of which reaches a height of about 310 feet above sea level. Out on the central summit stands the lighthouse, which was built in 1861. Its light, at a height of 224 feet above the sea, is visible up to 21 nautical miles out to sea.

Below the lighthouse, the cliffs are pitted with caves which can only be reached from the sea in ideal calm conditions at low tide. According to local tradition, in the past they were the hide-away of smugglers.

St Abb's takes its name from Princes Aebbe, daughter of King Aethelfrith, half-sister of Oswald, King of Northumbria, which lies only 12 miles to south. St Ebba's daughter, Ethelfred, founded a nunnery and archaeologists have discovered evidence of its remains nearby. With so much history around it is appropriate that the former village school has been converted into a small heritage centre, with the largest of its exhibits, a wooden-hulled fishing boat, parked in the playground. This is particularly appropriate, for St Abb's village has a distinctly salty tang to it and the buildings around its attractive wee harbour are often sketched and painted by artists. The harbour is the headquarters for a diving club, whose members take responsibility for maintaining a voluntary under-water marine nature reserve. Occasional fishing boats put into the harbour and a few local men still catch lobsters and crabs but nowadays it is at its busiest during the summer with holiday-makers. Inevitably, with so many visitors keen to enjoy water sports along this rocky stretch of coast there are occasional emergencies and the RNLI has based one of its inflatable Atlantic 21 class vessels at its local lifeboat station, where the volunteer crew raises funds during the holiday months by selling souvenirs to visitors.

In comparison with the fishing ports of the East Neuk of Fife directly across the Firth, this corner of the Borders is so far very little discovered by tourists, which is surprising considering how close it is to the English Border and the main A1 road.

In the Middle Ages one group of visitors who came to St Abb's by sea were most unwelcome, because they were the dreaded Viking raiders. From St Abb's, they stormed inland to the neighbouring village of Coldingham. There, in 870, they looted and plundered the monastery, slaughtered its monks and the abbess and nuns at the neighbouring convent and burned down the wooden buildings. Two hundred years later, King Edgar gave the lands of Coldingham to the monks of Durham Cathedral, which was dedicated to the greatest of the east coast holy men, St Cuthbert. Eighteen of the Benedictine priests came north and began the building of Coldingham Priory and, in 1098, the king graced the dedication service in its new stone-built church with his royal presence. For two and a half centuries Coldingham Priory flourished, but in the middle of the 1400s it declined. By 1461, the number of brothers had decreased to only two, and ten years later there were none. At this time, the Pope ordered that the priory's revenues be devoted to the Chapel Royal of Scotland. At the beginning of the 16th century, Coldingham's troubles continued when its convenient position on the main route into Scotland led to it being used as a base in the Borders by the invading English troops. In 1547, the Earl of Hertford proposed that the buildings should be demolished to stop them failing into Scottish hands. The church survived, however, and after the Reformation the local people who had previously been confined to worshipping at the altars in the three aisles of the nave, a part of the church so named because its roof resembled the upturned hull of a ship, celebrated the freedom of their new-found Protestant faith, by moving their services to the choir. In 1662 the south and the west walls of the choir, which were becoming ruinous, were rebuilt as they now appear. There are also traces of the east wall of the cloisters of the monastery and about 75 feet away from the church, the remains of the frater, the refectory where the monks ate their communal meals can also be found. 1998 marked the 900th anniversary of the priory and to mark it a detailed large-scale model of the monastery when it was at its peak was commissioned in the hope that it will soon be displayed in a new visitor interpretation centre to encourage visitors on a scale approaching the numbers who make annual pilgrimages to the other Borders' abbeys. An increase in tourism would be welcome to boost the local economy and provide more jobs, in the way that the successful Dunlaverock House Hotel has already done. Dunlaverock is a substantial, late Victorian villa and is a very comfortable, well-run, country house hotel, but with such superb sea-scapes from its dining room windows, right out over Coldingham Bay to the North Sea beyond, perhaps coastal house hotel would be a more appropriate description.

At Coldingham, our course along the shores of the Firth of Forth comes to an end. From here, it is very much a case of 'to Noroway, to Noroway, to Noroway o'er the faem', and so here is, indeed, an appropriate place to pause and think of that 'skeely skipper' of old Scots ballad renown, Sir Patrick Spens, and all the other sailors, who have navigated these waters. Roman galleys bound for Cramond, Viking long ships bound for plunder, *The Yellow Carvel*, *The Great Michael* and all the other ships of the early Scottish navy, bound to attack the English, all sailed past here. Some of their voyages, like that of the French sailing ship which brought Mary Queen of Scots back to the royal court at Holyrood and those of the Darien Company's expedition, which ruined the economy and led to the Union of the Parliaments, changed the course of Scottish history. In the 18th century there was the coming of the privateer John Paul Jones and in the 19th the trips to the Arctic by the Scottish whalers, whose efforts gave the country its first oil industry. Today instead of importing it, oil is a Scottish export, but still the Forth has its part to play as the giant tankers from Hound Point Terminal plough their way out into the North Sea. To reach that sea, the Forth has flowed over 103 miles from where it rises on the slopes of Ben Lomond to where we leave it on the coast of Berwickshire.

FURTHER READING

Discovering the River Forth by William F. Hendrie. John Donald.

Newhaven-on-Forth, Port of Grace by Tom McGowran. John Donald.

The Port of Leith by Sue Mowat. John Donald.

Queensferry in Old Picture Postcards by William F. Hendrie. European Library.

Bo'ness in Old Picture Postcards by William F. Hendrie. European Library.

Bo'ness in Old. Picture Postcards, vol 2 by William F. Hendrie. European Library.

Grangemouth in Old Picture Postcards by William F. Hendrie. European Library.

Cockburnspath Walks. Illustrated pamphlets by Sally Smith and Kenneth Wilson. Available from Dunglass Mill, Cockburnspath, Berwickshire.

Discovering Fife by Raymond Lamont-Brown. John Donald.

Discovering East Lothian by Ian and Kathleen Whyte. John Donald.

Discovering the Water of Leith by Hamish Coghill. John Donald.

Discovering the Borders, vol 1 by Alan Spence. John Donald.

INDEX

DISCOVERING THE FIRTH OF FORTH